My Date
with
History

My Date with History

A Memoir

SUMAN CHATTOPADHYAY

RUPA

Published by
Rupa Publications India Pvt. Ltd 2018
7/16, Ansari Road, Daryaganj
New Delhi 110002

Sales Centres:
Allahabad Bengaluru Chennai
Hyderabad Jaipur Kathmandu
Kolkata Mumbai

Copyright © Suman Chattopadhyay 2018

The views and opinions expressed in this book are the author's own and the facts are as reported by him which have been verified to the extent possible, and the publishers are not in any way liable for the same.

All rights reserved.

No part of this publication may be reproduced, transmitted, or stored in a retrieval system, in any form or by any means, electronic, mechanical, photocopying, recording or otherwise, without the prior permission of the publisher.

ISBN: 978-81-291-5046-2

First impression 2018

10 9 8 7 6 5 4 3 2 1

The moral right of the author has been asserted.

Printed in India by Replika Press Pvt. Ltd.

This book is sold subject to the condition that it shall not, by way of trade or otherwise, be lent, resold, hired out, or otherwise circulated, without the publisher's prior consent, in any form of binding or cover other than that in which it is published.

For Tupur and Sayar
Twinkling of my eyes

Contents

Preface ix
1. *Kolkata Ekattor* 1
2. The Turmoil Within 16
3. Campbell Sahib's Legacy 25
4. My Gurus 38
5. 'Aveek Wants You in *Anandabazar*' 52
6. Early Break 62
7. Delhi: Take It, or Leave It 72
8. Page One Singh 84
9. Prince Charming 95
10. The Bengali Patriarch 114
11. Pranab Da: The Comeback Hero 129
12. In the Tigers' Den 141
13. Of Bibi and Others 154
14. Kabuli Pulao 171
15. Moscow: Watching the Curtain Lift 189
16. Ayodhya, 6 December 1992 204
17. Kolkata Calling 228
18. The Mamata Blaze 239
19. Bengal's Chanakya and Chavez 251
20. Job Lost, Battle Won 263
Index 275

Preface

I have just turned sixty. Does that indicate the beginning of my life, as new research in the West seems to suggest? Or should I already have been contemplating in the woods for a decade, as our own sages had ordained? I don't know. Frankly I couldn't care less. Rites of passages have hardly ever bothered me. That's because all my life I have had only one identity: a journalist. And all the while I have passionately believed that for a journo, life is a ceaseless continuum, cascading from one dateline to another. In the meantime we also live. Indeed, a journalist is a journalist even before one is a journalist. Those growing-up days are but the period to mature, to sharpen the proverbial nose for stories, a continuum again.

Do I have regrets? Well, I have never had a dog. I have never had the occasion to worry about the bonsais in my balcony yellowing faster than they should. I have never been a member of any club either. Yes, it's possible to argue that in my sixty years I have missed out on the finer things, the subtler nuances that life has to offer to more discerning souls. My regrets have always been of a different kind. One of the most bitter regrets in my life, for example, has been my inability to extricate an interview out of Velupillai Prabhakaran, even though I was able to create, at great personal risk, an opportunity to meet him in his Jaffna hideout. I regret that although I was able to reach

Moscow, without a valid passport, to watch the Soviet Empire fall and the iron curtain lift, I was not present during the fall of the German Wall. I guess my regrets have always been more quantifiable, if you will.

How have I scored as a son, as a husband, as a father, as a friend over the past sixty years? I would be scared to even glance at such a mark sheet, if there were to be one. This much, however, I know: If I were to be given an opportunity to relive my life, at the end of it, yet again, I would be as scared to look at such a mark sheet as I am today.

Yet, age does catch up with you. Finally. Today, even as I keep one eye on the TV screen following the latest in the Gujarat Assembly election, I do have this urge to look back, with the other eye, and meet the Suman Chattopadhyay that has survived, for decades, the furious frenzy behind and beyond all the datelines. That's what this book is all about. Retelling some of the more memorable stories is just an excuse to meet the filer, for once. Nothing more. Nothing less either.

The book wouldn't have seen the light of the day without the constant support and encouragement of my friend Nilanjan Hajra. In more senses than one it was a journey we undertook together.

Kasturi, my wife, as always, has been a source of deep inspiration. Much of what I have written in these pages is actually what she has suffered quietly. She, however, wishes that the book would surely be my passport to immortality.

Suman Chattopadhyay

1
Kolkata Ekattor

'*Ei mal ta kon gram theke eseche re?*' (Where is this village bum from?) With those words ringing in my ears, I entered the classroom in my new school. That is how I remember my first brush with the city, which was destined to be my home for the rest of my life. Kolkata. That was 1971 and the city that the 'village bum', as a 14-year-old, confronted was Kolkata '71, a coinage later made famous by Mrinal Sen's eponymous film. The two words together, *Kolkata Ekattor*, carried within their subtext a heady blend of dreams and gunpowder, blood and poetry, unmitigated loss and courageous new beginnings.

The year 1971 was a turbulent one in South Asia. Events with far-reaching consequences were happening all around us: India fought its third war with Pakistan that culminated in the Simla Agreement; a new sovereign nation was born after a heroic and bloody uprising in East Pakistan; millions of refugees, having lost everything, crossed the border and poured into West Bengal, in one of the largest exoduses in world history; Prime Minister Indira Gandhi eventually stamped out the Congress old guard's machinations to clip her wings; the Indo-Soviet Treaty of Friendship to pre-empt President Richard Nixon's apprehended adventure of sending the Seventh Fleet into the Indian Ocean.

Much of this turbulence had strong Eastern connections.

Kolkata '71 was witness to a watershed in the history of this subcontinent: The birth of Bangladesh. The Provincial Government of the People's Republic of Bangladesh, formed following the declaration of independence from Pakistan, on 10 April 1971, had its capital in exile in Kolkata. None in Kolkata could remain unaffected by the tumultuous events unfolding daily before our eyes. I made it a point to be present at the mammoth rally at the city's fabled Brigade Parade Grounds addressed jointly by Sheikh Mujibur Rahman and Indira Gandhi. In terms of attendance, the rally created history of sorts, surpassing another historic rally at the same venue a few years before addressed by two Soviet leaders—Nikita Khrushchev and Nikolai Bulganin. Sheikh Mujib was a great orator and every time he thundered in front of the microphone, the crowd, numbering almost a million, roared back in one voice—'*Jay Bangla*' (viva Bangladesh). Even though I had little comprehension of the huge geopolitical importance of the event, the thrill and excitement gave me goosebumps.

Jay Bangla was the sacred slogan for thousands of brave young Bangladeshi women and men who sacrificed everything in the face of the bloodiest pogroms in South Asian history carried out by the Pakistani Army. Researchers of the strange idiosyncrasies of languages may find it interesting that Bengalis, with their unusual sense of wit, soon started using the term to mean a painful eye infection. Even today, most Bengalis would say that they have been afflicted with *Jay Bangla* to really mean conjunctivitis! Perhaps the contagious disease spread among the people of Kolkata as millions of people, uprooted from their homes, poured into the city in waves upon waves, as the war raged on in East Pakistan. 'With an estimated 10 million people leaving what was then East Pakistan for India between April and December 1971, this became the largest single displacement in the second half of the century,' observes a UNHCR report[1] in 2000. That was one of the many deeply unsettling realities of Kolkata '71.

They were everywhere. While a vast number of them settled in ghettos—known in Kolkata parlance as 'colonies', in the city's fringes, without even the least civic amenities—many sought out relatives and friends who had arrived in earlier years and had made good in Kolkata. None arrived in our home. Yet our family had a deep empathy with them, because they came from the land of my ancestors. My mother, Kalyani, came from a prosperous, land-owning family in erstwhile East Bengal, which was now being reborn as Bangladesh. She was born in Rangpur in 1925. My father, Sunil, came from Faridpur in erstwhile East Bengal, also the home of Sheikh Mujib.

A quaint town on the banks of the Ghagat River in northwest Bangladesh, Rangpur is said to have arrived on India's historical map in the late sixteenth century. It must have been quite a spectacle for my nengti (loincloth)-clad ancestors, when the great Mughal Emperor Akbar's trusted commander, Raja Man Singh, arrived on the banks of the Ghagat in 1575 with horses, elephants, soldiers, tents, cooks, concubines and all the paraphernalia that constituted the Mughal Army. The small town appeared on the global map when, in 1823, a Scottish trader and explorer, curiously named Robert Bruce, returned from Rangpur with a special plant that in subsequent years came to be known as Assam Tea, and changed the course of history in frontier Bengal. Also, it was Rangpur's late eighteenth-century Sanyasi and Fakir Rebellion (uprising of Hindu and Muslim mendicants), which had inspired a young civil servant, Bankim Chandra Chattopadhyay, to write a novel named *Anandamath* in 1882, which in turn gave India's freedom struggle its first pan-national slogan: *Bande Mataram*, a beautiful ode to the nation, which is now our national song.

---

[1]http://www.unhcr.org/3ebf9bab0.pdf

The family of my mother's mother—my Didima—came from Mymensingh, once again in East Bengal. Mymensingh was also Satyajit Ray's maternal home. The little zamindari run by the undivided family did not attract my Dadu (maternal grandfather) and the profligacy of his eldest son soon depleted its wealth. Instead of bothering with that, Dadu would frequently leave home to spend time at the local burning ghats (cremation sites near riverbanks) in the company of sadhus. He eventually renounced the worldly life to become a saffron-clad tantric and settled down as the high priest of a tiny shadowy temple, dedicated to Lord Shiva, in Varanasi.

I had three mamas (maternal uncles) and two mashis (maternal aunts) all of whom were elder to my mother. The eldest of my aunts chose to remain in Bangladesh and never crossed the border into India. So, my connection with Bangladesh was never severed.

In '71, my family, that is, my parents Sunil and Kalyani, my sister Suparna, three years elder to me, and I, had just arrived in Kolkata from Jhargram, a quaint nondescript town, deep inside the Jungle Mahal areas of western West Bengal. In the late 1960s my father was posted as a professor of history at Jhargram Government College.

My father was born in a lower middle-class family, with a dull life. His father, Prabodh Chandra, worked for the railways and spent a large part of his life in rail gumtis (small living quarters for staff members of the Indian Railways) along with his family. After his retirement, he settled in his own decrepit house in Liluah, a small, greyish town, some 10 kms from Kolkata, across Hooghly River, of which my first memories are that of an overpowering smell of dust and factory work sheds. Prabodh Chandra and Basanti Devi had nine children, six sons and three daughters, just two short of a regular football or cricket team. Curiously, first came the sons, one after another, and then the daughters. My dad was the second in the team. On completion of his Masters, he began his lifelong teaching career from a private college in Siuri, the district headquarters of Birbhum, close to Shantiniketan. It was also in this college that Pranab Mukherjee, our former President, and his brother Pradosh, came to study from a nearby village. I heard later that Pranab Da, with his alert and inquisitive mind, often badgered my father with endless questions on the Tudor and Stuart periods of British history. That also distinguished him from the rut.

I came to this world in October 1957, when my dad was still teaching in Siuri. Over the years, his profession took him from one small town to another. So I spent my entire childhood in deep rural Bengal, until my father was finally transferred, in the last leg of his career, to Presidency College in Kolkata '71. I, therefore, was a complete outsider to the huge, bustling metropolis, as I entered the classroom, clad in a doorman-like khaki uniform, in my new school: the famous Ballygunge Government High School. Among its illustrious alumni were Satyajit Ray and Rahul Dev Burman.

Sure, I was rattled, but by no means grounded. Soon my smart-ass classmates realized that 'the village bum' too had a trick or two up his sleeves. It was not for nothing that the authorities of my previous school in Jhargram had threatened to rusticate me. However, a few weeks into my new and alien environment, I realized there were some boys in the class who could easily outsmart me. They smoked in the classroom during the recess or before school hours. In the absence of matchboxes, they would often rub two live electric wires, hanging from a broken switchboard, against one another. The resulting sparks provided the fire to light cigarettes.

Soon, the batch got divided into various groups, each student choosing his own circle of friends. Even though I routinely topped in all the tests, I gelled particularly well with those who were poor, or at the most average, in their studies. I had a solid reason for this choice. These guys, unlike the goody-goody intelligent ones cocooned within good behavioural codes, were brave hearts. I believed they would stand by me in times of trouble.

Of all my friends—good, bad and the ugly—the only one who remained my dearest companion for a long time even after we left school, was Baninath Bose. He lived in Kalighat, then known for its famous Kali temple and one of Kolkata's oldest brothels. Bani lived in a small room, in a shabby building rented by his family, which lived across the street in another equally dingy building. His room soon became our rendezvous centre, where we ate, slept, drank, smoked, cried and exchanged our love stories.

It was through Bani that I was first exposed to another deeply disturbing reality of Kolkata '71: the Naxal movement, the Indian youth's most passionate engagement with Leftist ideology. In Kolkata '71, revolution was in the air. Bani was shy, handsome and well read. He had pronounced ultra-Left leanings. Even while in school he was the only one who openly sympathized with the Naxals and castigated the state Congress government for unleashing state terror against them. He kept in close touch with his neighbourhood Naxal friends, many years senior to him, and carried out their instructions secretly. When one of them was picked up by the police in a midnight swoop, he wept.

Surprisingly, his own maternal grandfather was a Congress MLA from Midnapore district. Bani took various advantages from his dadu—from cricket match tickets at the Eden Gardens to occasional free lunches and dinners at the MLA Hostel canteen on Kyd Street. But, neither did he ever compromise his political conviction, nor harbour any aspiration to carve out for himself a cushy political career in Congress using his family connections—hich has always been the order of the day in Congress, from top to bottom.

He grew up to be a professor in Midnapore College and continued to profess a just, egalitarian, classless society. And then we received the shock: Bani had been diagnosed with stomach cancer. The disease was at its last stages, his doctors said. I simply stopped seeing him. I just could not. Finally, I got the news that Bani had left us behind. He was barely 40. My dearest friend. Ever. An incorrigible dreamer.

I walked to the school from our apartment, a two-and-a-quarter bedroom, first-floor space behind a multistorey building on Deodar Street in South Kolkata. On coming to the city, my father rented it for ₹250 a month; in Kolkata '71, flats for rent at reasonable rates were aplenty. Obtaining them, however, was an ordeal. The landlord had to be convinced that the prospective tenant had not even the remotest connection with Naxals. Any family with a young person became an immediate suspect. By then, the state's law and order machinery had unleashed reckless, mindless and ruthless counter-terror against the Naxals. Having a young man as a tenant could often result in loud knocks on the door in the dead of night from policemen in mufti. Young men and women were taken away, often to disappear forever. Many would be asked to alight from police jeeps in desolate fringes of the city, advised to run away and shot from behind.

On my way to school, or returning home, I would pass by the home of the then chief minister: the flamboyant, pukka sahib Siddhartha Shankar Ray. It always appeared to be abuzz with people and was guarded by heavily armed policemen 24x7. Basking in Mrs Gandhi's glory, this corporate lawyer ruled the state in his own maverick style. Years later, I came to know him well enough to be able to call him Manu Da.

Deodar Street was a highly cosmopolitan neighbourhood, where multistoreys jostled with huge slums. In a way, the small lane in front of our house was a microcosm of India, where Hindus and Sikhs, Muslims and Christians, Bengalis and Biharis, Marwaris and Gujaratis, Malayalis and Goans, the rich and the poor, middle class and lower middle class lived side by side. When at home, I would keep myself locked inside for hours, studying, smoking, pondering and, when bored with everything else, watching for hours from my window the endless bustle of the slum life underneath. Subcity Kolkata throbbed with its own parallel, pulsating heart.

The vast Bihari basti, next to our house, had no sanitary facilities. Taxi drivers and darbaans at various small- and medium-sized industrial establishments, with their ever-expanding families, peopled the dark one-room shanties lined along an endless labyrinth of alleys, where it would be difficult for more than one person to walk side by side.

In this basti, I soon discovered Suresh. His father, who flaunted a lush black moustache and a shining baton, was the night watchman for Calcutta Chemicals, then famous for producing Neem toothpaste. My friendship with Suresh survived the demise of this once successful Bengali industrial establishment. With his father unemployed, Suresh soon had to drop out of school in class IX, as his family could no longer bear the luxury of his education. The equation was simple: If you wanted to survive, chip in with your two pennies.

Suresh's first job was that of a taxi helper. In those days, every taxi in Kolkata always had a driver and another person, the helper, who did all the errands for the driver, particularly if the car conked off. He would receive a pitifully meagre salary but the sop was that he got to learn to drive for free. And in good time, Suresh became a driver of a cab, owned by someone else.

On the periphery of the slum lived the rickshaw-pullers.

Tana rickshaws, hand-pulled by men till this day, are Kolkata's unique contribution to urban transport. Nowhere else have I seen babus and bibis, without an iota of discomfort, reclining across the seat while another man pulls them along. Nor have I seen a tana rickshaw-wallah who is not from some remote village in Bihar. They would stay in groups of eight to ten in a single dingy room. Their staple was sattu (gram flour) for both lunch and dinner, occasionally with a piece of onion. They bathed as well as washed their aluminium utensils at a common tube well on the street. After the long day's toil, late at night, they would play twenty-nine—a popular game of cards—for a paltry stake of four annas (i.e. one quarter of a rupee) per deal.

None of them could afford to live with his family. Their wives and children remained in 'dehat', the ancestral village. Once or twice a year, they would put on their only pair of clean dhoti and kurta to board a Bihar-bound train without ticket, offering a paltry bribe to the ticket checker. And, without fail, ten months later, a postcard would arrive from home, written with the help of some 'parha-likha' (literate) neighbour, announcing the birth of a child. They would rejoice if it was a boy, distributing laddoos; but, if it was a girl, such revelry would be considered unnecessary. They spoke the Bhojpuri dialect and sang Bhojpuri songs two or three days at a stretch during Holi festivities after consuming glasses of bhang.

Many of them were my friends and, during vacations, I spent a lot of time playing cards with them. All the rickshaws in our area were rented to them by Bihari Singh, an elderly landlord with high-powered glasses who lived nearby in his four-storeyed building.

Once in a while, patrolling policemen would extort from them their whole day's earning because, in most cases, the rickshaws they pulled did not have the mandatory civic licence. I still wonder how these people could still appear to be so happy and carefree.

On an adjacent narrow lane, there was another slum, again inhabited by the Biharis, but smaller in size and different in character. It was exclusively for the 'phuchka-wallahs'. The specialized art of turning a small 'lechi' (ball of dough) of semolina flour into a paper-thin yet firm, crisp and hollow ball of 'phuchka' used to be a mesmerizing event for me. They fried their phuchkas—in thousands and each of the exact same size—late in the night or early in the morning to keep them fresh. They would then apportion these among themselves, keeping them in large baskets. Half of the phuchkas consumed in southern Kolkata came from this slum. People were, of course, blissfully unaware about the appalling hygienic conditions in which these were prepared. But, unlike hooch and the prasad distributed after Pujas going bad, I have never reported or seen reports in my long journalistic career of mass sickness because of eating phuchkas!

Our street had two other huge slums adjacent to it. In one of these lived Oriya plumbers, and in the other, Bihari motor mechanics. One daily spectacle in the slums was that of women quarrelling over long queues to draw water from the common civic tap. In Kolkata, these are known as time-kol (tap) because the water supply is restricted to certain hours. Failing to procure water then might mean going without it for the day or having to draw it from a distant tube well.

Occasionally, the tranquillity of the neighbourhood would be violently disturbed at the dead of night when drunken hoodlums of the two slums clashed. From brickbats it would soon escalate to hurling petos (crude bombs) and firing from country-made pistols. Such rivalries used to be apolitical—more of an exercise in fruitless bravado than anything of real consequence—when I first arrived in Kolkata. Over time, however, they became easy recruits for political parties, whose patronage they needed to influence local police officials or getting bail quickly. But none of these hoodlums had anything to do with the Naxals, who seemed singularly absent from the mini-Bharat of the slums.

Of all these palpitating images of mini-Bharat, the sight of dehati young women bathing in the open was particularly addictive.

Among my immediate neighbours was a dedicated Communist Party of India (Marxist) (CPI[M]) supporter—a rarity in those days—whose son taught me how to make firecrackers, particularly tubris (flowerpots) at home. A Sikh family, with numerous children, lived in an apartment on the ground floor. The husband lived in Thailand as the head Granthi of a gurdwara there. Our neighbourhood had several other Sikh families as well as a gurdwara. We are proud that none of them was harmed during the massive anti-Sikh pogrom that was carried out in many cities after Indira Gandhi's assassination on 31 October 1984.

∽

We had a tight group of three: Sumantra, Surajit and Suman. In time came Partha. There was no liquor shop in our para (neighbourhood). Partha, a few years senior to us and from an affluent family, was our pathfinder in this regard. He was one of those who strongly believed that student life was valuable and must be prolonged as much as possible, and, therefore, had no qualms about failing in school. He was blind of an eye. Soon under his tutelage, we graduated from tea to beer. Since he didn't look like a school kid, he had no problem procuring beer. But we also realized quickly that the stuff was not really value-for-money and looked for alternatives.

Partha suggested we should shift to Bangla—a cheap country spirit. In Kolkata '71, you would not be much of an intellectual if you were not involved in drunken fracas after consuming a lot of this lousy stuff with an awful smell. I guess Ritwik Ghatak was the first intellectual brand ambassador of this cheap booze. He drank himself to death. Romantic anecdotes of his drunken escapades inspired many young antels[2], who did not have even an iota of Ghatak's talent, to turn Bangla into a trademark for being out of the ordinary in a superior sense.

Besides Ghatak, there were the Hungryalists of the Hungry Generation of the 1960s, a group of very talented poets and writers, albeit with no inkling of what real hunger meant, along with a similar group associated with the famous *Krittibas* poetry magazine. Two of the brightest names from these groups, Sakti Chattopadhyay and Sunil Gangopadhyay, were later my colleagues at *Anandabazar Patrika* (ABP) for more than a decade. And, of course, there was the unusually gifted Tushar Roy. His collection, *Bandmaster*, stunned Bengali poetry. They had turned Barduari—a dingy Bangla joint in central Kolkata—into a pilgrimage for the antels. The joint perennially smelt of vomit, and was frequented mostly by tana rickshaw-wallahs and labourers.

At the time, a pint of Bangla cost ₹5.50 and a full bottle ₹8. We, however, were never among the haloed customers of Barduari. Nearer to our home was another country liquor shop, almost hidden at the end of a small lane. The shop had its own tavern, big and sprawling, where people sat on wooden benches without backrest to consume the elixir of life. Inside the tavern, there was a small outlet that sold paan, cigarettes and a variety of fritters to go with the drinks. It was a poor man's joint, beyond the realm of most bhadralok.

At this joint, I struck friendship with two other guys: Both were named Munna, both were middle-class Marwari grocers. For me, the real point of interest was their insider knowledge of the brothel in Kalighat. One of them was a little senior to the other.

---

[2] Antel is a Bengali colloquial expression for half-baked intellectuals who have much pretention but little talent.

Senior Munna passed on to me the wisdom of masturbating about an hour before visiting a brothel. This, he explained, helps you 'extract all the bang for your buck'. The idea was not to have a premature ejaculation. It was, however, junior Munna who imparted us practical education. After our half-yearly exams in class XI, he suggested we accompany him to Kalighat.

The Kalighat brothel is a small, crowded and congested neighbourhood beside a throbbing bazaar situated on the eastern bank of the dirty Adi Ganga. The murder of Adi Ganga—a busy waterway till the early twentieth century, with a rich history of maritime trade—is a fascinating story of callousness and stupidity of Kolkata's town planners. But for me it has always been a mixture of myth and history, because since our childhood we have always seen it as a silted canal that regularly overflowed during high tides in Hooghly River, flooding vast areas along its banks with mucky water, emanating an awful stench.

Under junior Munna's courageous leadership, four of us headed for the slum right along this foul-smelling canal. Soon we were in a dark, filthy alley. Apparently, our destination was a shack on this lane. Munna was wearing a plain lungi and a vest. We were in our Sunday best. The lane was relatively empty in the afternoon and most of the girls were still not 'ready' for the evening. Munna brought us to a place that was locked from inside.

'She must be occupied. Let us leave,' one of us told Munna in a nervous whisper. But he ignored the advice and knocked loudly on the door. A drowsy middle-aged man emerged from the room, looked at us and left quietly. At this point my nerves gave way. I wanted to leave immediately. 'It's the girl's husband. He sleeps here during the day but leaves promptly once a "babu" comes. He knows me and also knows this is my regular hour,' Munna assured.

Munna's girl appeared within a few minutes. She wore a fresh sari and had a smiling face. She was short but plump, and seemed quite warm and affectionate. It was obvious she had just cleaned her face and put on some cheap talcum powder. She invited us inside and asked whether we would like to have a glass of beer or a cup of tea. Everyone felt too nervous to indulge in beer and opted for tea. Not Munna. He drank warm beer straight from the bottle and told us to wait outside. He wanted to be left alone in the company of his girl to negotiate the rate.

What Munna said, after his secret deliberations, seemed atrocious. 'She says we don't need to go to any other girl. She will entertain all of us herself, one by one.'

'Are you crazy? We will have to stand in a queue to f**k a woman?' Partha grumbled and everyone else nodded in approval.

I wanted to leave without wasting another minute. By this time my nerves were in tatters. Surajit did not seem to bother and Sumantra was still pondering. Only Partha readily agreed to accompany me back. Munna tried his best to convince us to take the plunge. Soon everyone became abusive and all of us were shouting at the top of our voices.

Suddenly, we noticed a kind of heightened activity along the lane. There were very few people on the lane, but within moments even those few people disappeared and we heard doors being bolted from inside one after another. Munna's girl reappeared on the door in a flash and literally dragged all of us inside. Once inside she commanded, 'Not a word. Not even a whisper. All of you go under the bed and don't come out unless I signal.'

We knelt down and slipped into the mosquito-ridden, roach-crawling and cobweb-wrapped darkness under the bed. And then Munna dropped the bombshell: 'Police raid.' The girl quickly left the room and then bolted it from outside.

Every minute down there seemed like eternity, with my father's face etched on it. All of a sudden, I felt terribly sorry for my mother and my sister and everyone else who loved me. Huddled under that prostitute's bed for the first and last time in my life I thought of ending my life.

After almost half an hour, the door opened and Munna's girl reappeared to triumphantly declare that the crisis was over. The police had come to collect their weekly dues. We surfaced into light, drenched to the skin with sweat. Our hearts went out to the lord almighty in great humility. The kind woman used her gamcha (thin towel) to clean our clothes and offered us tea again.

As we were stepping towards the door she cried in panic, '*Se ki, bosbena?*' (Won't you stay back?) She stood in front of us and tried to block the door. We forced Munna to pay her dues and disarmed her. Within a minute we were all on the main Kalighat Road, panting. We cursed our fate as well as Munna. I vouched not to repeat it ever. Beer and Bangla were all right. But no more visit to any brothel. Never.

Such was my initiation to Kolkata '71, which was neither just a city nor just a year, but a vivacious culture that bore within it everything that represented Bengal in an era which seems almost fantastic today.

2
The Turmoil Within

My personal space, from which I arrived in the stormy Kolkata '71, was no less turbulent.

My mother, I discovered quite late in my life, was my father's close relative. They had known each other for a long time even before their formal engagement. Unlike in the Muslim households, in a Hindu family, particularly among Brahmins, marriage between relations is considered sacrilege. More so in the 1940s when the Bengali bhadralok was petrified of society gossips: *'pachhe loke kichhu bole'* (lest people gossip), a quip immortalized by one of our first major women poets, Kamini Roy, who was also the first woman in India to obtain a graduate degree.

Surprisingly, they did not face any opposition from their families. One reason for that, I suspect, could be that there was no one—not even my grandfather—in my father's family who had the gumption to oppose his personal decision. By then my father had emerged as the de jure guardian of the household, overshadowing in the process his retired father. On the other hand, in my mother's family, which had by then fallen into penury, marriage of the youngest daughter was seen, perhaps, as a good riddance, a godsend opportunity.

After completing his formal education, in the early 1940s, my father took a temporary job with the military accounts department, an opportunity arising from the frantic defence activities during and following World War II. He did not enjoy the job and left it as soon as he got a call from a college in East Bengal. Immediately before the country's partition, he taught at Chandpur in erstwhile East Bengal, dominated overwhelmingly by Muslims. Even during the summer of 1947, neither he nor anyone living there had the slightest inkling of the cataclysmic turn their fate would take very soon. Instead, he saw and found Hindu families in the town happily building their residences and organizing grihapravesh—house-warming parties, which for Bengalis, is largely a religious ceremony.

According to him, the Partition was never inevitable as was later touted by the Congress stalwarts. It came as a shock, uprooting millions, creating mayhem and mindless human slaughter that, people like my father were convinced, could have been avoided. For him, the Mountbatten Declaration was a hastily crafted document by self-seeking politicians on both sides that was greeted by the affected masses with a helpless sigh of despair and gloom. While the whole nation celebrated independence, my father took a steamer and then a mail train to Howrah to land on the other side of the border in a land of total uncertainty. Since then, he could never return to his village called Ratandiah in erstwhile East Pakistan, which became Bangladesh less than three decades later.

In brief, we were dislodged from our moorings. We lost the soothing concept of having an ancestral home, the veritable gram (village), where one could go back, even if once in a while, to spend some happy hours in the lasting memory of our ancestors.

Of course my grandfather had settled in West Bengal, well before the Partition, in Liluah, which by default became our permanently temporary ancestral home! But then Liluah was no substitute of Ratandiah. Many, many years later, when I got the opportunity to visit my ancestral village in Bangladesh, taking time off my journalistic pursuits, I could not spot the house that I was told, once stood triumphantly as the happy abode of a happy family. It is difficult today to relieve the scars of those days, except for a few hours, perhaps, by watching some of the magical movies of Ritwik Ghatak.

The youthful exuberance of love between my father and mother, however, evaporated pretty soon after marriage, for the simple reason that my parents were not really 'made for each other'. My father was well educated but arrogant, almost ruthless at times when it came to enforcing his self-willed discipline. He was always full of himself, revelling in his small achievements both as a respectable professor and as a writer–commentator for ABP and *Hindustan Standard*, two important dailies published from Kolkata by the ABP Group. A miser to his bones, he never cared to spend money either for family days out or any other form of entertainment.

His only addiction was the radio, the only instrument of entertainment in the house for a long time, when there was news or live commentary of India's cricket matches played at home. He would pick up a quarrel with almost everyone and everywhere, it would sometimes appear, only to keep his pulmonary arteries effective. He thought riding in a rickshaw was an avoidable luxury and would walk miles at a stretch, forcing his family to do the same.

Thankfully, in matters of food he was not as stingy. He always bought the purest and the best for the family within his wisely calculated budget. In our childhood, he would often say, presumably with a sense of well-concealed guilt, 'With the salary I earn, I can do only one thing well—enjoy good food at home. And I do just that.'

That was indeed an honest statement. All his life, stretching over nine decades—he was never involved in any kind of corruption or unethical activity. He did not even succumb to the easy temptation of giving tuitions to students for a marginally more comfortable life. He was always a living embodiment of what an ideal and adorable teacher should be, now almost an endangered species in the self-seeking, and often dishonest, crowd that passes itself off as the teaching community.

My mother, by contrast, had no formal higher education, having passed just the intermediate examination, before dropping out of college. But she carried her family's aristocratic heritage and had a thoroughly cultured and cultivated mind. What she did not possess by way of academic degrees, she tried to make up with a healthy reading habit. She was reasonably conversant with the works of Rabindranath Tagore, Bankim Chandra Chattopadhyay and Sarat Chandra Chattopadhyay.

She had a lifelong love for Rabindra Sangeet. She was a prodigious singer, a quality that in her early days endeared her to almost everybody including her husband before their marriage. She could recite and sing from memory almost all of Tagore's few thousand songs and had almost a flawless sense of sur (melody) and tal (rhythm). A few years after her marriage, she was called by the organizers of a cultural event for a Rabindra Sangeet recital. The function was presided over by the redoubtable Niharranjan Ray—a giant among intellectuals. But my father refused to allow her to participate in it alleging in hushed tones that Niharranjan, notwithstanding his profundity and international acclaim, was a known womanizer. My mother suffered in silence, trying never to cross the ludicrous limits of a middle-class household.

In post-Partition Bengal, my father got his first opportunity to teach in a private college at Siuri. In the early years of their marriage, three of my parents' children, all male, died in succession in their neonatal stage. Soon, filthy questions began to be raised in the family about my mother's chastity and her 'mysterious' past in a crisis-ridden family. Someone even hinted that she could have contracted syphilis, thereby losing her ability to bear healthy children.

My mother did not lose her poise at these insinuations and prayed to god for another opportunity to prove them wrong. In October 1954, my sister was born. More importantly, she survived. Those days in Siuri were, by any reckoning, the happiest days and months in my parents' married life. My mother told me this later in one of her rare moments of tranquility. Her husband's stature continued to rise in the classrooms while she, besides babysitting, took personal care for the happiness and well-being of all her in-laws, turning her into their friend, guide and philosopher. None of them was as yet married and the younger ones were still at various stages of school or college education. All of them looked up to their sister-in-law for help and succour, until a fatal blow of fate, coming in the guise of an incurable disease, changed everything. For worse.

My birth, three years after my elder sister, was, in a way, the harbinger of a welcome change in my father's career. After a couple of private college jobs following the one in Siuri, he finally found the security of a government college in the year I was born. His first government teaching job was at Krishnagar Government College, established in 1846. I spent the first six years of my life in Krishnanagar, which the British tongue had simplified to Krishnagar. About 105.3 kms from Kolkata, located right on the banks of the Jalangi River, it is small, quiet and unusually moist and green.

Our life in Krishnanagar remained peaceful, by and large. The calm was periodically shattered, though, when my father lost his cool over either some trivial family issue or my 'delinquency'. Once, when I was five, I succeeded in charming and cajoling an elderly doorman of a neighbouring office first to gift me char anna (25 paise) and then to give me a ride on his new bicycle to

Ghurni. A few kilometres away from Krishnanagar, Ghurni was famous nationwide for its god-gifted potters, who churned out of their wheels amazingly beautiful clay figurines. I just wanted to buy a small idol of Saraswati, the goddess of learning, to celebrate, in my own way, her puja the following day. I knew that none in the family would permit me to travel such a distance with an unknown person; so I left silently.

As I disembarked from the doorman's bicycle, several hours later, clutching in one hand the small idol, I saw my father, pacing up and down the first-floor veranda, his ominous looks dropping clear hints of what awaited me upstairs. Unfazed, I smartly climbed the stairs, but the whacking that followed drew immediate attention of some of the neighbours, who came running and pleaded with my furious father to not beat his son to death.

He broke the idol, throwing it from upstairs, and just stopped short of breaking my bones. I cried but felt more miserable, first for the idol I lost and then for my mother who stood at the door in stoic silence, tears rolling down her eyes. The emotional distance between the father and the son had already started to creep in. By then I was my mother's son and hers only.

On the last day of 1964, we boarded a passenger train from Krishnanagar to come to Sealdah and then take a south-bound express train from Howrah to reach our new destination, my father's new posting: Jhargram College. We travelled first class, first time in my life, a luxury for me, provided by the government for its college teachers on transfer.

∽

Jhargram, located a little over 200 kms west of Kolkata, was then a small subdivisional town in undivided Midnapore district. In the mid-1960s, it was god's own little place where nature's bounties in all forms far outstripped the inconveniences of a semi-urban life.

Here was a place where, as my father often marvelled, all the six seasons of the Bengali calendar unravelled their natural mysteries in a way that could be seen, sensed and also suffered. Although we arrived in Jhargram in a bitterly cold winter, one of my more vivid memories of the town is its heat, with the mercury often threatening to touch 50 degrees Celsius in summer.

Nestled amid dense jungles of towering sal, simul, palash, mahua, kendu and several other varieties of trees, spring in Jhargram was a riot of colours dominated by myriad shades of red. I remember, besides jungles, I also saw tribal men and women—so distinctly different from us Bengali gentlemen—for the first time in Jhargram. Mostly Santhals, they came in large numbers in autumn to collect dry sal leaves, which they stitched into large plates and sold in the local market. A large number of Santhal women also worked as daily-wage labourers who assisted masons. The women were all very dark, lean and immaculately dressed in their clean white saris with red borders. They came in groups, spoke in an incomprehensible language and carried their own tiffin boxes, each neatly draped in a piece of clean cloth. They invariably shared their meals as they ate lunch under some huge tree. Although poor, their cleanliness and sense of hygiene was remarkable as also their sweet nature and temper. Sometimes they sang and danced in chorus, their bodies and steps flawlessly matching the drumbeats. It was a great spectacle.

For me, however, a far more curious sight would be a Santhal woman urinating beside the road, drawing their sarees up and bending the front of their abdomen forward to avoid spilling urine on their sarees. It was quite a regular sight. Obviously, they didn't find this a shameful act at all, just like lakhs of gentlemen who perform the same act in full view of others at the heart of every city in India.

By comparison, the Lodhas were poorer, nomadic and bare-bodied even in winter. They survived on small-time manual labour offered to them when everyone else had refused. They were known as a community of petty thieves. Every other morning we would hear exaggerated stories of thefts committed by them in some part of the town. However, in our long six-year stay we never experienced one first-hand.

My first close encounter with a Lodha was on an early spring morning under bizarre circumstances. In front of our house there was a huge drumstick tree which had become infested with caterpillars. Soon there were so many of them that the whole tree literally wore a fur coat of caterpillars. Frighteningly, when there was no space left in the tree, they marched in disciplined rows and invaded our house. Within days, they were all over the floors, walls and roofs of every room. Their stings had made life so miserable that my mother decided to shift to a neighbour's house. Thankfully, this was a strong enough signal for my father to finally do something about the menace.

One morning, he stood on the road in his lungi and vest, trying to catch passing labourers to clear up the mess by cutting down the tree. Each one of them quoted a price that my father found impossibly high, until, finally, a Lodha appeared with a brightly polished axe slung across his back. Without a word, he took to the job and after hours of hard work cleaned up the whole area, including the tree and the surrounding bushes. To my dad's great delight, he got the job done for just four annas.

In those days, three of my closest friends were three brothers, Bachchu, Pyanga and Ganesh. Their father was a small-time timber merchant, who looked like a one-eyed jackal and drank country spirit every night without disturbing anyone. Playing gulli-danda and marbles with them one fine morning, I stepped into my tenth year in 1967—a year that brought a tsunami of changes in Bengal, and in our home.

The overarching 'Congress Party System', a term political scientist Rajni Kothari famously coined to describe the party's countrywide uninterrupted domination, received a rude jolt in the 1967 Assembly elections. For the first time since Independence in 1947, some of the states, including West Bengal, passed into the hands of the Opposition parties. The only exception to this was the brief communist experiment in Kerala under a young, highly dynamic and heavily stammering E.M.S. Namboodiripad in 1957 which Pandit Nehru almost forcibly nipped in the bud.

In West Bengal, a dhoti-clad senior Gandhian from Tamralipta (now Tamluk)—one of the most ancient cradles of civilization and international maritime trade—revolted. He was Ajoy Mukherjee. Impeccably honest and a lifelong bachelor, he died in penury. But before that he shook the roots of the Congress in West Bengal by deciding to leave the party. In 1967, he joined hands with an assortment of Left and communist leaders to form the first United Front government—the first coalition rule in West Bengal's political history. On 15 March 1967, Ajoy Kumar Mukherjee became West Bengal's first non-Congress chief minister.

The turmoil outside soon reached our eventless home. My mother, suddenly, almost out of the blue, fell into depression and quickly turned into a patient of violent schizophrenia. Our home came to be known as a madhouse, ridiculed by the neighbours in whispers and sympathized by a few well-wishers. The existential foundation of my sister's childhood and mine was shaken to the roots. The insufferable agony continued for years even after we shifted to Kolkata, only to end with my mother's premature passing away, leaving a gaping and incurable wound in our minds. Schizophrenic patients, I learnt much later, normally live twelve to fifteen years less than an average healthy person.

3
Campbell Sahib's Legacy

George Campbell, the lieutenant governor of Bengal from 1871 to 1874, the son of George Campbell of Edenwood, had annoyed George Campbell, the Secretary of State for India, in the early 1870s, by siding with the peasants of Pabna district during their rebellion against the local zamindars' tyranny in 1873. He was a man of sharp intellect and, as a Civil Service officer, was a cut above most of his contemporaries. He was a Doctor of Civil Law from Oxford University and penned tomes, like *Modern India* (1852), *Ethnology of India* (1868) and *Tenure of Land in India* (1870).

Campbell Sahib was also, in a sense, the architect of the Bengal Tenancy Act, 1885, that sought to reverse many of the disastrous clauses of the Permanent Settlement Act and considerably improved the legal rights of the *ryats* (landowning peasants).

It was, therefore, quite befitting that this man gave Bengal's most revered educational institution a permanent address by inaugurating a new building for Presidency College on 31 March 1874.

Exactly a hundred years later, I walked through the gates of the same building on College Street to collect admission forms for graduate courses in history and political science. The idea was to take tests for both, hoping to qualify for at least one. I qualified for both and chose history. Within weeks, with a pounding heart, I was standing before the grand staircase that led to our department on the first floor: the same flight of stairs had quietly borne the weight of such persons as Jagadish Chandra Bose, Prafulla Chandra Roy, Ashutosh Mukhopadhyay, Swami Vivekananda, Subhas Chandra Bose, Satyendranath Bose, Rajendra Prasad, Meghnad Saha, Prasanta Chandra Mahalanobis and Amartya Sen, to name just a few of the stalwarts who, in many senses, shaped the course of history of not only Bengal but also of the whole of India in the nineteenth and twentieth centuries.

This is the college that was the cradle of the nineteenth-century Bengal Renaissance, from which dawned India's sense of modernity. No other single educational institution in the country has produced so many pioneers in every imaginable field—from the pure sciences to literature to religion to politics, the social sciences, statistics and economics.

If Presidency College gave modern India many of its wisest minds, it was also the hotbed for the Naxal movement—the most radical challenge to conventional wisdom in India following independence. Some of the movement's sharpest brains debated within the precincts of this college and decided to kill and die for a cause they passionately believed in. If Siddhartha Shankar Ray was a product of the college, so was Timir Baran Singha, who was brutally murdered by the police for being a Naxal, but has been immortalized in a heart-rending poem by one of our finest contemporary poets, Sankha Ghosh, again, a Presidencian.

Forty years down the line, while arguing over such an institution, I received, perhaps, the rudest snubbing in my life. 'You are suffering from an ill-timed nostalgia,' my daughter, Tupur, told me. She had just decided to opt for St Stephen's College, in Delhi, ignoring, disdainfully, her father's alma mater. The Left Front regime's suicidal ideological war against 'bourgeois elitism in government-funded educational institutions' had turned Bengal's academia into desolate ruins. Even Presidency College could not stand the onslaught of the arrogant stupidity that was the hallmark of the CPI(M)'s educational policy. And the last rites of the colossal institution have been read over the past few years, under the Trinamool Congress amid tumultuous celebrations over upgrading it to Presidency University. The off-the-record anecdotes of nepotism, incompetence and spineless surrender of the institution's highest administrative heads in the face of rude interference of the ruling political party, which reach my desk through my able reporting team regularly, are shocking. Indeed, today's Presidency has nothing more to offer other than nostalgia.

∽

Our History (Honours) class had twenty-six students, twenty-two of whom were girls. Once again, I felt like a stranger in my new educational institution. The first thing that I noticed on entering the classroom was that all my fairer gender classmates came from English-medium backgrounds and preferred to 'taak Inglis, waak Inglis, laaff Inglis and run Inglis', a la Amitabh Bachchan in *Namak Halal*. Most of them also dressed 'Inglis'. And there I was, marooned in that anglophone world with a spoken English that could barely convey my thoughts.

It offered me some comfort to see the remaining three boys huddled on the last bench, visibly nervous as the girls chirped away in the 'funny language'. The sense of alienation and the crisis of identity, however, did not last very long. Of course, a few of them were quick on the uptake and were brilliant. But most of the others, academically, were on par with me, at best. Moreover, their cloistered upbringing in sanitized environments at their homes and schools had left them innocent at large, just beginning to decipher the myriad colours of life beyond the strict vigil of guardians. In this adventure, I soon became their pathfinder.

Most of my classmates, for example, were so polite and well-mannered that their repertoire of Bengali khisti (abuses) did not travel beyond 'shala', i.e. 'sala' in Hindi and brother-in-law in English. Again I leave it to researchers into the strange idiosyncrasies of languages to explain why in certain Indian languages such an innocuous relative as the brother-in-law should be made to symbolize an ass! Do they do that anywhere else in the world? I don't know! Anyway, as I soon realized, the vast world of Bengali expletives lay before them unexplored. But soon I also discovered that behind their 'Inglis' dazzle many of them had warm hearts and long-suppressed carefree minds, itching to take the plunge into the bustle of the real world.

With some of the girls I became as close as a family member. I taught them Bengali abuses, dirty Bengali parodies of famous songs, little-known secrets about politicians, inspired them to bunk boring classes to accompany me either to Kolkata's legendary Coffee House, just across the street, or a film show, and helped them prepare for the Bengali exam that we had to take compulsorily along with our honours courses. In return, they paid much of my bills everywhere, protected me in my hours of crisis and helped me generously with their notes.

All this, however, was strictly within the limits of friendship. Only once did I overstep that limit and wrote a passionate love letter in Bengali to a beautiful girl in my class. The very next day she spurned my offer so charmingly that I could neither feel the hurt nor got angry. Towards the end of my college life though, I found my love, not in Presidency, but in Scottish Church College. I married Kasturi in 1982. I was 25 and she, 24.

Our faculty was no big shake: a motley combination of good, bad and boring. My father, Sunil Chattopadhyay, shouldered the heaviest responsibilities, teaching over three years, two papers carrying one-fourth of the total marks. For the first two years, he taught ancient Indian history, and in the third year ancient Greece.

He was a disciple of two of his legendary professors, Kuruvilla Zakaria and Sushobhan Sarkar, and emulated them while teaching. Unlike many others, he would not sit while delivering his lectures and would always use the blackboard to explain unfamiliar words or jargon. As a result, he would always get a full captive class. I felt proud to be his son.

Among our other teachers, I particularly remember Hirendranath Chakraborty, a fascinating human being. For a while he was also at Krishnagar College with my father and then left for England to do postdoctoral research. His wife and only child stayed back in London and got domiciled there but he came back to continue with his teaching job. He smoked an English briar with English tobacco from which emanated a heavenly aroma. He allowed us to smoke and drink in his presence, brewed and served fine European coffee in huge mugs and often accompanied some of us to various drinking joints. Once I brought a bottle of Bangla to a friend's place where Prof Chakroborty was also present. To our great surprise, he finished off the bottle and got so drunk that I had to carry him back home in his car.

Ajay Bannerjee was the other professor all of us loved and adored. Unlike my father, he sat while teaching and explained to us complicated historical phenomenon in elegant, lucid English. He looked like a 'Glaxo baby', loved to eat and feed others and had a brilliant sense of humour.

ങ

The first person with whom I struck an almost instant camaraderie in college was Somak Roy from the physics department, three years senior to me. A few days into college, I picked Somak Da as my guru.

Somak Da had the build of a Santhal man—athletic—straight out of some Ramkinkar Baij sculpture. He had a set of Colgatewhite teeth and a laughter that would unsettle a gecko from the wall. He came from St Lawrence High School, a Jesuit institution located in my neighbourhood. No one could remotely remember when Somak Da was last spotted, either in class or the laboratory. He headed straight to the canteen and, on many occasions, left it bodily carried by his friends and crouched into a taxi for home well past midnight. He was impressed with my forays into hooch dens and became particularly pally when he found out that I had enough willing girlfriends who would fund our drinking bouts.

This was all fun for us, his chelas. For his girlfriend, Aparajita Di, however, it was an endless nightmare. Her love for Somak Da was pure and her commitment to him unflinching. Contrary to many doomsday predictors, their marriage has been a complete success, thanks primarily to the wife.

But then Somak Da was brilliant in more senses than one. He had a sharp mathematical brain, which was at the same time a huge repository of the finest of contemporary Bengali poems. He had the rare talent of drawing pencil sketches of anyone he saw. He was a great debater in both English and Bengali and an avid chess player. He was an astute political strategist. And he had the most devastating punch during drunken brawls. Surprisingly, none of this brilliance was reflected in his later life and career. He had a decent job in a bank, from which he took voluntary retirement, and now earns his living by offering tuition in mathematics to senior students. In his drawing room he has built a bar counter, where he ceremoniously fills a glass with liquor, sets it on the countertop, walks to the other side of the counter, drinks it and walks back to pour the next glass with equal aplomb.

To the college union run by the Chhatra Parishad (West Bengal is the only state in which the students' wing of the Congress is not the NSUI), Somak Da was the guiding light but never an office-bearer. I loved and adored him but he never invited me to join student politics.

My invitation to join the Chhatra Parishad college unit came from two other seniors—Bhaskar Chakraborty and Arunava Ghosh. While the former is now a professor of history at Calcutta University, Arunava is the only one among our college contemporaries who continues his flirtation with politics, besides being a prominent and influential advocate at the Calcutta High Court.

Once a bastion of the ultra-radicals, Presidency in the mid-1970s was under the unassailable influence of the Congress's student wing. Once in a while, the Chhatra Parishad strongmen would bash recalcitrant students with pronounced Left leanings. If a Naxalite, even of yesteryears, could be spotted anywhere on the campus, he would be either chased out or brought to the union's common room and given merciless 'third degree'. I was too young to have any active role in this and scrupulously stayed away from these ugly episodes. Naxalism was stamped out from the campus and Presidency students had no sympathy for parliamentary communists like the CPI(M).

At long last and after much debate it was agreed that we should have a free and fair student union election. So it was. Only Somak Da took charge of the college telephone in the bursar's office and kept calling those girls who we suspected might have the audacity to vote against us. Every time their parents picked up the phone, he had a simple message: 'Do you want your grandchild to look like me? If not, please do not send your daughter to college on the day of the election.'

Arunava, on his part, flexed his muscles outside and gathered a large number of fellow student leaders from various other colleges, principally from the Hardinge Hostel nearby, ostensibly to provide us 'moral support'! That was the day I was introduced to a tall, handsome, turbaned Sikh youth from Hardinge Hostel who spoke fluent Bengali. A lad from Asansol, he was already a known face in the Congress and earned notoriety for all kinds of 'dadagiri', which, it was rumoured, also involved revolvers. Much later, I found him in Delhi as a prominent member of Rajiv Gandhi's shouting brigade before he switched over to the BJP and became the party's vocal Rajya Sabha member. He is Surendrajeet Singh Ahluwalia.

Anyway, the 'free and fair election' passed off smoothly for us in which I too became a class representative, winning my seat with a thumping majority. I was made the secretary of the Rabindra Parishad, the college's cultural affairs body.

But then came June 1975. Fissures began to appear within the Chhatra Parishad. On 26 June, Indira Gandhi forced Emergency on the nation. Many of us felt obliged to oppose such a draconian action. The factional feud within the Congress had already come to the surface. Now it invaded our campus too. The rise of Sanjay Gandhi changed the course of politics both within the Congress and outside, definitely for the worse.

Nationally, Indira Gandhi stood discredited and humiliated after the Allahabad High Court nullified her election victory in its verdict on 12 June. Jayaprakash Narayan's Navnirman agitation captured the popular imagination across India. He became a national icon, the Mahatma's reincarnation, almost overnight. JP, as he was called, started his own version of non-cooperation and civil disobedience movement against the Congress government. He even appealed to the armed forces to respond to his clarion call. During his whirlwind countrywide tour before the Emergency, he also came to Kolkata and led a mammoth anti-Congress procession that passed through the College Street. On the Presidency campus we felt uncomfortable and our confidence began to be shaken with every unfolding event in national politics.

In the student union, we debated and then decided to oppose Indira Gandhi's continuation in office calling the decision brazenly undemocratic. We also decided to show black flags to Sanjay Gandhi when he came to the adjacent Calcutta University campus and stood in an open jeep with his wife, Maneka, by his side. He was showered with flowers and a huge procession of khadi-clad Congressmen followed him into the university.

Dr Satyen Sen, then vice chancellor, shamelessly vacated his official chair for Indira Gandhi's son to sit and address a gathering of the so-called intellectuals handpicked and rehearsed by the party. Five of us stood in front of our college gate and unfurled our black flags as Sanjay's convoy came very close. The sight created a momentary flutter among those walking in the procession and they looked at us as if we were animals of an unknown species.

Somak Da, among the five of us, was already dead drunk and stood there for a longer time than necessary and we had to drag him inside. Our token show of defiance to the emerging villain emboldened our spirits and we decided to oppose Sanjay by all means, even if that invited retribution from the police or the state authorities. Soon we found a mentor and guide in Priya Ranjan Dasmunsi, who, despite being so close to Indira Gandhi, was falling quickly from Sanjay's grace and was, at the same time, emerging as an alternative power centre within the Congress.

Dasmunsi hated Sanjay, opposed his Maruti misadventure and his authoritarian style of functioning. Every evening, Arunava would take me to his small office in Bhawanipore to seek guidance in those troubled times. Soon, he asked me to write for his popular Bengali weekly, *Dakshini Barta*. I wrote several signed articles as well as the unsigned editorials in which I tore apart Sanjay and his hoodlum brigade. I soon discovered, to my utter amazement, that such journalistic pieces came to me quite effortlessly. Priya Da, as we called him affectionately, became my hero. When he chose to part company with the Congress and joined the breakaway faction, we stood by him as his intellectual assistants.

In college, we started our own bilingual magazine, called *Presidencian*, and began visiting all those who, like us, opposed the Emergency and collected their articles for our publication. Among them was Gour Kishore Ghosh, then a senior journalist for ABP, and my would-be guru in journalism. While in jail, after being arrested for opposing the Emergency, he had complained of chest pain. He was kept in a state hospital for treatment under police protection. Among the established journalists he was the most vocal and fearless critic of the Emergency. He lampooned Indira Gandhi and her son in his inimitable satirical columns under the pseudonym, Rupadarshi. I visited Gour Kishore just once and he gave us a small piece that we smuggled out in connivance with a friendly hospital employee.

Barun Sengupta, another celebrated political journalist of ABP, was also arrested by the Siddhartha Shankar Ray government to teach him a lesson. He was beyond our reach as he was then kept in various small-town jails.

Jyotirmoy Datta, a brilliant journalist of *The Statesman*, went underground, changing shelter every night to evade arrest. Both Gour Kishore and Jyotirmoy believed strongly in symbolism. Gour Kishore shaved his head and walked publicly with a dog leash around his neck to mourn the demise of democratic rights. Jyotirmoy vowed to walk bare feet everywhere until the Emergency was lifted. His cat-and-mouse game did not last long as he was soon trapped by Lalbazar (headquarters of the Kolkata Police) detectives. Gour, Barun and Jyotirmoy cast deep shadows on me. I soon started nurturing the ambition of following in their footsteps.

Leela Roy, wife of Annada Shankar Roy (one of Bengal's leading intellectuals and an ICS officer from the British era), encouraged us, but, at the same time, stuck a note of elderly caution. Annada Shankar was then in his seventies but did not hesitate to air his grievances against desecration of democratic institutions all around. In those days, because of strict press censorship, no mainstream newspaper could afford to carry any news or views that in any way opposed the government. Annada

Shankar, therefore, chose a well-respected Bengali trimonthly, *Alekhya*, to unequivocally ventilate his grievances, writing a series of scathing essays. Khitindra Chandra Ghosal, the editor of the journal, happened to be my uncle, my father's first cousin. He was a staunch nationalist and taught English literature at the reputed Narendra Ramakrishna Mission College. The imposition of Emergency disturbed him so much that he regularly boarded the suburban trains to hawk his periodical, encouraging passengers to read them. In brief, the intellectual and political resistance to the Emergency was overwhelming in Bengal.

The police did not harass us till we called an indefinite strike and closed the Presidency College in April 1976, drawing huge attention from the media. Till then, Presidency College never allowed admission tests except in English, a colonial elitist hangover that did not provide a level playing ground for aspirants from Bengali-medium schools. Consequently, many bright students, weak in English but very strong in their subjects could not compete fairly with their English-medium counterparts. I took the initiative to motivate the student union to support the cause as the admission season drew closer.

We petitioned to the principal to change the rule and gheraoed him several times till police intervened and dispersed us. The principal, a good-natured chemistry professor, sympathized with our cause but pleaded his helplessness. He needed a nod from Writers' Buildings, the administrative headquarters of the state government, to change such a time-honoured policy and tradition. As soon as the admission process started for the year, we called an indefinite strike and sat in dharna in the college portico. Arunava, true to his wont, started a fast-unto-death and further aggravated the crisis. The college ground to a complete halt.

After a couple of days, Chief Minister Siddhartha Shankar Ray, known to be one of Indira Gandhi's closest advisers, swung into action. Several Congress leaders and ministers came to the college as his emissaries to persuade us to withdraw the strike and come to the negotiating table. We remained defiant. After a week, Ajit Kumar Panja, then health minister, came to announce an invitation from the chief minister. He told us to form a delegation and accompany him to meet Ray at Writers' Buildings. At the venue of the demonstration, Somak Da lay hidden somewhere in the crowd, half-asleep. Hearing the minister, who spoke to us using a microphone, Somak Da stood up and shouted back, 'Tell that playboy he will have to come here to talk to us. We won't go.' A humiliated Panja left immediately amid wild cheers and booing of the students.

Soon rumours spread that some of us would be picked up by the police to break the strike. None of us panicked. We stayed wide awake, singing in chorus, smoking, and Somak Da drinking, as usual.

It was illegal to organize a strike anywhere during those black days of Emergency. The chief minister thundered many times in his press conferences threatening us. Yet we remained unfazed. Throughout the day the portico of the college remained crowded with student sympathizers. We spotted in the crowd some known faces from the detective department. We offered them tea, biscuits once in a while, and even booze during their and our night-long vigils. After a few days, they turned into double agents and gave us all necessary tip-offs about what was happening in the two red buildings, the police and the administrative headquarters, in BBD Bag, the city's administrative district. One of the detectives was a talented singer and a fan of Kishore Kumar. During his night duty, he entertained us with all the popular songs of Rajesh Khanna. Winning over the police was easier than breaking the chief minister's arrogant resolve.

The war of nerves that continued for almost two weeks finally ended when, pitted against our resolve and united determination, Siddhartha Shankar Ray was forced to blink first. The helpless and harassed principal came down to the portico to announce our victory. The colonial edifice stood breached. Did Campbell Sahib turn in his grave? Or did his spirit chuckle at the thought that finally even the Presidency College gates were open to the ryats' sons and daughters?

4
My Gurus

Among various other things, he was a small-time electrician, 'rescuer' of air-raid victims in the British government's Air Raid Precaution Unit that was formed in 1941 after the Japanese bombing of Kolkata, private tutor, temporary contractor for a timber merchant, foreman at a military aerodrome, salesman, insurance agent, dishwasher at a restaurant, proofreader and clerk at the land customs office.

The *Asiaweek* magazine described him as 'a rare tiger' after he received the Ramon Magsaysay Award in 1981. He was the quintessential rebel among journalists in Bengal. He was Gour Kishore Ghosh. And exactly as the great conservationist Jim Corbett had described the tiger, Gour Kishore was, above all, a 'large-hearted gentleman with boundless courage'.

He was my first guru in the profession.

Even though I managed to get a first-class postgraduate degree in modern history from Calcutta University simply by diligently mugging up answers to all predictable questions, the only thing I was good at was Bengali prose writing, an ability I put to good use during my undergraduate years in Presidency College. Thus, for me joining vernacular journalism in Bengali was a natural call.

Then there was my professor–father who wanted me to follow in his footsteps and take up teaching, a suggestion I could not readily disregard. However, I was delighted when the West Bengal College Service Commission found me suitable for a lecturer's job in a college in the distant railway town of Kharagpur where Mahendra Singh Dhoni worked as a ticket collector before embarking on a successful cricketing career. My mother was keeping indifferent health and, as the only son, my presence at home in Kolkata was a necessity. Even my father saw no merit in my leaving home for such an inconsequential job. It was 1981.

Destiny intervened. I landed up at a lecture by Gour Kishore Ghosh, organized by the United States Information Service (USIS) at its Chowringhee office. Post lecture, during the interactive session, I entered into a heated argument with the speaker over an issue I have now forgotten. My angry rebuttals didn't antagonize him. At the end of the event he called me aside and asked about my antecedents. 'I see. So you are Chhabi Da's son. Meet me at my office tomorrow. Since you are interested in journalism let me inform you I am starting a newspaper soon,' he said before leaving. My father Sunil's nickname was Chhabi and he was a close friend of Santosh Kumar Ghosh, arguably the doyen of modern Bengali journalism and the main architect of ABP's commercial success. He contributed regularly to both ABP and the English daily, *Hindustan Standard*. Gour Kishore, for a long time, was Santosh's colleague at the ABP.

Soon Gour Kishore asked me to appear for an interview for the position of a junior subeditor in his new-found daily, *Aajkaal*, which had its office at one of Kolkata's famous mansions known as the Laha Bari. There, on the ground floor I found the editor banging away on an old typewriter only with the index finger of his right hand, behind a nondescript wooden desk in a corner of a huge room. For several minutes there were no visible signs of him noticing my arrival. Finally he looked up. Then followed a long narration of the hurdles I would be asked to overcome before I could be considered for the coveted job.

I was told that I have to take a written test. If I passed that, I would be asked to submit a dissertation of around 5,000 words. If that was found impressive enough I would be called for an interview. If I cleared that too, I would have to face yet another interview with the editorial board of the newspaper. Emerging out of that unscathed would mean a job as a journalist in the paper with a princely salary of ₹650 per month. That I was 'Chhabi Da's son' and that it was he who had asked me to meet him for a job would be of no effect in this regard, he told me bluntly. The only criterion was merit.

I wasn't seeking any favour from him using my father's name as a calling card. So his weird, impervious and arrogant behaviour strengthened my resolve. And I did top the list of applicants for the job who took the written test, which took me one step closer to my first journalism guru.

Gour Kishore was an amazing human being besides being a great journalist of his time. He was born on 23 June 1923, in Jessore district of what is now Bangladesh. His father left home for good when Gour Kishore was 18 and had just cleared the intermediate examination in science securing a first division. He became, per force, the only breadwinner for his family, which included his mother and unmarried sisters. That marked the end of his student life.

Job hunting began. Even as he was shifting between all kinds of sundry jobs, trying his best to make two ends meet, Gour Kishore also became deeply involved with the Communist Party of India (CPI). Sometime in 1945, the party sent him to Lalmonirhat in north Bengal. After being constantly harassed by the police, he was asked by the party to go and work with the Darjeeling Himalayan Railway workers. While living with and organizing the railway workers, Gour Kishore met a sincere, honest and dedicated local leader, who later metamorphosed in one of his stories into the famous Sagina Mahato, which was adapted into a wonderful film by one of our leading directors Tapan Sinha, with Dilip Kumar and Saira Banu in lead roles.

His experiences as a trade union worker steadily disillusioned him with the CPI. Instead, he gradually became a disciple of M.N. Roy, and for the rest of his life remained a radical humanist. Manabendra Nath Roy, whose real name was Narendra Nath Bhattacharya, was one of the main founders of the communist parties of Mexico and India. During his days in the Soviet Union, he engaged himself in frequent debates with Vladimir Lenin and later became disenchanted with Stalin's excesses and formed the Radical Democratic Party in India. It attracted many young politicians including S.R. Bommai, who later on became Karnataka's chief minister. In Kolkata, several intellectual stalwarts such as Shiv Narayan Ray and Amlan Dutta were deeply influenced by Ray.

Gour Kishore's first foray into journalism began in 1949 as a proofreader at *The Times of India*'s first Bengali daily, *Satyayug*. In 1950, he began writing a column in *Desh*, a weekly magazine published by ABP. His pieces in these columns are scathing testaments of his times. He also wrote a fair bit of literature. But first and foremost, he was a satirist. All his columns were accompanied by cartoons drawn by Kutty, a Malayali artist who studied Bengali politicians brilliantly. One of his cartoons still adorns a wall in former President Pranab Mukherjee's Kolkata residence. With Gour Kishore's death, the glorious genre of satire writing died in Bengali journalism. And the brilliant genre of cartoons in Bengali newspapers died with Kutty's retirement.

For him, freedom of expression and espousing democratic values were non-negotiable for any civilized existence. No power on earth, no allurement of any kind could influence or restrain him from acting on his faith when the situation so demanded, a glowing obstinacy that cost him dearly on many occasions.

Gour Kishore was a visionary. He was also an activist

journalist dedicated completely to the causes he championed, individual freedom and secularism topping the list. He was one of the few Bengali intellectuals who devoted all his life trying to understand the Muslim life, their problems and aspirations, their sense of alienation, their social behaviour and customs as also the reasons for frequent communal strife.

His much acclaimed trilogy, *Jal Pade Pata Nade, Prem Nei* and *Pratibeshi*[3], a moving saga of Muslim life before and after the Partition, was based entirely on arduous ground research. The Bhagalpur riots in the late 1980s shook him so vigorously that he kept on visiting the place over and over again to chronicle the incidents. His research continued till he breathed his last. In December 1992, when parts of Kolkata witnessed predictable communal tension following the demolition of the Babri mosque, he promptly took to the streets and organized peace marches in the affected areas, despite a serious health condition.

Till his death on 15 December 2000, Gour Kishore represented Bengal's fearless journalism. He spared no one. He maligned no one. He feared no one.

He was beaten up by the Congress government's police in 1953. In 1967, after he wrote a satire on Karl Marx and Mao Zedong, CPI(M) supporters ransacked the ABP office. While most employees fled, Gour Kishore stayed unmoved amid the vandals with his proverbial umbrella. Thankfully, the goons did not recognize him.

In July 1970, at the height of the Naxal movement, the radicals issued a death threat against Gour Kishore, for a scathing piece on their leader Charu Mazumdar. They conveyed to him the verdict in a letter that detailed the charges against him. Gour Kishore printed the whole letter and with it an even more scathing sarcastic piece.

---

[3] 'Leaves quiver with raindrops', 'There is no love' and 'Neighbours'

Just before Emergency was declared, Gour Kishore blasted the Congress government police again for their criminal treatment of the Naxal youths. The moment Emergency was declared, in a unique protest he shaved his head. He also wrote three articles opposing Emergency in *Kolkata*, a little-known magazine that used to be published by yet another fearless journalist, who was then with *The Statesman*, Jyotirmoy Datta. One of these three stirring pieces was addressed to his 13-year-old son, and explained why he had no choice but to put his family at great risk by opposing the Emergency.

Soon Gour Kishore was arrested and imprisoned in an eight-by-eight foot cell. But he kept writing from jail and smuggled the pieces out with the help of friends who visited him in jail.

Among those to whom Gour Kishore wrote regularly was Aveek Sarkar, then the de jure editor of ABP. Another brilliant journalist from ABP was also arrested during the Emergency: Barun Sengupta. He too wrote regular letters to Aveek Babu. Confiding in me, many years later, Aveek Babu had contrasted the two sets of letters he received during those days. The letters, he said, revealed the fundamental difference between the two persons: the former, a relentless crusader and the latter, a comfort-loving, successful journalist. While Gour Kishore, in his letters, urged him not to lose poise or patience in those hours of grave crisis, Sengupta mostly pleaded with Aveek Babu to pull the strings to secure his early release. Aveek Babu had preserved these with care in the drawer of his office desk. The fire that engulfed almost everything in the ABP office destroyed these letters too. 'Gour Babu belonged to a different genre, always upright and unwavering in his faith even under the most trying circumstances,' Aveek Babu had told me.

Gour Kishore suffered a third heart attack in jail, and was released from the prison in September 1976, on health grounds.

He returned to ABP but left it soon enough as he found the paper's brand of journalism politically partisan, stale and out of date. He floated *Aajkaal* after he found a non-resident Bengali promoter to bankroll his adventure. It was while appearing in the multi-layered tests for securing a job in this daily, that I met my second guru. Having cleared the written tests, I was asked to appear for an interview.

My examiner was a dark, bald, toothless, frail and angry-looking creature who seemed mightily bored and irritated with life. He did not bother to exchange greetings or pleasantries. As soon as I entered his small glass cubicle, he gave me an English newspaper with some paragraphs highlighted. 'You have just ten minutes to read it and answer my questions on the piece,' he said. It was a *London Times* post-editorial on some complicated environmental problem. I went to an adjacent, even smaller, room to read it as carefully as I could.

After ten minutes, I returned to my examiner's room only to find him snoring loudly on his chair, his mouth wide open, exhaling an unmistakable odour of alcohol, consumed last night. I stood there stunned for a while, not knowing what to do next. I tried to make all kinds of noises that are to be made in such situations: I cleared my throat again and again, indulged in a few bouts of mock coughs, rearranged the chair in front rather noisily and even tapped the table. Nothing happened. Finally, mustering all the courage I had, I caught him by his shoulders and shook him vigorously. Hamdi Bey emerged out of his deep slumber with a smile that will remain with me all my life.

'How did you find the passage?'

'Very boring. Also I found the author's pontificating tone rather disgusting.' I spoke my mind, encouraged by the examiner's friendly and warm behaviour. At this point he broke out into a loud laughter and offered me a Charminar—that hard-roasted filterless Vazir Sultan brand without smoking which you couldn't be intellectual enough in our times. Satyajit Ray's bright sleuth Feluda smoked nothing except Charminar, remember?

I hesitated. 'Tell me if you smoke or not,' he retorted rather angrily.

'Yes I do. But I am not sure whether I should smoke in your presence. You are almost my father's age.'

'In a newspaper there are only colleagues, no father-mother business. You should call me by my first name.'

I was surprised he was not asking me any questions about the passage I read and had almost forgotten by then. He lit my cigarette and said, 'You may go now. On your way out ask the next man to come in.'

On 9 February 1981, on the auspicious occasion of Saraswati Puja, I joined *Aajkaal* as a trainee journalist. A month and a half later, on 25 March, the newborn daily hit the stands. Satyajit Ray did the calligraphy of the paper's masthead. Our voyage began with Gour Kishore as the captain of the ship and Hamdi Bey as his first mate.

Between the two of them, Gour Kishore and Hamdi Bey had quite a few things in common. They were contemporaries in the profession, loved classical music, alcohol and the warm company of women. Hamdi, much more than Gour Kishore, whom he occasionally called Mahatma Gour. They were both self-taught, virtually having no worthwhile academic degrees. Gour Kishore, because of penury could not pursue his education beyond the Intermediate level, and Hamdi was just a matriculate when he left Chhapra district in Bihar and came to Kolkata to make a living.

Hamdi also in his early youth had become a disciple of M.N. Roy. He started his journalistic career with *Quest*, a party organ of the radical humanists, edited by Roy himself. Thereafter, he worked for various English newspapers, but was mostly with *The Statesman*. He was posted in Ranchi and Shillong and fell for the charm and natural beauty of the two towns. His articles on these places were later compiled and published under the title, *Small Towners*.

Hamdi was a heavy drinker and an avid bar-hopper. He also wrote a fascinating book on Kolkata's bars, describing their history and evolution, their individual attraction and also the connoisseurs who frequented these joints.

Hamdi regularly wrote *The Statesman*'s editorial pieces. These he used to write over lunch and drinks in one of the adjacent bars. 'I would write on any piece of paper I found in front of me, including the table napkins. A bearer from the newspaper would come in time to collect the copy and get it typed. Once proof-checked, he would return to the bar to show me the final copy. That was our regular routine,' Hamdi told me once to explain *The Statesman* culture of those days. His English was elegant but precise. His no-nonsense character reflected in what he wrote.

Hamdi's knowledge was encyclopaedic and interests varied—ranging from history and politics to gardening, trees, birds, volcanoes and cuisines. Surprisingly, he had no interest in sports. Hamdi's tailor-made copies were a treat first to read and then translate. A few days into my job, I became the undeclared translator of the 'Bey of Bengal'.

Hamdi was a quintessential bohemian and did not believe in the institution of marriage. He had lived with three women—separately, of course—but married none of them. He had a daughter by his third girlfriend who was our age, who also became a journalist. During his last years, he stayed with Jyotirmoy and Minakshi Datta in the same locality. When he died he left only his broken pair of glasses and soiled clothes.

Gour Kishore's decision to choose Hamdi as our trainer in the new newspaper, despite his scarce knowledge of Bengali, limited to broken conversation, was a master stroke. As a hands-on professional teacher and a valuable resource, Hamdi was irreplaceable. He taught us the basics, the grammar and the craftsmanship of journalism that transcended language barriers. He was able to inculcate in young minds the spirit of enquiry, an essential prerequisite of a successful career in journalism. More than anything else, his encyclopaedic knowledge was for us an easily accessible reservoir we could fall back on in the fledgling newspaper, without any worthwhile library services.

Late one night, when I was the shift in charge at the news desk, the teleprinters started jumping, violently ringing the bells. The paper had already gone to bed and we were enjoying a drink sitting on the courtyard staircase. I ran to the machine. I found a small two-part 'take' from the Agence France-Presse (AFP) announcing the deadly eruption of a volcano that was feared to have killed several thousand people. The story carried the dateline Chiapas. Then the machines fell silent and did not bother to wake up that night.

I was flummoxed and helpless. I realized it was a big story, but I did not know how to dig out more information to put the story in perspective. Also I did not know whether I should ask the press to stop printing and await the details. Delayed printing meant delayed distribution, a totally unwelcome prospect for a small newborn newspaper. My guts told me to take the risk and I stepped into the next room without wasting time.

Hamdi was sitting on a chair, his head reclining on the back, and he was snoring like an ox. I woke him up and told him my predicament. He went to the washroom, came back to his chair, put on his glasses and then asked me to take a dictation. In less than fifteen minutes he dictated a complete story indicating the exact location of the volcano in South America, the history of volcanic eruptions in the past half a century and how it could affect not only human lives but also the weather. Next morning we were flooded with the same story and its various versions all indicating what Hamdi had told me the previous night, which we had already printed. That afternoon I took him out for a drink and paid the cheque.

But then it was not always easy to work with Hamdi. In some cases he would be irritatingly obdurate. On one such day, Bangladesh President and Army General Ziaur Rahman was assassinated. Hamdi came to the office with his version of the story and insisted we carry it. Zia was killed by gunshots and everyone in the world said it. But Hamdi insisted he died in a mine explosion on his way to Dhaka, the country's capital.

Gour Kishore was not in town and there was none who could convince Hamdi to fall in line with conventional wisdom and follow agency reports. 'I have got the version from a source who can never go wrong. Just carry it. Else I will fire you right away,' he insisted. I had to oblige and the next morning all of us looked like fools. But Hamdi remained quite nonchalant, not even bothering to own up to his mistake. He just said, 'I have told my source that you are a son of a bitch, a scumbag.' Much later, I learnt he got the story from his friends in the US consulate. I felt reassured.

Training over, Hamdi started getting tremendously unpopular in an office environment dominated by inhibited Bengali middle-class mindset and sentiments. Ranjan Bannerjee, a well-known film critic and columnist, left the job on the very first day after encountering Hamdi in an informal interview. His intimidating behaviour, laced with choice four-letter abuses, appalled Ranjan so much that he went back to his college to reclaim his lecturer's job. He came back after Gour Kishore took it upon himself the difficult task of reassuring Ranjan and providing him immunity from Hamdi's overarching clutches.

Hamdi just did not understand what discipline meant in a newspaper office. He was one of the firsts to reach office every morning but would disappear any minute without bothering to inform anyone. No one knew whether he would come back or even if he did, exactly when. When the editor brought it up with him, Hamdi did not protest. But from the next day he started carrying his bottle of gin to the office. He would pour it in his glass brought from the office canteen and drink it intermittently—undiluted. When drunk, he would not disturb anyone, but straightaway go off to sleep on the chair. Often, he would doze off with a burning cigarette dangling from his lips. At other times he would piss in his trousers.

The spectacle shocked many and complaints against Hamdi started piling up on the editor's desk. Gour Kishore knew his friend better than anyone and continued to ignore them till it reached the employer. The editor was asked to summarily sack Hamdi. Gour Kishore agreed but added a condition: along with Hamdi his resignation too should be accepted. Hamdi survived, though not for long. When his editor friend departed he was left with no other choice but to quit silently.

After Gour Kishore left *Aajkaal* and rejoined the ABP, I was also suspended twice for drunken behaviour. On the first occasion I was at fault since I picked up a stick to beat the imbecile chief reporter and chased him out of office. The second time round, I just fell unconscious in the slippery toilet with my nose bleeding profusely.

My ties with Hamdi almost snapped after I joined ABP, more so after I was transferred to its Delhi Bureau in 1985. During my short and occasional visits to Kolkata, I enquired about him from Gour Kishore. One day, during one such visit, I was told that Hamdi was suffering from terminal throat cancer and counting his days.

Along with Gour Kishore, I went to see him. We left the office in the same car and Gour Kishore asked the driver to stop in front of an old wine store in Esplanade that used to be Hamdi's favourite when he was with *The Statesman*. He bought a bottle of Blue Riband gin to gift it to the ailing Hamdi. I was more shocked than surprised and found the gesture weird. Hamdi was looking like a skeleton, his throat covered by a soiled piece of paper. His eyes lit up as soon as he saw us and smiled. He was no longer in a position to talk, with a deep hole right in the middle of his throat. Gour Kishore smiled back and then asked an attendant to pour a few drop of gin in a glass. Hamdi looked more delighted. He took the glass, closed the cut on his throat with his fingers and gulped down the drink, some of it oozing out soiling his shirt. He then coughed for a while and wrote a note for Gour Kishore in Roman script but in Bengali. '*Sara jiban tumi khele cigar aar amar holo cancer?*' (You smoked cigar all your life, and I got cancer?) I could not hold my emotions and started to weep.

By the time Gour Kishore decided to leave ABP, the stranglehold of the ABP Group on mainstream Bengali literature and journalism was complete. Like a loyal Congressman in his party, in the ABP too, one could easily bask and prosper in the family-led and controlled feudalism, though enlightened and benevolent. You would be patronized for your talent and, once in the good books, you would be looked after even after you had turned into a fossil. The Sarkars were the best paymasters in the industry. Every act of omission and commission would be condoned and forgotten if you remained unwaveringly loyal. When time comes to call it a day, take a bow and fade out.

Once you have received such patronizing, never, however, commit the mistake of leaving the organization, driven by dreams or ambitions. If you do so, you would be immediately dubbed a 'gaddar', a veritable betrayer. The empire would strike back with all the force at its command.

Santosh Kumar Ghosh, another of the doyens of modern Bengali journalism and arguably the principal architect of ABP's commercial success failed to rebel even after his total marginalization in the establishment. He chose to languish for years in his own little chamber with a regular pay rise and all the trappings of power intact. He died in harness, in his superannuated borrowed times, a sad and broken man. But his patronizing masters picked up every tab of his expensive cancer treatment in the high-end hospitals of Mumbai and Kolkata.

Only two men of consequence had been able to quietly rebel and refused to embrace, beyond a point, this glorified slavery— Gour Kishore Ghosh and Barun Sengupta. Both left the ABP in the early 1980s. First Gour Da and then Barun Da. Many years later, I followed them. Like my guru, I too failed.

Barun Da did a V.P. Singh of sorts—launched his own Bengali daily, *Bartaman*, a success story from the beginning. But Gour Kishore followed Pranab Mukherjee and returned to the ABP fold leaving all of us, his recruits and dependents, almost in the lurch.

Yet when Gour Kishore left the ABP, he indeed had a dream, one of experimenting, to the extent possible, with a kind of alternative journalism that would be low on political overtone but rich in matters affecting human life in the contemporary world. In other words, he wanted to initiate in hackneyed Bengali journalism, a paradigm shift, quite in tune with the changing nature of problems and aspirations of the newer generations.

His model was hardly wrong. But he was a stubborn individual, uncompromising even in matters of day-to-day business. Consequently, he incurred the displeasure of the management of *Aajkaal*, regularly fell sick, had to be hospitalized and gradually found himself in a blind alley. His dream ended in a whimper. He resigned without a fuss.

Aveek Babu, having known the value of the man, promptly took him back in ABP.

5

'Aveek Wants You in *Anandabazar*'

A fragrant smoke mingled with the aroma of the best-quality imported coffee, which I later learnt to be Blue Mountain; huge dumps of books and periodicals, scattered and dusty; a large mahogany secretariat table; a cup and saucer of exquisite bone china; and behind it, on an expensive leather chair, a man in spotless snow-white dhoti–kurta, holding a Montecristo cigar between the index and middle fingers of his right hand. Every time I close my eyes to remember my first encounter with Aveek Sarkar, then editor-in-chief of ABP Group, this is the picture that conjures itself in my mind.

That was 2 May 1983. I had been summoned to his room, on the third floor of the office of the Group's flagship Bengali daily, *Anandabazar Patrika*. Besides a host of other weekly, fortnightly and monthly Bengali and English magazines, the Group had begun to publish, some fourteen months ago, an English daily—*The Telegraph*—with the country's youngest newspaper editor, M.J. Akbar, at the helm.

When I came out of Aveek Babu's room, I should have been arranging my future plans with joy, because it was a job interview and my mission had succeeded. Instead, I headed for the nearest cheap bar and downed several pegs of rum to steady my spinning head. That's how being with Aveek Babu in a closed room for an hour, for the first time in my life, had left me. That was not the last time, and I was not the only person to experience that spin.

I was told later that Aveek Babu, my would-be boss for the next twenty-two years, had very recently changed his attire from Western to impeccably Eastern, after taking charge of the Group following the sudden death of his father Ashok Sarkar. Family tradition, he had decided, must not be tampered with. The role model of the quintessential Bengali bhadralok is something that he inherited along with the reins of the Group.

During the interview, Aveek Babu didn't ask me any question about my educational background or my limited journalistic experience at *Aajkaal*. It was kind of a breezy monologue that touched upon various aspects of Bengali life, history and culture. Most of his views were unconventional and to unaccustomed ears seemed bizarre, almost shocking. He made it clear he did not subscribe to Bengalis' 'blind adulation' of Rabindranath Tagore, Subhas Chandra Bose or Satyajit Ray. For him, Tagore was just another poet. Tagore's experimental university, Shantiniketan, according to Aveek Babu, reflected pure retrograde thinking. Even though he acknowledged Ray's prowess as a film-maker, he did not think much of his films after the Apu trilogy. He was even more dismissive of Bose who, Aveek Babu felt, was no match for Mohandas Karamchand Gandhi and his shrewd brand of 'baniya politics'.

I liked his irreverent avant garde attitude but hated his dismissive tone and convoluted logic. Yet, suppressing the call of all my nerves, I suffered his arrogance and pomposity in silence as was prudent for a jobseeker.

Over the years, as I got to know him better, I realized that was an integral part of the man's argumentative character. He loved to shock his visitor with outrageous comments on events and personalities. For him, presenting a counter-narrative to conventional wisdom, as long as I knew him at least, was an interesting pastime. He enjoyed the baffled look on the listener's face. Gradually, I also learnt the art of suffering his eccentricities.

Twenty-two years later, on 1 October 2005, I quit the Group which by that time had been renamed as the ABP Group. Over this period I had been part of the process by which a fairly large newspaper group emerged into a media empire shaping, besides Bengali journalism, the average Bengali's taste for art, literature and culture. On the personal front, these years also took me to places and gave me opportunities to meet persons at national and international historic moments. I blossomed into a journalist under Aveek Sarkar's tutelage.

Initially, I was appointed for a periodical that was to be named *Sanando*, but it never saw the light of day. I spent six months for the aborted exercise before being transferred to ABP in December 1983. During this leisurely period, I came into close contact with a number of literary luminaries and got an insight into the working of 6 Prafulla Sarkar Street, the most coveted and sought-after address for anyone wanting to pursue literary or journalistic ambitions.

However, I neither felt excited nor had a sense of déjà vu as I climbed the marbled staircases to be part of Bengal's hallowed cultural Mecca. The idea of joining a magazine was hardly tempting as I always wanted to be a newspaper journalist. Also, I greatly missed the warm, friendly, informal working atmosphere in the company of colleagues of my age in the palatial atrium-centred Victorian building that housed *Aajkaal*. For the unintended and untimely break in my career I could only curse Gour Kishore, who, after having lured me into this profession, suddenly left his paper without any prior notice. Even as I followed him to ABP, Gour Kishore did not have any role in my new employment. I could not even make out if he felt happy seeing me there.

In the building packed with honeycomb cubicles on every floor I felt uncomfortable and claustrophobic. In the new and virtually alien atmosphere I could only draw comfort from the fact that Santosh Kumar Ghosh, the editor of the proposed magazine was well known to me, being the closest childhood friend of my father. Badal was his pet name and I called him Badal Kaka. In no time the close personal bond developed into a closer filial relationship.

My father and Santosh studied together in Rajbari High School in Faridpur district of erstwhile East Bengal. Santosh was a bright student. Bengali language was both Santosh and my dad's forte. The love for language and literature brought the two friends closer and the friendship lasted till Santosh died in February 1985. He was only 64. At Keoratala, the city's famous crematorium, my father wept like a child.

While my father took to teaching, Santosh, forced by his family's acute financial difficulties, started his journalistic career pretty early in life, working for two newspapers simultaneously in day and night shifts. In 1951, he went to Delhi as the news editor of *Hindustan Standard*. Seven years later, he came back to Kolkata to take charge of the Group's flagship Bengali newspaper, turned it into a behemoth and took it to unassailable heights. By any reckoning, Santosh Kumar Ghosh was the architect of what we know as modern Bengali journalism.

He was also bilingual, a distinction quite common among Bengali elite in yesteryears. Legend has it that Santosh Babu could dictate two editorials simultaneously in Bengali and English on two different subjects for ABP and *Hindustan Standard*. In the era of letter press, he would stand between two tables to oversee the pages of the two newspapers being 'made' at the same time. His English was Victorian, but his Bengali, although somewhat stiff for the uninitiated, bore the stamp of his genius.

Both Gour Kishore and Santosh wore two hats, one of a journalist and another of a littérateur. Both had authored a number of novels and short stories. Santosh took particular care to bring into ABP's fold eminent authors, creative writers and poets who lent a literary aura to even the journalistic content of the newspaper, making it so much more readable, leading to its wide acceptance among literature-loving Bengalis. However, that presentation style bordering on fictionalization, although popular, robbed the paper of much of its credibility. The change came after Aveek Babu succeeded his father as the editor-in-chief of the Group.

Even in 1983, when I joined the Group, among my new colleagues were Sunil Gangopadhyay, Shirshendu Mukhopadhyay, Shakti Chattopadhyay, Syed Mustafa Siraj, Moti Nandi, Ramapada Chowdhury and Nirendranath Chakraborty: a virtual who's who of contemporary Bengali literature. The office, it seemed to me, was a paradise for autograph seekers.

When I joined ABP, Santosh was well past his prime, virtually a drag on the Group's owners. When Ashok Sarkar died in February 1983 following a massive cardiac arrest while delivering a lecture at the city's celebrated book fair, Santosh hoped to be the paper's editor. To many, it was a legitimate ambition for the most deserving person in the Group. He was shattered to see Aveek Sarkar's name instead in the next morning's edition. In order to appease the grand old man, the Sarkars dangled before him the challenge and promise of launching a new periodical that would carry Santosh's name as the editor. Predictably though, that periodical was never printed.

Many years later, I had asked Aveek Babu why Santosh had been denied his due. He smugly replied, 'How can an alcoholic be trusted with such an important responsibility?'

Alcoholic he was. I have a childhood memory of Santosh landing at our home in Jhargram one late evening so drunk that he could barely stand on his feet. My father was not at home and my frightened mother shut the door on his face. The next morning he came back sober, totally oblivious of the previous night's incident, to stay with us for a few days. My father, otherwise a teetotaller and a stern disciplinarian, strangely found no fault with his friend's erratic, inebriated behaviour. Suffering a drunk Santosh used to be quite an ordeal.

As children, my sister and I, however, always looked forward to his rare visits while we were in Krishnanagar and Jhargram. His visit meant a joyous ride with all the family members to some nearby place as Santosh always came in his chauffeur-driven car. It also meant loosening of restrictions and prohibitions on my movements as my father would remain immersed in conversation with his friend all the time. A well-known author and journalist, his visit would temporarily enhance our prestige in the neighbourhood as also among my friends. For a few hours I could bask in his reflected glory.

Santosh Kumar Ghosh was also my first childhood hero. I must have thought, why not become a hack if that makes you so rich and famous?

Following my appointment in the Group in 1983, my job was to give Santosh constant company in office and outside, an experience I loved when he was in a cheerful mood and dreaded when he was drunk or agitated. It was difficult to keep pace with his mercurial temperament at a time when he felt neglected, left out, nourishing a grudge against the owners for quietly ignoring his claims to the paper's editorship. He used to tell me often, 'I am living on borrowed times.'

I sympathized with Santosh as I was aware of his importance in the Group as long as Ashok Sarkar was alive. Between the two, they shared a unique relation based upon mutual trust and respect. With anecdotes of their joint trips and sharing of hotel rooms, he strove hard to explain how he considered Ashok Babu as the guardian of the publishing house as indeed of him. The power and freedom that Ghosh wielded would not have been possible without the benevolent patronage of his mentor; the two men together scripted the success story of Bengal's most popular, influential media venture.

Three of Ashok Babu's four sons—Aveek, Arup and Adhip—took charge of ABP's affairs after their father's demise. Santosh always had a soft corner for Arup, who saw to it that the old man, shorn of powers and responsibilities, continued to enjoy his fat salary and perks. The admiration was mutual. Arup often went out of his way to accommodate Santosh, who was becoming increasingly cantankerous. I was present during one such incident.

One morning, just as I was entering his office, he stormed out of his room and screamed at me, 'Sanando is never going to happen. You look for a job elsewhere.' On most other days, he would take me along when he left office, be it to some bar or the myriad social events that he had to attend. But not on that day; I feared that he might never return. I did not have the guts to call his residence to find out, so I wandered about listlessly and finally went home.

The next morning, to my great relief and surprise, I found that Santosh had arrived at the office before me. His man Friday for forty years, our office peon, Gunadhar Da, assured me that all was well. With a broad smile, Santosh himself filled the missing links of the jigsaw. Apparently, on learning about his fiery exit, Arup traced him at a bar and personally drove down to the place. 'Do you know, Arup told me that I was like their father and had no business to contemplate leaving ABP. He is right. They are indeed my children. I cannot leave them.' This man, I told myself, would never resign.

Notwithstanding his unpredictable behaviour, Santosh still had sparks left in him. For example, after much thought he came up with an idea of serializing in Sanando a novel that would be written by twelve authors. Yet, to my surprise, when he drew a list of possible authors, none of them were from the Group. It would be a community novel—a long-lost tradition in Bengali literature.

I was also witness to his unmatched brilliance as a professional. After Sunil Gangopadhyay won the Sahitya Akademi award, M.J. Akbar approached Santosh with a request to write for the *Sunday* magazine of *The Telegraph*. I watched bemused, sitting at the other end of the table, how M.J. coaxed him into writing this piece.

'Santosh Da, you are the best man to write on Sunil,' said M.J. 'Who else is there in this office with such an equal command over both Bengali and English?'

'When is the deadline?'

'Tomorrow morning,' said M.J. 'You know how hard-pressed we are on deadlines.' Ghosh was beaming even after M.J. left his room. 'You heard for yourself what he said. After all, Akbar is no fool!'

The piece had to be based on a conversation with Sunil. It was arranged that Sunil and Santosh would meet at a restaurant in Great Eastern Hotel that evening. 'Stay back in office. I will come back and dictate the piece to you,' Ghosh said as he left for the conversation.

That evening was a test of patience for me. It was scheduled to be a short tête-à-tête that ideally should not have taken more than an hour. He came back close to midnight, drunk to the gills. As I rushed to his room, famished and tired, Santosh blurted out, 'I will sleep for three hours. Wake me up after three hours and take notes,' and curled up on the small sofa in one corner of the room.

I called a neighbour to inform my family that I would stay back in the office, had dinner in a shack outside the office and went to the page make-up room to spend the next three hours. As I entered Santosh's office at the stroke of three, he was already awake, browsing through some scribbled notes on some pieces of soiled yellowish paper napkins.

Then he dictated to me the entire piece, commas and semicolons included, which paid a glowing tribute to Sunil, and

I remember, described him as having the 'face of a lama'. As he finished dictating, Santosh brought out a bottle of perfume from the drawer and sprayed it profusely all over his body. And then, to my surprise and disgust, inside his mouth.

'What are you doing?' I asked.

'This is to ensure that Nihar does not smell the alcohol when I reach home,' he explained, alluding to his wife Niharika, whom I had always known as Nihar Aunty. I have never seen a more ludicrous thing in my life. The entire city of Kolkata knew Santosh Kumar Ghosh loved his drinks. Yet, at the age of 63, the old man still had the illusion that his wife did not!

His article on Sunil came out as a cover story on the following Sunday. Santosh received many congratulatory messages and also a personal, confidential letter from Sunil's wife Swati. Curiously, Swati chided him for being all praise for a congenital womanizer. Santosh let me read that letter, upon the condition that I won't disclose this as long as he lived. I did not.

He once saved my job after I got involved in a brawl with one of the finest poets of our times, Shakti Chattopadhyay, who was himself notorious for being a drunkard.

Shakti Da had invited me to dinner, and I landed up with a friend. I had no second thoughts as the host was Shakti Da. By the time we reached his home, Shakti Da, Santosh Kaka, Buddhadeb Guha and Tarapada Roy were already halfway through a bottle of Dimple whisky. A woman, known to the friend of mine, was also one of the invitees. While we were at our drink, my friend and the woman cuddled up in a corner. Suddenly, as we were about to have dinner, Shakti Da yelled at my friend and asked him to get out of his house. I was drunk too and could not take my friend's humiliation lying down. During the next half an hour we were locked in a pitched battle. The next day I heard that Shakti Da had complained to the bosses about me. This was probably the first time that a complaint regarding a drunken brawl was not about Shakti Da, but by him. Santosh took my side and I escaped unscathed. Later on, both Shakti Da and I buried the hatchet.

Santosh had another trait which is rare among authors and journalists. Whenever a piece drew his attention, he would shout from the rooftop how good it was. If it was an in-house piece, he would summon the writer and praise him. To outsiders, he would either make a telephone call or write a letter. He was a compulsive reader and used to read anything that he could lay his hands on. He was always on the lookout for a good piece of poem or short story or an essay in small-time magazines and nothing worthwhile would ever escape his eyes. I have no count of the number of writers he had discovered, nourished and helped establish themselves.

One of my great regrets is that although I was successful in convincing Santosh Kaka to write an autobiography, it never went beyond the first instalment that was published in Jyotirmoy Datta's magazine, *Kolkata*. Incidentally, the number also carried the only novel that I dared to write, largely at the behest of Jyoti Da! This was my first and last literary attempt.

At office, days rolled on without much work. Six months into my job, when my confirmation letter was due, Santosh made me sit across the table and wrote a letter of recommendation to Aveek Sarkar telling him that I was the most promising young journalist he had ever come across. Nirendranath Chakraborty, another renowned poet of our times, once told me, 'If he wishes, Santosh can publish a newspaper on his own, sitting in a small room. None of us has that talent.' The recommendation that such a man gave me, to this day, continues to be the most treasured award I have ever received.

Soon the Sarkars announced officially that the idea of the magazine had been shelved. Santosh Kaka himself called me and said, 'Aveek wants you in *Anandabazar*.'

And I entered Aveek Sarkar's room for the first time in my life.

6
Early Break

'Jyoti tells me his finance minister lies through his teeth.' If a chance encounter with Gour Kishore Ghosh, my guru, drew me into my lifelong vocation, this sudden angry outburst from one India's most important post-Independence political figures catapulted me to the front rank in Bengal's most important newspaper by far—*Anandabazar Patrika*.

This was Indira Gandhi. Venue: Ranchi's Raj Bhavan. Date: a few days after the Kolkata All India Congress Committee (AICC) session in December 1983. This AICC session especially drew national attention because of Rajiv Gandhi's participation in it as the party's new general secretary. Although Indira Gandhi presided over the conference, Rajiv emerged as the cynosure of all eyes.

I accompanied two senior colleagues when Rajiv gave them a long interview for ABP. That was the first time I saw and sat in the company of India's future prime minister. His charm, politeness and sense of chivalry stood in sharp contrast to the arrogant, imperious nature of his mother that was in full display a little later in the customary concluding press conference.

Indira lost her composure hearing an innocuous question from an *India Today* correspondent who wanted to know her assessment of Rajiv's performance as the party's general secretary.

Rajiv sat next to his mom greeting the question with a pleasant smile. But the mother snapped at the top of her voice, 'Are you from *India Today*? I hate to respond to an anti-national paper.' As I sat quietly in one corner of the media room, I remembered having read somewhere that Rajiv was more of his father Feroze Gandhi's son than Indira's.

Just a few days later, I saw Indira Gandhi in a similar cantankerous mood at a small press conference at Ranchi's Raj Bhavan where she stayed overnight after inaugurating the annual Science Congress at Birla Institute of Technology. This time, however, I had asked the question and my paper, known even in Delhi for its Congress leanings, could not be easily dubbed anti-national.

What prompted me to ask Indira an uncomfortable question was an ongoing spat between Rajiv Gandhi and West Bengal's then Finance Minister, Ashok Mitra, over the state of Bengal's economy. In his address at the Kolkata AICC session, Rajiv had described Bengal as an economic laggard blaming the ruling Marxists for its slow and tardy progress. Ashok Mitra, true to his acerbic style, made fun of Rajiv, saying he would not learn economics from an airline pilot. The verbal duel was the talk of the town when I left Kolkata for Ranchi to cover the Science Congress.

Mrs Gandhi listened to Mitra's remark and then called him a liar. Since there was no other Kolkata correspondent in that evening press conference, my story appeared as the front-page lead story the following morning. I was surprised as Jyoti Basu did not contest the prime minister's accusation to stand by Mitra in public. Both Basu and Mitra shared a close personal relationship with Indira; the former, being her friend from the London Majlis days and the latter, being her former chief economic adviser. It was a clear indication of Basu's growing displeasure with Mitra who soon quit the state cabinet over irreconcilable policy differences.

Indeed, the AICC meeting in Kolkata turned out to be *the*

event in my journalistic career, giving me an unexpected early break in an office where newcomers were generally treated like ragpickers collecting news that, with much luck, might make it to a single-column brief on the fifth page.

I was particularly unwelcome because somehow the news about my being an arrogant and irreverent brat had preceded me.

In 1981, when I joined the profession, I wanted to be a reporter. Many who joined with me did, but Gour Kishore Ghosh vetoed my wish, insisting I spent at least the first couple of years on the news desk.

'I know,' he said, 'you will curse me now. But someday you will remember me for giving you the correct advice. A stint on the news desk is essential for the wholesome development of any journalist.'

Twelve years later, in 1993, when I returned from Delhi to take charge of ABP's news operations, I thanked him indeed. My experience of running a news desk at the beginning of my career helped me weather many a storm in hostile surroundings.

Yet, when I crossed over to ABP's reporting department, I felt truly sad leaving Santosh Kumar Ghosh, for I knew how lonely he was. He was diagnosed with cancer soon thereafter and died on a day I was away from Kolkata on an official reporting assignment. I have never seen a braver soul who accepted the inevitable with such perfect equanimity. From his deathbed, Ghosh regularly wrote letters to his friends that bore not a hint of impending death or melancholy. Instead, in his inimitable Bengali prose, he poked fun at life.

To begin with, I was an unwelcome intruder into ABP's reporting department where a bunch of quarrelling old fogies far outnumbered colleagues of my age. I found the atmosphere thick with an air of mutual suspicion where people spoke in high decibels, indulged in constant chest-thumping braggadocio and lectured on every conceivable human folly. The one factor that bonded this motley group of self-seeking individuals together was their common hatred for the state's communist rulers. In no time, I could make out that the place was nothing more than an extension of the city's Congress office, and most of the reporters owed personal allegiance to the party's one faction or the other.

ABP, in those days, was the government's number-one adversary. For the communist leaders, on the other hand, the paper stood for bourgeois ideals and represented the interests of their class enemies. Berating ABP in every public meeting happened to be their favourite pastime.

In the Kolkata of the 1980s, such communist jargon still formed the staple of political discourses—revolution was still in the air. In the red bastion, capital was considered a dirty word, and capitalists, objects of unmitigated hatred. Even state-sponsored bandhs were called at the drop of a hat, often against one or another decision of the central government and occasionally to demonstrate solidarity with the victims of US imperialism in Cuba or Nicaragua. The city would remain crippled and paralysed for hours together when on every other day a long procession would be taken out through the major thoroughfares in support of either the working class or the toiling masses. They painted the city red with slogans of *'Cholchhe na, cholbe na'* (It's not working, it's not going to work), exhorting comrades to declare war against the Tatas and Birlas of the world. Even Moscow, Havana or Beijing seemed less enthusiastic about revolution.

In ABP's newsroom, only one person had iconic stature who rose to the pinnacle of fame through political reporting—Barun Sengupta. Those days he was called the Uttam Kumar—Bengal's unchallenged screen idol till date—of Bengali journalism because of his enviable popularity that was resented by his peers but exploited by the owners to the hilt. His attributes were twofold—wide-ranging political contacts in Kolkata and Delhi, and his ability to communicate in simple, conversational prose. He was arrested during the Emergency, as Chief Minister Siddhartha Shankar Ray bore personal grudges against him. Sengupta, already a household name in Bengal, emerged overnight as a cult figure that he put to good use when he launched his own daily, *Bartaman*, in late 1984.

With Sengupta, I could never strike any personal rapport as I found the man shallow, and hated his condescending, patronizing attitude. In office, he behaved like a know-all messiah, cracked poor jokes about state politicians and often fell asleep in his chair. He wrote a weekly political column, made predictions like an astrologer, sometimes peddling gossip as truth. His popularity endeared him to all the owners, particularly Aveek Sarkar, who used to accompany Sengupta on his daily rounds in the city to meet important ministers, bureaucrats and high-ranking police officials. While Santosh Kaka was Aveek Babu's journalistic guru and mentor, Sengupta ushered him into the hurly-burly of life beyond his cloistered, protected environment.

I admired Sengupta more as an entrepreneur for scripting a fascinating success story with his own newspaper, turning it over in a short period of time into the state's undisputed number two Bengali daily. The feat was rare for a man who came to Kolkata in the wake of Partition as a member of an uprooted Hindu refugee family struggling hard to find his place in a city ravaged by communal riots and population explosion. His was a rags-to-riches story that was built upon struggle, perseverance and indomitable ambition, a rarity for a regular Bengali, normally seeking moksha in secure and stable employment. The magnificent *Bartaman* building on the city's Eastern Metropolitan Bypass stands as a testament to the man's courage and business acumen who showed the guts to leave a cushy, comfortable job to pursue his own dreams.

Many years later, I tried the same thing inspired by Sengupta's success and launched my own newspaper. It did not take me long to realize that running a newspaper business against all conceivable odds required different kinds of skill sets that came naturally to Barun Sengupta but eluded me despite my best efforts. Like him, I was also the son of a refugee though.

Both Gour Kishore Ghosh and Barun Sengupta were imprisoned during the Emergency and by strange coincidence both left ABP to start their own newspaper venture—one succeeded, and the other left in a huff. Yet, measured on the yardsticks of courage, conviction and idealism, Gour Kishore, compared to Barun Sengupta, would always occupy a much higher pedestal.

Bidhan Sinha, an elderly cantankerous gentleman was my first chief reporter. His working mantra was simple, to be His Majesty's most loyal and obedient servant. He was a reformed Leftist, had strong political opinions that he painstakingly subordinated to Aveek Sarkar's wishes and instructions. He would countenance arguments up to a point and then conclude the discussion with a clear fatwa: 'What you say or feel may be important to you. For me, however, the editor's wishes are the last words.'

Post superannuation, he was rewarded with a long spell of extensions, much to the envy of his contemporaries. For him, I was a useful hand as I wrote readable prose effortlessly, without ever refusing an assignment.

In the initial days, I routinely moved like a shuttlecock between the two imposing colonial buildings that respectively housed the headquarters of the city police and the civic corporation. Once in a while I would also be sent hurriedly to cover an accident or a political clash. I cannot claim that I enjoyed my apprenticeship as a reporter doing boring routine stuff but I chose not to complain. For I knew I would easily carve out a place for myself as and when opportunity came my way. It dawned upon me soon enough that barring a few, ABP journalists were an ordinary lot, most of them being extraordinarily stupid and mediocre. In terms of intrinsic worth my young colleagues in *Aajkaal* were of much superior breed.

There were historical reasons for this. ABP, like most other important vernacular newspapers, was born in the 1920s as a vehicle for nationalist movement against the colonial rule. The paper remained avowedly Gandhian till Subhas Chandra Bose, the local Bengali hero, was forced by Gandhi to relinquish his elected post as the president of the Indian National Congress. In the late 1940s, the paper had a distinct Hindu communal overtone much like a publication of today's saffron brigade. The paper recruited freedom fighters as journalists during the British Raj and nominees of the state Congress stalwarts, post Independence. The tradition continued unabated till Aveek Sarkar changed the rules of the game, initiating a process of recruitment based not on political reference but merit and academic excellence. The seniors I met in 1983 were the remnants of an earlier era, an incongruity in the changing climate of the newsroom.

I drew Aveek Babu's attention fortuitously through an assignment that came as a much welcome windfall.

However, I felt ecstatic as, upon return from Ranchi, I found a perceptible change in the office atmosphere. Henceforth, I would not be asked to do errands but would be given important assignments regularly. Apparently, Aveek Babu had praised my reports and my enterprise openly in an editorial meeting. That ended my marginalization almost overnight and it did not take me very long to emerge as the editor's blue-eyed boy.

The year 1984 came with a series of disasters. Failing to tackle the militancy in Punjab, Indira Gandhi took the outrageous decision of sending the army into the Golden Temple, a sacrilege for which she herself was killed by her two Sikh bodyguards just a few months later. Mrs Gandhi's assassination triggered a countrywide anti-Sikh pogrom, mostly in Delhi, that left thousands of innocent Sikhs dead. Kolkata's Sikh community too felt the heat, though bloodshed could be avoided thanks to the deft handling of the charged situation by the state administration.

In my locality, some of us formed a vigilante group to provide round-the-clock protection to our frightened Sikh neighbours.

The ABP office, however, had remained closed during those dramatic days of Operation Blue Star because of an indefinite strike clamped on us by a handful of our trade unionist colleagues owing allegiance to the ruling CPI(M). The illegal strike opposed by an overwhelming majority of the employees continued for fifty-three days at a stretch with the tacit support of the rulers who found, in the situation, a godsend opportunity to teach their bourgeois adversaries a lesson. The ugly face of Left militancy shocked the media world, forcing the Editors Guild of India to send a delegation to Kolkata. But Jyoti Basu and his comrades maintained a gleeful distance, provoking their supporters to lay a siege around the ABP office to prevent anyone coming even close to the office premises.

The strike could be broken only after the Calcutta High Court decreed it illegal. Amidst showering of brickbats and empty bottles, the employees led by the owners came in a huge procession to resume work in the office. A few of them got badly injured and had to be hospitalized. In the melee I saw M.J. Akbar throwing bottles in the direction of strikers assembled on the other side of the street. The anti-strike agitation of the ABP employees brought me close to many unknown colleagues working in various other departments. The agitation was remarkable for the spirit of oneness and solidarity that could take on the might of the seemingly invincible Left.

Rajiv Gandhi lost no time to call fresh general elections after his accession to power. Although a language daily with only statewide circulation, ABP, as a rule, sent its correspondents everywhere within and outside the country to cover important events. For over fifteen years, I was the biggest beneficiary of this wise policy as I went to every site of important occurrence during this period. It started with the 1984 general elections when

I was sent to Gujarat.

Two snapshots from that trip are still fresh in my memory. The first was spending a day in the company of the Maharaja of Baroda who was contesting the election on a Congress ticket and the second was a long conversation at Rajkot with Morarji Desai, camping and campaigning there for Janata Party candidates.

Desai was nearing 90 then, but his gait and cheerful appearance belied his age. He was straight as a ramrod, slim as a cane and his skin had hardly any wrinkles. He was sporting his famous Gandhi cap. Speaking with him, I realized he was angrier with the BJP than with the Congress. Referring to the party's lamp symbol (changed later to lotus) he commented, 'How do you use a lamp? You use oil. Take it from me, son, the lamp of the BJP does not contain oil. It is Gandhiji's blood.'

In the 1984 elections, the Congress recorded its highest-ever victory with 413 Lok Sabha seats. Predictably, the party swept Gujarat too, winning all but two seats in the state. Even in the Left bastion of West Bengal, the election threw a lot of surprises, returning 16 Congress candidates out of a total of 42 seats, some of them from traditional Left strongholds. The elections marked the triumphant return of Priya Ranjan Dasmunsi into electoral politics after a life in hibernation post the Emergency. It also heralded the arrival of a firebrand woman leader, Mamata Banerjee, who, over a period of time, would emerge as the Opposition's most credible face and finally unseat the Left from power.

The results came as a surprise to all including the Left leaders. Even some of the winners did not believe it.

I am not quite sure how Indira Gandhi would have fared in this election if she had not been killed. Punjab was in flames, so was Assam. Sensing danger, Indira Gandhi had begun to play the Hindu communal card rather openly. Even before she deployed the army to storm into the Golden Temple, she spoke in favour of the Kashmiri pandits while on a tour to Jammu. Her campaign was a precursor to what we saw in later days as the BJP gradually rose into prominence. That way her tragic death saved the party, as her son could readily cash in on the sympathy wave.

Rajiv's new dispensation after the elections radically altered power equations in West Bengal Congress. Pranab Mukherjee was summarily dropped from the Union Cabinet while Barkat Ghani Khan Choudhury was accommodated with an inconsequential, powerless department. A few months later Pranab was sent to his home state as the president of the state Congress Committee. In the elections for Kolkata Corporation, the Congress did remarkably well just falling short of majority. Even that could not save Pranab from further disgrace and humiliation, ultimately leading to his expulsion from the party. In no time, Dasmunsi re-emerged as the most powerful Congress leader, enjoying Rajiv's total confidence.

On 2 September 1984, as I was holidaying at my in-law's place in Balurghat, a sleepy town bordering Bangladesh, my mother Kalyani died in Kolkata. She was only 59. By the time I came back home making an overnight journey, the cremation was over. In more senses than one, I was my mother's son. Memories of times that I spent with her, before and after she was devastated by schizophrenia, kept haunting me for a long time after she was gone. I was desperately looking for a break to start everything afresh. Thankfully, I did not have to wait long. In May 1985, Aveek Babu decided to transfer me to ABP's Delhi bureau.

7
Delhi: Take It, or Leave It

'What you have done amounts to anti-national activity. Important ULFA commanders have fled their camps frustrating our efforts because of this exposure'—that was Prime Minister Chandra Shekhar blasting me in his office. What had I done? I broke, in ABP and *Business Standard*—then ABP Group's business organ—a story about how the Centre was going to impose President's Rule in Assam to combat the United Liberation Front of Assam (ULFA), an insurgent outfit, hours before it actually happened. On being reported about my story, the prime minister promptly got me hauled up to his office. The angry and agitated dhoti-clad, bearded Thakur from Uttar Pradesh's Balia then gave me a brief lecture on the 'abysmal depths' to which the standard of journalism had fallen. In reply, I politely informed him that I stood by my report.

This was certainly a memorable incident in my long stint in Delhi as ABP's correspondent. But it happened a good five years after I went to Delhi, accompanied by my wife, two worn-out suitcases and a black-and-white TV travelling by Rajdhani Express. Till then it was quite a dream of sorts for me to travel in this elite train. My office gave me two chair car tickets and since I had no other belongings, I never asked for any transport allowance. My father chose to stay back in our rented flat on

Deodar Street all by himself. Kasturi and I decided to start our life afresh in an unknown land amid unknown people.

Going to Delhi in June 1985 was not my choice after all. Nor was my return to Kolkata to take charge of ABP in September 1993. As is the rule everywhere, in such cases, the boss decides for you and he can never be wrong.

Initially, all important assignments in my reporting career came to me when others declined or failed to deliver. In early 1985, I got a chance to cover the Gujarat disturbances when a senior colleague for some reason opted out at the last minute. I ended up travelling on his round-trip air ticket. Despite Indira Gandhi's assassination and the consequent nationwide anti-Sikh pogrom, security was still very lax at Indian airports and no one had to carry a photo identity card.

Similarly, three other colleagues, almost all my contemporaries and rising stars, were tried out for Delhi before me. Surprisingly, all of them returned to Kolkata citing one excuse or another. One of them talked of homesickness, a trait quintessentially Bengali. I was, therefore, not given any choice. Aveek Sarkar's untold message was loud and clear: take it or leave the institution.

I took it and remain, till date, beholden to Aveek Babu for offering me the opportunity. My fairly long stint in the country's capital during the cataclysmic years of the late 1980s and the early 1990s changed my life forever. I never had to look back.

It did not take me long to understand why so many of my predecessors did not, or could not, survive in the nation's capital. In Kolkata, an ABP reporter would be treated as the first among equals by everyone. In Delhi, by contrast, most of the relevant people would not care a fig about a reporter's language brand identity. In the mid and late 1980s, nine out of ten of them would confuse ABP with *Amrita Bazar Patrika*, a better known brand in that part of the country for historical reasons. It almost became a routine job for all of us to correct the mistake every time we spoke to someone. It was natural, therefore, for language journalists to suffer from an identity crisis in a land where only two languages pervaded and dominated virtually every walk of life—English and Hindi. Punjabi came a close third.

Language journalists in Delhi were not treated as anything more than second-class citizens by the powers that be, and as poor cousins by the 'Angrezi' scribes masquerading as the 'national press'—the self-styled champions of the nation's conscience—even though they knew precious little about the real India: the 'Bharat.' A language journalist in Delhi in those days was important only to the handful of politicians and bureaucrats representing their state and those who spoke their language. Even though Delhi has a substantial Bengali population, running into several lakhs, most of them neither speak nor read their mother tongue. Even in Chittaranjan Park, the most well-known Bengali ghetto in Delhi, very few people, mostly elderly, read Kolkata's Bengali newspapers in the afternoons. They have retained their culinary habits as also the practice of celebrating the annual Durga Puja festival with great fanfare, yet most have nothing 'Bengali' left in them.

I resolved not to remain cocooned within the company of a handful of Bengali politicians and bureaucrats. I was excited to spread my wings to unchartered territories not required by the call of my duties. Of course I felt sorry, particularly on those days when I broke stories for my paper that did not create even a ripple in the capital. The same stories, translated the next day by my colleagues working for English newspapers, often created sensation.

However, there were some perks as well. The single-storeyed apartment provided by the company in Gulmohar Park, a plush South Delhi locality, came as a pleasant surprise to me. Besides two spacious bedrooms, it had a huge drawing-cum-dining room, courtyards, both in the front and in the back of the house, with some space for gardening. The owner was a god-fearing Tamil journalist who rented the house to the ABP after he retired and shifted to Chennai. True to his belief and prejudice that one should not bathe where one relieves himself, he kept the bathroom and the Indian-style toilet totally separate. A small tulsi plant stood right in the middle of the courtyard. By the time we moved in the plant had dried and my atheist wife never replaced it with another one.

In the Nehruvian era, Gulmohar Park was designated as a journalists' colony, where many scribes and scholars were given plots to build their own houses. In the late 1980s, the neighbourhood still retained its demographic character, although some of the houses were already sold to non-journalists. Our immediate neighbour was a Bengali family with whom we struck intimate relations. Two of my other colleagues, including Sunit Ghosh, our chief of bureau, also stayed in Gulmohar Park. Poet Harivansh Rai Bachchan too had his house in the same locality, where his son, Amitabh Bachchan, would visit his mother regularly. Amitabh was then a khadi-clad star among the newly elected Congress parliamentarians, having trounced heavyweight Hemwati Nandan Bahuguna in Allahabad by a huge margin. Despite being a first-time parliamentarian, Amitabh was allotted a sprawling bungalow on Motilal Nehru Road, where he stayed when he came to Delhi. In our locality, speculation was rife about the ownership of a huge three-storeyed mansion close to the Bachchans'. It remained closed most of the times. The gossip was, Rekha owned it.

The ABP had its Delhi bureau in a single room on the first floor of the Indian Newspaper Society (INS) building on Rafi Marg. Another room, slightly bigger, was shared by *The Telegraph* and *Business Standard*. Later on, our room was renovated to accommodate our *Business Standard* colleagues, leaving an entire room for *The Telegraph*. Those were the days when M.J. Akbar's writ worked like magic in the ABP. Sometimes I wondered who actually owned the ABP Group, the Sarkars or Akbar.

One afternoon, Aveek Babu was in our room chatting with his ABP colleagues. A *Telegraph* reporter came to him to get the sanction for a foreign trip to attend a youth festival. His request was turned down. Surprisingly, Akbar too was in *The Telegraph* bureau at the same time. Soon he too came to our room with the same application and virtually ordered Aveek Babu to sign his approval.

The INS building, where I spent eight years, had its own charm and character. Most of the important outstation publications had their Delhi bureaus in the building. In the early 1980s, an annex was added to the main building to accommodate a large number of other outstation newspapers, overwhelmingly language dailies. As a result, journalists working out of the same premises developed a sense of camaraderie and a relationship of mutual dependence on each other.

In 1985, the ABP's Delhi bureau had just four members. By virtue of his seniority, Sunit Ghosh succeeded Ranjit Ray as the bureau chief. In terms of education, erudition and journalistic prowess, however, there was no comparison between the two. Ray was a card-holding member of the CPI and had shifted to the ABP from *The Statesman*. During his interview with Ashok Sarkar, he minced no words about his own political association and vowed never to change his ideology. Much before the Left in Bengal started its anti-Centre campaign, Ray had launched a battle against Delhi for what he called its discriminatory attitude towards his home state. His weekly column, 'Rajdahani Rajneeti' caught the imagination of contemporary Bengali readers as he gradually became a household icon along with Barun Sengupta. He was personally known to all the political bigwigs of the capital including Indira Gandhi. Many years later, he disappeared—just vanished into thin air—under mysterious circumstances. Despite all-round efforts, Ranjit Ray could not be traced.

By comparison, Sunit Ghosh was a lightweight, shy, withdrawn, constipated and a veritable shirker. Since he never cared to closely supervise the bureau's functioning, we got enough freedom to go our ways. I used it to the hilt. Wandering around Lutyens' Delhi in the scorching summer fascinated me. I went from door to door, from one Bhawan to another, from one political party headquarters to another, meeting politicians, bureaucrats and whoever I came across in the corridors of power.

The Telegraph's Delhi bureau, by contrast, was an all-woman affair presided over by the white-haired Kewal Verma, who was also my neighbour in Gulmohar Park. We called the team Kewal Sahab and his Rani of Jhansi regiment that included Tavleen Singh, Seema Mustafa, Rita Manchanda, Tania Midha and Manini Chatterjee. All of them were known and respected for their courage of conviction, strong and distinguished personalities (I remember Tavleen slapping a foul-mouthed Sikh politician right on the face in Amritsar without batting an eyelid), sharp political views (which is what, I suspect, drew Manini to P.C. Joshi's son Chand, so many years older to her, and marry him briefly), writing abilities and willingness to compete with men in any kind of seemingly hazardous assignment.

A Hindu Punjabi by birth, Kewal Verma was a communist in his youth and was fairly well read and well connected. Manmohan Singh, among others, was his longtime friend. More than anything else, he was an affectionate and argumentative person who loved to talk, debate and gossip about contemporary events and political bigwigs. He engaged all his women colleagues into high-decibel debates and arguments that fascinated me as a newcomer to Delhi. When he got angry, Kewal Sahab used choice Punjabi abuses either to denounce a counterargument or debunk his opponent. His memory was sharp and he was a storehouse of anecdotes.

Talking about corrupt Indian politicians during the Bofors scandal he once narrated an interesting incident about Partap

Singh Kairon, the first post-Independence chief minister of Punjab. The Bhakra-Nangal dam that changed the face of Punjab and made possible the Green Revolution was Kairon's biggest contribution to his state. But the construction of the dam also brought him a great deal of disrepute as corruption charges were levelled against him and some of his family members regarding the award of contracts. The charges rattled Jawaharlal Nehru in Delhi, who summoned Kairon to the capital to explain his position. Before meeting the prime minister, Kairon summoned a handful of known Punjabi journalists based in Delhi to his room in Punjab Bhawan. Once the journalists were inside, the chief minister bolted the room and quickly undressed himself. Before anyone could realize what was happening, Kairon showed all the journalists his naked backside and said, '*Lena hay to ek ek karke le le, lekin Bhakra Nangal hone de mere bhai.*' (Should you wish, take turns to screw me here but for heaven's sake don't disrupt the construction of the dam). Kewal Sahab's contention was simple. Corruption of a deliverer might be condoned. But not otherwise.

As a student of history I should have spent my time in Delhi, marvelling at the relics and monuments reminiscent of the great empires. Yet I did not. I visited the Qutb Minar barely twice. I went to Agra just about once, that too grudgingly, to keep the home front quiet and the visiting in-laws happy. I never went inside the Safdarjung Tomb that lay on my daily route. I plunged head on into my daily work, often travelling out of Delhi on assignments. Soon I became a workaholic who would not say no to any call of duty. This endeared me so much to Aveek Babu that he started calling me, 'Chautala', in reference to Haryana's Devi Lal and his efforts to pass on power to Om Prakash Chautala.

Officially, my beat was covering the Left parties and playing second fiddle to a senior in matters related to the Congress. But unlike in Kolkata, where the choices were limited and office hierarchy clearly delineated, Delhi seemed like a vast ocean for a daily voyage into the unknown. Individual enterprise that was hardly encouraged in a Bengali organization pervaded all levels by constipated broken hearts and high-sounding braggadocios. But for me at least, it was not discouraged either. For an aspiring newsman of any language, Delhi was, and still is, the veritable Mecca. For me it soon became the be-all and end-all of my life. Given a choice I would have remained in Delhi till the last day of my working life.

But the story has its flip side. If you are a journalist, Delhi also injects into you, like slow saline drips, a false sense of self-importance and a distorted notion about life beyond the city limits. The constant exposure to the country's movers and shakers, personal intimacy with many of them and their dependence on you for either favourable coverage or suppression of embarrassing facts often give one a heady feeling as if you are also a part of those who define the destiny of the nation. Instead of contempt, in Delhi, familiarity with political bigwigs and influential officials breeds allurement, temptation and corruption. In a city where wheeler-dealers cast their lengthy shadows over almost every echelon of power, ill or at the best modestly paid journalists too often find it difficult to remain immune to corrupting influences. Like the highest number of BMWs or Lamborghinis, Delhi also has the highest number of crooks masquerading as journalists.

I soon found out that in the capital's corridors of power there was a price tag for everything as most of the 'sarkari Bhawans' swarmed with favour-seekers, starting from two-penny fixers to well-attired middlemen who came in their expensive cars. The more discreet and influential among them visited the ministers' houses or set up exclusive appointments with them in the members-only exclusive clubs of various five-star hotels. Many small-time Congress party functionaries made a few extra bucks by bringing prospective clients from their states to Delhi. While in the capital, they stayed at luxury hotels, liberally entertained friends, drove expensive hired cars and smoked imported cigarettes. Their income varied with the nature of the job: a particular price for fixing an appointment with the minister, another for doing the same with a senior bureaucrat in the ministry. Even a minister's promise of delivering a job often fetched a windfall if the hapless client was new and uninitiated in the intricacies of back-room deals. The personal attendants of ministers too expected money from the visitors as if it was their birth right. I know of such an attendant who made a couple of thousand rupees every day working in the Commerce Ministry.

In time, I came to know one such Congress party functionary who made frequent trips to Delhi accompanied by Kolkata's small- and medium-level baniyas. He was Dipankar Gupta. A district committee leader from North Kolkata, he was a pot-bellied man who loved his food more than anything else in the universe. He could laugh loudly at himself and had no pretensions whatsoever about his activities in Delhi. While in the city, he made it a point to visit our office every afternoon to read the morning Kolkata newspapers and share party gossip with us. I could easily gauge from Dipankar Da's mood whether or not his trip would fetch him the expected booty.

On one such afternoon I found him quiet, circumspect and unhappy. It was an unusual sight that made me somewhat anxious about the state of his health.

'What's wrong with you Dipankar Da? Are you feeling unwell?' I asked in a sombre tone that reflected my concern.

'No, I am upset and worried for other reasons. I think I will have to stop coming to Delhi.'

'Why?' I asked.

His reply was simple and unambiguous. 'Ah! Dear, baits are reducing by the day. Earlier I used to travel to Delhi by flight, later it was scaled down to Rajdhani Express, first class. This time I had to travel in a three-tier rake in Kalka Mail. Can you imagine?'

'Where are the "murgis" (chicken baits) going?'

'Everyone is now flocking around either Subrata Da or Somen Da. I am not even getting the feathers.'

Even as I burst out laughing, I sympathized with him and took him out for a Mughlai dinner at a Pandara Park restaurant.

In my days in the hurly-burly of the capital's political life, Bengalis had an insignificant role but they played a stellar one in Delhi's journalism. Every newspaper had a sizeable number of 'Bongs' (as Bengalis are called in northern India), some of them occupying very important editorial positions. The owners of the city's two most important newspapers, *The Times of India* and *Hindustan Times* had their roots in Kolkata and, perhaps, had an undeclared bias for Bengalis.

The two most striking Bengali journalists who I befriended during my Delhi days were Subhas Chakrabarty and Dwijen Nandi. Subhas Da was a *Times of India* veteran, loud-mouthed and full of himself. He loved his evening Scotch and covered and treated the External Affairs Ministry almost as his personal fiefdom. He had amazing contacts in the ministry, wrote and pontificated almost every day on the front page of his daily about various aspects of foreign relations. He was also a close friend of Jyoti Basu and invariably spent one evening with the chief minister during the latter's trips to Delhi. He was also like a father figure to young Bengali journalists like us, always ready and willing to lend a helping hand. Aveek Babu too maintained cordial relations with him and enjoyed his company.

Dwijen Nandi, on the other hand, was a freelance journalist who covered the same ministry for two papers but limited his activities and curiosities only to the official briefings at Shastri Bhawan. A senior communist and a self-declared Sinophile, he once wrote extensively against Muzaffar Ahmed, better known as 'Kakababu' to his Bengali comrades transcending generations. Kakababu is considered a doyen of the communist movement in Bengal. The CPI(M), in a rare exception, celebrates his birthday every year. In his exposés, Dwijen Da showed, with the help of unimpeachable archival evidence, that Kakababu was also a British agent. Predictably, this infuriated his party comrades who lost no time to ostracize him. But Dwijen Da took the expulsion with perfect equanimity and lived the rest of his life in a quiet and saintly manner in a government accommodation. A lifelong bachelor, he led a remarkably frugal life, cooked his own food, washed his own clothes and always wore white khadi half shirts and white trousers. He was a regular visitor to our office and shared with us many unknown anecdotes about the communist stalwarts.

Outside my work, life in Delhi really had no charm for me. I loved my share of booze and the Press Club, where drinks, I knew, were dirt cheap, and was a stone's throw from our office. Yet it was out of bounds for me for many years. Before my departure from Kolkata, Aveek Babu, during a private conversation, had extracted from me a promise that I would stay away from the Press Club. His concerns were genuine. He too was aware of my weakness for alcohol. I kept my word and became a member of the Club a good five years after I first came to Delhi.

Also, the concept of 'para' or 'mohalla' (area marked by camaraderie among those who live in it) was unimaginable in my Delhi neighbourhood. Besides my immediate Bengali neighbours and some resident journalists, I hardly knew anyone and never visited anyone's home. The surrounding environment was enchanting with beautiful houses, manicured parks, winding lanes and huge rows of trees. Almost every houseowner had a car that was invariably parked overnight in front of the house. In that affluent locality no one was bothered about petty theft and there was hardly any. In many ways I found myself a misfit in a lifeless, selfish surrounding, although staying in Gulmohar Park was a signature statement of cosiness, comfort and affluence. For many Delhiites, obsessed with money and material gains, that was, however, a big deal.

8
Page One Singh

'*Is halat mein abhi andar jaoge to bachke laut nahi paoge*' (If you go inside like this you will not return alive), said the tall and lanky Sikh gentleman, stretching his hands to block our way. We could vaguely make out his sharp shape in the pitch darkness. I, along with my friend from *The Statesman*, Chandan Mitra, was trying to sneak into the Golden Temple in Amritsar, the heart of Sikh nationalism that had taken Punjab by storm in the 1980s. It was midnight. 29 April 1986. The day had begun with tense uncertainties. Several militant groups in association with the Panthic sympathizers had organized a Sarbat Khalsa (assembly of Sikhs) in the Golden Temple premises and declared Khalistan as their goal. Chandan and I had rushed from Delhi to be in the right place at the right time. Ever since I was posted in Delhi, a significant portion of my major assignments involved the turbulence in Punjab.

The congregation at the temple was indeed a spectacle. Thousands, mostly young men, almost all wearing saffron turbans came from all over Punjab to attend it. Many of them had guns slinging from their shoulders in a show of open defiance to the authorities and the security forces posted in good numbers just outside the Darbar Sahib. All of them sat on the marble floor in an orderly manner and cheered enthusiastically as speaker after speaker waxed eloquent about Delhi's betrayal and the miserable condition of the Sikh 'qaum' in a Hindu-dominated India. The speakers included militant priests and youth leaders of All India Sikh Students Federation. When the resolution on Khalistan was put to vote, every attending member raised his hand in spontaneous endorsement.

By late evening, the word went around that security forces would enter the temple complex to put an end to the militant activities. The tension in the city was palpable. Would this result in another Operation Blue Star? After downing enough number of pegs to be smelt out from quite a distance, at around midnight, Chandan and I had this sudden urge to visit the temple and find out first-hand what was happening inside the Akal Takht. We avoided the main gate and entered the temple from a small alley just opposite. As was the custom, we took off our shoes and cleaned our feet before entering. The complex that was swarming with people till evening now wore a deserted look. As we moved a few steps forward, an elderly Sikh gentleman appeared from nowhere, and with his stern but polite warning saved us from grave danger. We felt ashamed, promptly understood his message and took an about-turn.

The next morning, the Surjit Singh Barnala government, already under pressure from New Delhi, sent in a huge police force to mop up the 'Khalistanis'. The operation was peaceful as the police faced no resistance from the militants.

Politically, the chief minister found himself in a corner as his party soon split vertically over his decision to send police to Darbar Sahib. Personally, he was excommunicated from the Panth and declared a 'tankhaya' by the high priests for defiling the temple and acting against the interests of the community. Barnala's government survived the initial shock, though its popularity and legitimacy soon plummeted to abysmal depths.

In simple terms, 'tankhaya' means chastisement or punishment that is meted out to persons found guilty of religious misconduct. Of course Barnala was not the first Sikh leader to face such religious stricture. Maharaja Ranjit Singh, arguably the most influential Sikh leader in history, had to face 'tankhaya' following his marriage to a Muslim woman and had to appear before the Akal Takht to seek forgiveness. Zail Singh and Buta Singh, two Congress heavyweights, faced the same discomfiture soon after the Operation Blue Star.

Operation Blue Star, the army operation launched on 1 June 1984, through which Prime Minister Indira Gandhi neutralized militants led by Jarnail Singh Bhindranwale operating from the Golden Temple, certainly marks a watershed in the post-Partition history of Punjab. My association with the troubled state began post Operation Blue Star. To be more precise, it began with the historic Rajiv Gandhi–Harchand Singh Longowal, of Shiromani Akali Dal, agreement, signed on 24 July 1985. I reached Amritsar, for the first time, the very next day. The most enduring memory of that visit is of a man whom the hacks called 'Page One' Singh. No one knew his real name. No one really cared. He was a tall man with a flowing beard that had just about started greying. In those days, a flowing beard was supposed to be the hallmark of a god-fearing, religious Sikh gentleman, just like his 'kara' on the wrist and his turban. If any one of us at the Amritsar Central Telegraph office handed him a news copy for dispatch, he would ask just one question: '*Yeh keya page one story hai?*'(Is it meant for the front page of your paper?)

Of all the operators, he was the fastest on the telex machine. The question he asked was his own peculiar way of proclaiming superiority over his colleagues. Not for him were those inconsequential stories that would be dumped by the night editor in the inside pages.

At work, Page One Singh hardly talked. But when he came to our hotel rooms late at night, after duty hours, he seemed a different man—jovial and forthcoming with a dry sense of humour. After a couple of Patiala pegs of Old Monk rum, he would narrate to us, in minute details, stories and gossip about Bhindranwale and his henchmen in the Golden Temple. While he made fun of the gun-toting extremist leader using choice expletives, he was equally bitter about the Gandhis who, he felt, were responsible first for the Operation Blue Star and then unleashing a pogrom against the Sikhs following the assassination of Indira Gandhi. Nine months later, the wound was still raw. Tears rolled down his cheeks when he narrated how his brother was butchered by armed goons outside his New Delhi home. Every Sikh, everywhere felt the same. The Punjab story was far from over.

While in Delhi, I routinely saw how every Sikh on the road was seen and treated as a veritable suspect by the state security agencies. Anyone with a turban and beard would be subjected to humiliation and rigorous body search at every 'naka' (security roadblock). Those nakas were set up to inspect every passing vehicle and the sight of a Sikh sent the security forces into over drive. At every such stop he would be dragged out of the vehicle, questioned, interrogated and frisked. After the anti-Sikh riots that claimed thousands of innocent lives, the Sikhs lived a harrowing life in a charged atmosphere of suspicion and terror. Many of them chopped and trimmed their hair and beards out of sheer trepidation in an effort to hide their identities. One of them was my friend and colleague, Hardev Singh Sanotra, who worked in the Delhi bureau of the *Business Standard* and lived in the same locality as mine. Many months after I first met him, I came to know that he was a Sikh when Hardev himself volunteered this information during one of our numerous 'spirited' addas.

The Punjab Accord between Rajiv and Longowal in July 1985 was the first attempt to turn the tide and restore sanity and normalcy in Punjab. More than a year had passed after the dreadful Operation Blue Star and it was business as usual on that sultry July afternoon when I entered the desolate premises of the magnificent temple. The only sign of activity was in the 'langar' (community kitchen) where a handful of pilgrims were finishing their late lunch. Most of the rooms on either side of the 'parikrama' (pathway) were closed. There was no trace of even a Sikh Students Federation leader. The all-pervading silence seemed unsettling.

A sweet young lad ushered me into a room on the ground floor of a building adjacent to the Akal Takht when I enquired about Baba Joginder Singh who was still camping there. The room was small and dark and Bhindranwale's father was lying on a bed enjoying his siesta. The old man looked unremarkable and was visibly annoyed that I had breached his privacy without any notice. He reprimanded the person who brought me to him using four-letter words but soon regained his cool when he learnt I was a visiting journalist from Kolkata. I found it extremely difficult to engage him in any fruitful discussion as he spoke halting Hindi with an incomprehensible rural Punjabi accent. Two things, however, emerged clearly. He refused to talk about his slain son and called Longowal a 'traitor' for compromising the 'Panthic' honour and interests. When pressed for an answer he could not elaborate the reasons for his opposition and it seemed he never even bothered to read the text of the Punjab Accord.

Baba Joginder Singh's opposition had symbolic importance as his only claim to fame was entirely for biological reasons. The real trouble arose when other than the sundry, scattered militant groups, two heavyweight Sikh leaders—Prakash Singh Badal and Gurcharan Singh Tohra—refused to endorse Longowal's Accord, calling it a sell-out. On the afternoon I was meeting Bhindranwale's father inside the Golden Temple premises, Longowal called an extended meeting of his party colleagues in Shiromani Akali

Dal at Anandpur Sahib in another part of the state to discuss and ratify his agreement with the prime minister. The euphoria over the Accord died and gave rise to all-round cynicism almost immediately after it came in the public domain. The only question was—would the Accord hold?

Tohra, arguably the wiliest of all, was the head of the Sikh Gurdwara Prabandhak Committee (SGPC), the apex controlling body of all the Sikh religious shrines, that also had its headquarters in the Golden Temple complex. Badal, on the other hand, was the most well known of the Sikh politicians who wielded considerable influence both within and outside the party. Both of them were consciously bypassed during the hectic parleys in both Punjab and Delhi preceding the Accord, presumably on the assumption that they were unlikely to fall in line and would scuttle the efforts. Instead, Longowal and Arjun Singh (then governor of the state) roped in the support of Surjit Singh Barnala and Balwant Singh, both relatively lightweights. The virulent opposition by the Tohra–Badal duo acted as a damper and robbed the Accord of its political legitimacy to a great extent. On the other hand, the sharp division in Akali Dal leadership lifted the sagging morale of the militant outfits that regrouped themselves gradually and started returning to Darbar Sahib in Amritsar. They announced their re-emergence when Longowal was killed in his own district barely a month after the signing of the Accord.

His death dealt a crushing blow to the peace process but Delhi decided to go ahead with the assembly polls nevertheless. The process of implementation of the Accord also started in right earnest. As expected, the Akalis won the polls and Barnala was made the chief minister. Balwant Singh was given the finance portfolio. The government barely lasted a couple of years as the ugly face of mindless militancy resurfaced in the state and soon the situation spiralled out of control. A new chapter started unfolding in the Punjab story and I ran to the state again and again till violence and killing became such a routine affair that most of the outstation newspapers lost interest in them—just as it was to happen in Kashmir several years later.

Among other things, the Accord conceded the Sikhs' legitimate demand that Chandigarh should be handed over to Punjab in lieu of certain Hindi-speaking villages contiguous to Haryana. A commission headed by a retired judge was quickly set up and it was to give its verdict expeditiously. We were told the official transfer would take place on 26 January 1986. In Punjab we saw and felt an unmistakable mood of expectancy.

For the Punjabis who were forced to migrate as a result of the Partition, the loss of Lahore was like a festering sore in their collective psyche. Their desire and yearning for a capital of their own went unheeded as Chandigarh, a union territory, was used as the joint capital of both Punjab and Haryana. Le Corbusier's Chandigarh, although a modern, well-planned city, was dull and monotonous compared to the grandeur of the historic city of Lahore. Much later, when I visited Lahore, I realized what the loss could possibly mean to the erstwhile Lahoris and why the Punjabis on our side of the border were prepared to settle even for a poorer substitute.

The official enumeration of the villages meant to be transferred to Haryana turned out to be a much publicized farce. Critical in the process of enumeration was a small village called Kandu Khera that shot into prominence because of the Punjab Accord. A large number of journalists landed near the village on 26 January, the morning of enumeration. The whole village was cordoned off and declared out of bounds for the angry reporters. Balwant Singh was also on the spot, supervising the arrangements from outside. There was no way to find out whether the enumeration process was free and fair and whether the villagers were declaring their choice independently. A group of Delhi journalists led by Seema Mustafa and Sankarshan Thakur of *The Telegraph* somehow sneaked into the village but were quickly spotted by the security forces. After a bout of heated exchange, the security men lost their cool and went berserk. All the intruders were dragged out of the village, put into a prison van and dispatched to an unknown destination. Hardev and I felt nervous after we heard the story upon our arrival on the spot a few minutes later. The security forces in Punjab were known for their notoriety and recklessness and we sought Balwant Singh's help and intervention. He smiled mischievously and told us not to worry. After a while he instructed a police officer to take us to the place where Seema and Sankarshan were in detention. As it turned out, it was a beautiful, sprawling state guest house. As the police jeep entered the premises we saw Seema and Sankarshan enjoying steaming cups of tea in that cold winter morning sitting in the sun-baked garden.

I was part of a large number of journalists who arrived in Chandigarh on 25 January to witness the official transfer of the city the following day as per the terms of the Accord. We were kept waiting by officials in their secretariat building till about midnight when reports came from New Delhi that the appointed commission had failed to identify any Hindi-speaking areas adjacent to Haryana. If it wished, the central government could still have gone ahead with the transfer as the findings of the commission were binding on all the parties. But Rajiv Gandhi's government dragged its feet ostensibly under the influence of Bhajan Lal, the indomitable Congress chief minister from Haryana who threw a lot of tantrums, virtually blackmailing Delhi. Instead, the Centre appointed a second commission that went beyond its terms of reference and further complicated the matters. Finally, a third commission was set up that was told to give its findings within twenty-four hours. In other words, the whole process turned into a joke raising new and legitimate questions about the

Centre's sincerity. The promise remains unfulfilled as Chandigarh's status remains unaltered as the joint capital of both Punjab and Haryana even today.

During my repeated tours to the trouble-torn state, I developed a great deal of respect and admiration for Surjit Singh Barnala, the man in charge of Punjab's destiny. He was a perfect gentleman: warm, affable and always cooperating. Unlike Badal or Tohra he was not a crafty, scheming politician and had a wide range of interests including art, painting, literature and travel. He abhorred militancy from the core of his heart and denounced Khalistani aspirations in no uncertain terms. Let down by the Congress leadership in Delhi and hemmed in by problems on all sides, Barnala, however, failed to deliver as chief minister as the state gradually slid into chaos and all-round uncertainties yet again, culminating into the showdown of 29–30 April and the 'tankhaya' stricture on Barnala.

Barnala made an appearance before the Akal Takht in December 1988. As per the custom, he made a short confession owning up the charges brought against him. The five priests chosen from among the congregation then deliberated among themselves to decide on the nature of punishment. While the priests sat on the floor, the accused was made to stand silently in one corner. After a while, it was decided that Barnala would have to clean and polish shoes of the pilgrims sitting near the main gate of the temple. He accepted the order without a word and carried it out smilingly for a few hours at a stretch. I was astonished to see that no one made a fuss and the pilgrims treated it as virtually a non-event. For a while, I sat next to him to elicit a response. He said, 'I feel blessed. I do not see it as a punishment but an opportunity to serve the Guru Granth Sahib.'

In May 1987, Barnala's government was dismissed by Delhi on grounds of the deteriorating law and order situation and the rise of militancy. It was a few months after Siddhartha Shankar

Ray went to Chandigarh as Punjab's new governor in place of Dr Shankar Dayal Sharma. In his gubernatorial avatar, Manu Da, as we called Ray, made no attempt to live up to his image as the chief minister of West Bengal in the early seventies. He gave K.P.S. Gill, the state's then director general of police, the carte blanche to tackle the extremist problem the way he liked. Ray, on the other hand, made conscious efforts to keep the process of dialogue going with anyone who wanted to say something about Punjab. The gates of the Governor House in Chandigarh were thrown open to the common men where Manu Da held regular durbars. At the same time, he travelled extensively throughout the state to keep abreast of ground realities. As a result, human rights activists never got a chance to criticize Ray for his role as governor of Punjab. Many years later, when he breathed his last, Punjab fondly remembered him in state mourning. But in his home state, he died virtually unsung.

I met the 'super cop' of Punjab, K.P.S. Gill, just once at his official residence in Chandigarh, soon after Operation Black Thunder that flushed out the militants once and for all from the Golden Temple. Unlike Operation Blue Star, this operation was a completely transparent one as the authorities allowed the media to be a witness. Even foreign journalists were allowed inside. There was continuous television coverage that brought out even the minutest details of the operation. However, it took Gill and Co. a few more years to wipe out militant violence from Punjab.

Chandan Mitra, along with whom I went to meet Gill, was almost a fawning admirer of the super cop and regarded him as the saviour of the troubled border state. I did not share his opinion as I thought Gill often abused his freedom and authority and indulged in avoidable excesses. More than that, after our long tête-à-tête over two bottles of imported Scotch and delicious dinner, I came back unimpressed. I found him smug, arrogant and intellectually pretentious. He came across as a man too full of himself with scant regard for human rights or civil liberties. He made no secrets of his preference for all good things in life often boasting about his superactive libido even at that age. Years later, the super cop became notorious and controversial because of a 'bottom-pinching' case.

9
Prince Charming

Mani Shankar Aiyar did not like my questionnaire. Not without reason. Many of the questions were sharp and uncomfortable. He dictated a new set of questions, which would flatter the interviewee more than clarifying issues that I wanted to raise, and ordered me not to be too ambitious. In an hour's time, I boarded the helicopter, humiliated, helpless and with my heart pounding like a hammer, to interview Prime Minister Rajiv Gandhi. That was the first and the last time I interviewed anyone with a set of questions that was not mine.

Soon after landing in Delhi in May 1985, I was asked to cover Left politics, a coveted beat in Kolkata but of much lesser significance in the country's capital where the Opposition in general was in a hapless state following Rajiv's landslide victory in the 1984 elections that overshadowed even Nehru's performance in the immediate aftermath of India's independence. The BJP was reduced to just two seats, the Left fared somewhat better. It was Rajiv, Rajiv and Rajiv all the way.

I found out that none in ABP's Delhi bureau covered the Prime Minister's Office (PMO) as a regular beat, a negligence borne out of fear and a sense of inferiority. I went for the jugular, put in a lot of effort to break the glass ceiling and finally succeeded.

With hardly any opposition to confront, Rajiv, egged on by

his inexperienced coterie of friends, declared war against his own party's old-timers, his mother's close associates, in order to establish his image as Mr Clean. In the centenary session of the AICC held in Bombay in December 1985, he startled the nation by calling some of his colleagues 'power brokers' in his presidential address. As he finished his speech amid deafening applause, I saw a red-faced Pranab Mukherjee hiding his face from the prying photographers in disgust. Everyone present there understood the deposed finance minister was the Congress president's principal target.

As the old guards of Indira era got marginalized in the new regime, two groups surfaced to flex their muscles in Lutyens' Delhi—those who opposed Indira during and after the Emergency and a handful of Rajiv's anglicized friends, some from his Doon schooldays. Mani Shankar Aiyar was one of them. Although a serving Foreign Service officer, he always wore khadi kurta-pyjama a la Congress style and treated the prime minister as his private possession. In the PMO, Mani was singularly unpopular with his colleagues for his brash arrogance and abrasive style of functioning. Mani could not care less, because the friend-turned-boss had brotherly affection for him and valued his genius.

Of all the PMO officials, I had the closest personal relation with Mani, then working as the joint secretary. I visited him regularly at the South Block and even went to his residence once to have dinner with him and his family. He was a live wire; I admired his erudition, enviable command over Queen's English as also his acerbic sense of humour.

But that day I was appalled by his rude behaviour in the VIP lounge of Kolkata airport as he denied me my legitimate professional freedom to ask the prime minister what I wanted.

That was the last day of Rajiv's whirlwind electioneering for the 1987 West Bengal Assembly elections that raised a storm in the state's placid political weather.

I was the only media representative in his entourage in every trip he made to my state that year. In 1987, he came to Bengal more often than he visited Amethi, his parliamentary constituency. His frequent visits, his travel by road to various places in rural Bengal, his encounter with the villagers and his decision to lead the state election campaign from the front turned it into a battle royal between Rajiv Gandhi, the young prime minister, and Jyoti Basu the seasoned communist patriarch and the chief minister of West Bengal. The two locked horns in a manner the nation had not seen before. Hence Bengal's election story in 1987 drew the ready attention of the country's media who came in droves to find out what was really happening in this godforsaken Left citadel.

Rajiv set his eyes on West Bengal quite early, many months before the Assembly polls. He was desperately seeking an electoral victory to refurbish his image as a vote catcher following the Congress's poor performance in a few state elections before that. Egged on by Priya Ranjan Dasmunsi, then the Pradesh Congress Committee (PCC) president and a union minister, Rajiv thought the Left could be dislodged from power after a decade if he took the reins of the campaign in his own hands. How mistaken he was!

Rajiv's first political strategy was to try and neutralize the most effective propaganda in the communists' arsenal: that West Bengal suffered because of the hostile Centre's indifference towards the state. West Bengal had indeed been given a bad deal on various issues, which had contributed to the downfall of its economy. Priya Da, my long-time friend, impressed upon his leader that any meaningful counter-offensive against the Left in West Bengal would have to first address the state's nagging and legitimate economic grievances.

In September 1986, eight months before the state was to go to the polls, Rajiv descended in Kolkata with a planeload of central ministers and secretaries to have a marathon meeting with Jyoti Basu at Raj Bhavan, the governor's residence. The initiative took everyone by surprise, more so the state rulers who had to hurriedly prepare themselves with a credible charter of demands. In a joint press conference after a daylong meeting, Basu and Gandhi announced a host of decisions to address and alleviate Bengal's economic woes. Most of them, however, remained on paper.

I found a place in the prime ministerial helicopter at the initiative of Priya Da who introduced me to Mani Shankar Aiyar. Rajiv Gandhi needed widespread publicity in West Bengal and in those days of pre-24x7 news television he could not have chosen better than ABP, by far the leading Bengali newspaper in West Bengal. Mani had good rapport with Priya Da and agreed to take me in the entourage with one rider: 'At Priya's insistence I have been hedging a bet on you. Please do not disappoint me.' Since then I was a regular co-passenger in every trip Rajiv Gandhi made to my home state.

I took full advantage of travelling with the prime minister to write exclusive stories, giving graphic details of whatever unfolded before my eyes involving the country's prime minister. For me it was a once-in-a-lifetime experience that I have cherished.

For the three days following the Raj Bhavan meeting in Kolkata, Rajiv criss-crossed Bengal on road. He drove his own Jonga, gifted to him by the King of Jordan. Sonia sat next to him on the front seat like a Barbie doll draped in a dupatta, waving occasionally at the cheering crowds waiting at the roadsides. Priya Da sat behind, with a well-built SPG commando who lost his life in the blast at Sri Perumpudur in Tamil Nadu that claimed Rajiv's life on 21 May 1991. I was accommodated in the fourth car of the convoy along with some officers of the PMO. During the journey, however, I took the liberty of hitching a ride in one of the cars closer to Rajiv's Jonga.

Rajiv was always in spotless white, a pair of Lotto sneakers and expensive sunglasses. He drove like a Grand prix driver on the state roads, sanitized, well in advance, by the security forces. As a result, the official white Ambassador cars trailing him often fell far behind, unable to keep pace with the prime minister's breakneck speed.

Once, somewhere in North Bengal, the prime minister's Jonga came to a screeching halt, as if to avoid an imminent accident. The cars following him almost crashed into each other causing a flutter and minor injuries to some. I ran close to his car to find no encumbrance to warrant such an emergency brake. The next thing I saw was a senior official alighting from his car and walking across the road to pick up an empty food packet from the street. As it transpired, Rajiv saw in his rear view mirror the elderly gentleman throwing the lunch packet from his car window. The sight irritated him so much that he decided to teach the senior civil servant a necessary lesson in civic senses. The official put up a brave face despite the drubbing he got from the prime minister and I got a good snippet for my diary on Rajiv's Bengal safari.

The purpose of Rajiv's road journey was to meet villagers impromptu without giving any notice to anyone in the local administration. The road map of his tour was shared with the Intelligence of course, but not where he might stop, simply because no one knew that. As a result, none could predict where he would slow down his vehicle and take a turn to enter a village. He chose them at his own free will after getting a general background of the area from Priya Da. That meant I had to stay alert and vigilant so that I could run and quickly reach the spot to witness the drama. After a couple of such stopovers, the prime minister's security guards became friendly and allowed me to stand close to Rajiv inside the security cordon.

The reactions and facial expressions of the villagers as they saw the country's prime minister walking to their doorsteps braving broken and muddy roads, littered with animal waste, clearly varied from being amusing to bizarre. Some cried out in utter disbelief, calling upon neighbours to come out quickly and share the unexpected spectacle. Some wanted to touch Rajiv Gandhi to be reassured they were neither dreaming nor hallucinating. Women in many Hindu villages blew conch shells and held impromptu arati to greet him. Everywhere, the villagers took quite a while to come to terms with reality before striking conversation with the prime minister. Priya Da acted as the interpreter between Rajiv and the villagers, occasionally distorting their answers so that a horrific picture of Bengal's rural life and economy emerged before the prime minister.

Rajiv asked simple and pointed questions, often very personal. He also tried to dig out facts about the implementation of various central welfare projects meant for the rural poor. He heard complaints everywhere, natural and predictable, from those living on the margins, often without basic amenities. Most of the respondents were vocal against the partisan behaviour of their local panchayat functionaries belonging to the Left parties. Doles and benefits, they said, were only for those who swore allegiance to the rulers. Once in a while, Rajiv lost his cool when he heard complaints of rampant corruption.

Sonia stood beside her husband all the while without uttering a single word. In a small village, dominated overwhelmingly by the lower castes, a newborn goat caught Rajiv's eyes. He picked it up, put it on his lap and called Sonia aside. The couple patted the baby goat affectionately, admired its fur while enquiring from the houseowner the details of their livestock. As he handed it back to its owner, Rajiv said, 'Take the poor thing to its mother. Looks like it was born only today.'

In another Muslim village in West Dinajpur, on the third and last leg of Rajiv's Bengal tour, the couple walked straight inside a dirty, dingy and dimly lit cowshed, infested with swarms of mosquitoes. Perturbed and embarrassed, the security guards did not know how to protect the prime minister and his wife from such alien invasion. The hosts produced a few handheld fans and I grabbed one of them to give Sonia Gandhi a little comfort. Convinced she would be mighty pleased with my gesture, I mustered the courage to ask her a pro forma question about her experiences on that trip. Sonia turned and gave me such a stern look that my confidence wilted. I stepped aside leaving her in the company of friendlier insects.

Seventeen years later, I narrated the experience to Sonia Gandhi at a dinner hosted by her at 10 Janpath for a group of language editors before the 2004 Lok Sabha polls. I went from Kolkata to attend it. Manmohan Singh, still recovering from his second heart surgery stood at the gate to greet and receive the guests. After the introduction, when he learnt I represented *Anandabazar Patrika*, he said smilingly, 'Aveek offered me a job with an astronomical salary. I told him I did not want so much money as a retired person.' Hardly did he or the world know then that the same man would be chosen to become India's prime minister for two consecutive terms just a few days later.

I chose a table where two of my favourite 'dadas' were sitting—Pranab Mukherjee and Priya Ranjan Dasmunsi. As a gracious host, Sonia was moving from table to table spending time everywhere. She came and sat next to me; she looked relaxed and charming. I could not resist the temptation of recounting my encounter with her in that mosquito-infected cow shelter and said, 'Madam, that morning you had cast a tigress-like glance at me, as if I was committing an act of sedition.' Sonia burst out in laughter so loudly that it bewildered many of the guests at other tables.

There was hardly any room for such laughter, however, back in 1986, with political tension reaching a crescendo. Mani Shankar Aiyar took copious notes of the villagers' comments, based on which Rajiv Gandhi blasted Jyoti Basu and his government before his departure. He tore apart the much-touted rural development initiatives during the Left regime, calling them nothing more than hogwash. It started a verbal duel between Gandhi and Basu that continued unabated till the results of the Assembly polls were out.

A few days after Rajiv left Bengal, Basu called the prime minister a liar and his party brought out a well-prepared information sheet on the villages Rajiv visited, giving details of development projects. Aveek Babu saw in this high-decibel slanging match another story opportunity and called me over from Delhi. He asked me to revisit the same villages to find out who was telling the truth. I did so and wrote a series that evoked a lot of interest in the state. I found both guilty of committing excesses and indulging in lies. As a result, I declared the game drawn and returned to Delhi.

The monsoon that year brought floods in several districts of West Bengal. Rajiv did not miss the opportunity to pay a visit and announce central help for the victims. In December 1986, he went to Darjeeling amidst a bandh called by Subash Ghising, the then supreme commander of the Gorkha National Liberation Front (GNLF) which was demanding separate statehood for the Gorkhas. Rajiv went to Bagdogra from Delhi and took an Air Force chopper to reach the Lebong Race Course grounds, very close to Darjeeling. The second chopper carried his officers and security personnel. Thanks to Mani again, I was accommodated at the last minute.

In the history of post-Independence India, no prime minister had ever made a similar journey to an area so politically hostile. The bandh was total and not even a dog came out on the street to greet Rajiv Gandhi. Undaunted, Rajiv gave a long speech in an empty school ground, in the presence of a few hundred deployed policemen and a handful of hacks. Some of the local security constables were told to quickly get out of their uniforms and into civilian clothes to avoid a total embarrassment for the prime minister. Next, he went to the Himalayan Mountaineering Institute where a small Lepcha delegation, escorted by armed policemen, called on him to submit a memorandum. I went to see the GNLF supremo, who refused to say a word either about the bandh or the boycott call. Instead, he made me sit in his cold, freezing office chamber and read out one after another his lousy patriotic poems written in Hindi. I could make out he felt mighty happy seeing his own people showing exemplary solidarity with his cause.

Once the poll dates were declared for April, Rajiv started his aerial blitzkrieg, coming to Bengal half a dozen times to cover almost every nook and corner of the state. Again, I accompanied him as the solitary media person.

Rajiv could hardly be blamed if the public response he received during his intensive campaigns made him supremely confident of dislodging the Left from the Writers' Buildings. Wherever he went, he created a storm as people came out to see him in thousands on the roads or to hear him in the public meetings even during midnight or the wee hours of the morning. In every meeting, he raised slogans in Bengali coined by Dasmunsi. He chose Jyoti Babu as his target of attack and midway through the campaign exhorted him to gracefully retire from politics.

The success of the prime minister's campaigns took his political opponents by surprise and his personal attack infuriated Basu so much that he went on a public counteroffensive. In every meeting Basu thundered, 'I do not understand what this prime minister is up to. Would he renounce his prime minister's post to become the chief minister of West Bengal should the Congress get a majority?' The heated duel between Gandhi and Basu over an Assembly poll was unprecedented, more so because of the personal overtone in their attacks. Basu was hurt beyond measures as the sniper was the son of two of his close friends—Feroze and Indira Gandhi.

Basu, of course, had the last laugh. The results demonstrated unmistakably that the grassroots support for the communists remained intact. It also proved that a massive turnout in campaign rallies should not be equated with either political support or votes.

During my tours with Rajiv I felt the rare charm and warmth of his persona when I sat next to him in his helicopter to interview him. I quickly realized that because of his inhumanly hectic schedule, these helicopter rides were his only opportunity to catch up on lost sleep. Midway through our conversation, I could feel, he could no longer resist shutting his eyes. I felt awkward and did not know what to do. He took out from his kurta pocket a small bottle and poured a few drops into his tired eyes and continued with the discussion. His replies were all predictable and boring but not the warmth he exuded. It seemed to me he was a quintessential gentleman dragged into the quagmire of politics, a place where he was singularly a misfit.

However, in late 1987 or 1988, it was difficult to find a hack in Delhi who would say two kind words about Rajiv Gandhi, perceived to be the Peter Pan of Indian politics only a few days earlier. His government's decision to overturn the Supreme Court's historic judgement granting alimony to Shah Bano, the hapless old lady from Indore, created a shockwave among the secular brigade which saw it as an opportunistic and ill-conceived capitulation to the mullahs. Arif Mohammad Khan, the Congress MP from Bulandshahr and a minister in Rajiv's cabinet, resigned in protest signalling the first wave of internal revolt in the Congress. Further, the Bofors scandal that the Swedish radio broke and followed up zealously by *The Hindu* and *The Indian Express* put Rajiv on the mat, making him a suspect largely because of his inconsistent remarks and behaviour both within and outside the parliament. Ram Jethmalani, the flamboyant criminal lawyer, started taking potshots against the prime minister asking him a set of ten embarrassing questions about Bofors every day, continuously for a month.

Rajiv's affable nature again came to the fore when he lost no time to make up with his 'Jyoti Uncle' after the 1987 Assembly polls in West Bengal. A seasoned politician and a family friend, Basu also reciprocated the gesture and accepted Sonia's invitation to have dinner with them. Basu also supported Sonia's entry into politics publicly when the saffron brigade launched a personal attack against her, calling her a 'foreigner'.

Rajiv took no interest in West Bengal's affairs afterwards. He remained hassled and embroiled in Delhi, facing crises, one after the other, almost turning him into a brooding King Lear. In 1988, the AICC held a session at Maraimalai Nagar, a satellite town of Chennai. I travelled with Rajiv in the same compartment of the local train that took him from Chennai to the venue. All the way he stood on the door like a daily passenger greeting curious onlookers on the way. He was still the Prince Charming, yet he looked tired, pensive and worn out. It was not the same prime minister I had travelled with in my state only a year ago.

And then came 1989. Aveek Babu banged the phone on me and ruined my morning. He was very annoyed with me. Reason? My coverage of the Lok Sabha elections in 1989. In my dispatches from Uttar Pradesh I had been consistently hinting a possible rout of the Congress. Aveek Babu, I knew didn't quite agree with me, but was still giving me a long leash, even though the West Bengal Congress leaders and a section of my office colleagues had been labouring overtime to discredit me before my editor for what they called my 'partisan political position'. In reality, I had none. I wrote in simple language exactly what I saw.

For example, in Amethi, I saw a number of Congress goons vandalizing a small public meeting of Kanshi Ram, the Bahujan Samaj Party architect and supremo, who was also contesting from the same constituency. In those days, the Bahujan Samaj Party was hardly a recognizable political force in UP and Kanshi Ram, notwithstanding his relentless campaign against the 'Manuwadi parties', posed no real challenge to Rajiv Gandhi. Yet in my dispatch I narrated the incident in detail which was, to me, an ostensible indication of panic and nervousness that gripped the Congress even in the prime minister's constituency. In the 1989 elections, Amethi seemed like a tottering Gandhi family borough amid all-round Congress retreat.

With this, Aveek Babu lost his cool. In ABP, members of the Gandhi family were untouchables. Period. After a long and gruelling field trip lasting several days, I had returned to Varanasi with a view to take a day's break in the city that was teemed with memories. Just as I woke up to a nostalgic idle morning, came Aveek Babu's phone call. After a shouting bout for several minutes he banged the phone down.

For a moment, I felt insulted. Then came a flood of anger, and finally a strange calm: f**k the office, f**k the editor, f**k my colleagues and f**k the Congress leaders, I told myself. I had a hearty breakfast and headed straight for Devnathpura, the place where, during the Puja holidays in our childhood, my sister and I would come with our mother to visit our ageing grandparents in our maternal uncle's home. It may be difficult for non-Bengali readers to appreciate this, but for every Bengali the maternal uncle's place—the Mamar bari—signifies a very special space. A common rebuke in Bengali for anyone making absurd demands is '*eki Mamar bari?*' (Is this your maternal uncle's home?) Truly unfortunate is that Bengali child who never had the indulgence of a Mamar bari. Luckily, my sister and I were not among those. Indeed we were perhaps doubly lucky because our Mamar bari was in Varanasi, arguably the world's oldest living city!

After some difficulty, I did locate the house. It was a strange feeling that I have no words to describe. A hardcore newsman, I am not a sentimental guy. The same house was standing there, the locality hadn't changed much either. Only, it had new occupants, with whom I had nothing to do. Memories choked my voice.

My maternal grandfather was tall and slim, unusually fair, with a flowing white beard just like Rabindranath Tagore. He was a practising tantric and a priest in a small local temple. The saffron he wore had a deep reddish glow that distinguished him from other sanyasis. The rudraksh beads (brown seeds woven into a rosary) he wore were unusually big but went well with his imposing built. Even when he sat at home on his bed, he held a trident in his left hand. Towards the end of his life, he lost his voice, seeking refuge in sign languages. Most of the time he could only manage to mumble. Only my Didima's trained ears could decipher the sound, depending on the time of day and night.

Even though he was very fond of my sister and me, we felt nervous, uncertain and speechless in his presence. His appearance, his clothes, his trident, his beard, the deep red tilak on his forehead, all combined to create a mysterious aura. I would invariably run for cover when he called me and urged me to sit on his lap.

When my grandfather became an invalid, one of my mamas, who stayed with his parents and remained a lifelong bachelor, succeeded him as the temple's new priest.

The three of them lived in a one-and-a-half-room first-floor apartment in a dilapidated old building surrounded on all sides by Muslim weavers of Banarasi silk. They simply could not afford anything better.

One of the rooms had two beds on two sides which my Dadu and Didima occupied. The other room was used during the day as a kitchen and as a bedroom at night for my Mama.

The building housed some poor Hindu tenants on both the floors. On the first floor, bang opposite my Dadu's, there lived a Bengali couple with five children, all packed inside one midsized room. The steep staircase was dark and broken, littered with thick red paan spit and food leftovers from the kitchens of the residents.

The most frightening aspect of that building was its toilet

that the residents on the first floor shared. It was what we call in Bengali a 'khatapaykhana', a small, suffocating, slippery room where one had to squat over a pit and listen to the excreta landing on a huge mud container several feet below with a nauseating thud. When full, a sweeper (a lower caste untouchable) from the local municipality would come and replace the mud container with a new one.

During our brief visits to Varanasi in my childhood in the mid-1960s, I screamed and cried every morning insisting that my mother accompany me to that horrible toilet. I was scared of falling through the hole and finding myself half-drowned in faeces in that dreadful pit. I felt relieving myself on the railway tracks was preferable to visiting that death chamber.

One of the families living on the ground floor bought old newspapers and worked all day and night making 'thongas' (paper bags). All the children—seven or eight boys and girls, old and young—were employed in the thankless job, because hiring labour would have made the little family business completely unviable.

The kids sat cross-legged in the open courtyard on rat-eaten mattresses performing their duties according to allotment and specification. Some cut the newspapers into proper shapes—the most delicate part of the job—to pass them on to the second group which would paste the cut pieces with glue made out of wheat flour to finally pass on to the last group which cleaned and stacked the packets, ready for use. The whole day the house buzzed with their shrill, loud chirrups adding some life to that otherwise depressing habitat.

The other place where some signs of life in the building could be found was in the grocery, which had an unmistakable odour of spices, mustard oil, gur and rat-poop. Located in the corner of the building's ground floor, the shop opened early in the morning and closed well after I went to sleep upstairs. Dhiren, a fair and charming young man, owned the shop and extended a warm hospitality whenever I visited. He was a devout Hindu Brahmin and proudly wore a sacred thread to constantly remind him the world of his purity and superiority of birth in a locality swarming with 'mlecchas' (foreigners).

Normally, he wore a fresh lungi and a white fatua (loose cotton waistcoat) with two front pockets. In summers, during the day, he sat bare-bodied and in winters he would wrap an ordinary shawl. A god-fearing soul, Dhiren would invariably visit the adjacent Shava-Shiva temple twice: once before opening his shop and again after closing it. He was almost a member of my Dadu's family. We called him Dhiren Da. Dhiren Da acted just like a family guardian, a position deservedly earned. He also had the right to tweak my ears if I was caught doing some mischief. During the day, I spent a lot of time in his shop expecting biscuits, chocolates and, on days when transactions were abysmally low, at least a handful of sugar. Once he took me to see a football match of Mohammedan Sporting, a premier club from Kolkata, which was visiting Varanasi to play an invitation match.

When my Mama returned home every afternoon from the temple, he carried two treasures: pranamis (donations made by devotees) in coins and small denomination notes, and prasad in the form of sweets, mostly dry, such as sandesh and chamchams. He kept the coins in a baby food container that stayed hidden in one corner of the kitchen cabinet, lost among an assortment of various other containers of different sizes and made of all kinds of metal. The discovery of the hidden treasure kept me perpetually happy during our stays at my Dadu's as I often stole a few annas (50 paise) and sikis (25 paise), quietly slip outside, walk a few paces down to the nearby market to buy and enjoy a few chamchams and rabri. Experimenting for over god knows how many years—perhaps a thousand—the confectioners of Varanasi had achieved a culinary height in the form of rabri that could not have been very far from divinity.

The quick depletion of the treasure drew my uncle's attention in no time and I became very cautious thereafter. He, however, was an indulgent uncle. He often took me to the temple with him. I would sit next to him, watch his elaborate puja carefully, but became particularly watchful when visitors came with prasad and pranamis and threw the coins in front of the idol. I was not particularly impressed with the way he performed the daily puja, mumbling the mantras instead of chanting them loudly. I thought he was either bored with his priestly duties or did not know the mantras well. It seemed in his inaudible whispers he was actually cursing his own fate rather than offering prayers to the almighty. The idol in the small brick-coloured temple was tiny, black, with a peculiar shape that I have not seen anywhere else. The uniqueness of the idol added a degree of importance to the temple as the visitors and devotees kept coming in regular streams all through the day and round the year. This in turn was a divine blessing as the earnings from the temple was the only source of income for my Dadu's family. Occasions such as Kali Puja and Diwali brought the annual bounties including some small pieces of low-carat gold that my Mama used to pawn for a few hundred rupees.

Varanasi, Kashi or Benaras—as the holy city is variously known—was also home to a vast litany of old crippled men and women, widows or widowers, awaiting to breathe their last at the feet of Lord Vishwanath, the city's presiding deity. Let alone the cow, even the bull was considered as holy as the city's waters (of the Ganga). It could be hooted, cajoled, caressed and even twisted by its bushy tail, but could never be hurt. In Bengali, we call it the proverbial 'dhormer shanr', literally meaning the 'holy bull'—it is a metaphor for a lazy, good-for-nothing person. In Varanasi, however, its position was just second to the gods and goddesses in the numerous temples scattered over the whole city.

Cows and bulls are considered sacred all over India. There

is nothing special about it. But the holiness of the bovines of Varanasi has left an unusually lasting impression on me. While covering the Kumbh Mela at Haridwar as a young journalist I watched a frail village woman sucking the udders of a newly mothered cow as a man keenly watched her from a distance. The man later told me that his wife had failed to conceive for years. He was confident that after sucking milk straight from the cow's udder she would be blessed with children.

The Muslim men and women, who also lived along the serpentine lanes of Devnathpura, offered a strikingly different cultural flavour. The women came out on the lanes all draped in black, their faces hidden behind veils, looking at the world outside, including the bulls, through the nets in front of their eyes. The bearded men mostly wore lungis and skull caps, and spoke a totally incomprehensible language. Many years later I was told it was a curious mix of Urdu and the prevalent Hindvi boli (dialect). While at home, especially during the day, the young and elderly among the men kept themselves busy in front of the looms weaving, thread by thread, exquisite designs with Banarasi silk.

Generally, we were not encouraged to visit their homes nor were we much welcome there. Yet, I always felt tempted to peep into their houses through the ground-floor windows. They never asked me to come inside nor did I dare to do so, especially after watching them in a huge Muharram procession wielding open swords and inflicting wounds on their bare bodies at regular intervals. They were neighbours—indeed, next door, close and immediate—but the two communities lived separately in their own worlds as if in two different countries: the Hindus with their pujas, mantras, cow dung, Ganga snan (dip in the Ganges) and an assortment of menial jobs and the Muslims with their weaving, Friday namaz, burqas and skull caps, and occasional family revelries closely guarded from the outside world.

Not far from my Dadu's place was the eternal Dashashwamedh

Ghat. Since eternity, people from all over India have been taking dips into the water flowing past this ghat to cleanse themselves of all their sins. During our brief visits to Varanasi, I had the opportunity to cleanse myself very frequently.

For me, however, visits to the temple of the holy town's presiding deity were far more appealing. The busy and humming long and serpentine lane that led to the Vishwanath temple was simply fascinating. I wanted to go there again and again not so much to offer my prayers but just to be dazzled by the spectacle all around and, if possible, do some shopping for my own little world.

On both sides, the lane had numerous little shops displaying all kinds of trinkets, including small wooden utensils, that to me appeared to be godsend for our khelna-bati (doll's house). The little plates, mugs, cups, kettles, stoves and almost everything else that we needed, were on offer, neatly packaged in baskets made of palm leaves. Most importantly, they were dirt cheap, well within my mother's small shopping allowance.

ო

All these came back in cinematic sequences as I roamed around the mohalla that day in 1989. However, I could not enter my Mamar bari as the dilapidated structure stood locked and abandoned almost as an archaeological relic. There was no sign of Dhiren Da anywhere. A neighbour told me the condemned building would soon come under the municipal hammer. On the way back I entered the Shava-Shiva temple to seek blessings in my hour of crisis. As the grandchild of the temple's most celebrated priest, I claimed special favours from the deity.

My prayers were answered a few days later as the results clearly demonstrated a Congress rout in UP and North India. I was in the Kolkata office on the counting day having had a sleepless night before. In Delhi, the day belonged to Vishwanath Pratap Singh and in the Kolkata ABP office, to me. However I took my success in my stride and before returning to Delhi, politely told my boss to trust his reporter's instinct on the spot. Aveek Babu patted my back with a chuckle.

On the night of 21 May 1991, I was sleeping like a log at my sister's house in Kolkata after a long working day and consuming gallons of badly brewed beer. I was bodily shaken by my brother-in-law to wake me up as if burglars had breached into the house. It was a few minutes past midnight. A phone call had come to their landlord's home (my sister didn't have a landline) asking me to rush to office immediately. I turned on the television and saw the news. Rajiv Gandhi had been killed in a suicide bomb attack.

It did not take me more than twenty minutes to reach office and my taxi driver was still blissfully unaware of the earth-shaking incident. The city looked calm just as it should be during that hour and the atmosphere outside seemed sultry and humid. In the newsroom, I saw both the Sarkar brothers sitting face-to-face. Aveek Babu told me to leave for Delhi by the first flight before disturbances started. He told me that he was to meet Rajiv in a few days and hand over a packet of his favourite chocolates he had just brought from England. For once in my long association with him, I saw Aveek Babu not being able to hold his emotions.

Notwithstanding all his shortcomings, Rajiv Gandhi was indeed a nice man to know.

10
The Bengali Patriarch

Jyoti Bosu namaskar, panch bachare ekbar

Even in my wildest nightmares I hadn't apprehended that these two innocuous lines would upset the last grand old man of Bengal politics. 1987. My editor, Aveek Sarkar, had asked me to temporarily shift base from Delhi to Kolkata to cover the Assembly elections. One day, I was following Chief Minister Jyoti Basu's convoy to his constituency, some 30 kms from Kolkata. In one of the villages I was amused to see a group of children running after the cars chanting these two lines, meaning 'Salute Jyoti Basu, once every five years we do see you!' That was a common whinge drummed up by the Congress, indicating that even though the people of Satgachhia voted for Basu repeatedly, he had no time for them. Of course, the voters themselves never took it seriously, and returned to him consecutively, five times, between 1977 and 1996, until the patriarch bid goodbye to electoral politics. I am sure the children were chanting it just for fun. Judging that it would provide an interesting colour to my copy, I had begun my report with it.

Next morning, it resulted in a reprimand from Aveek Babu, who told me Basu was upset with my copy for giving credence to what a bunch of children were shouting for fun. That was so unlike the septuagenarian political boss of West Bengal. Basu never took to heart anything that the media reported about him, least of all the *Anandabazar*, for him and his ilk, a 'bourgeois crap'. He treated reporters as nothing more than irritating insects, ignored them royally, occasionally speaking to them in his typically incomprehensible monosyllables. Why would such a man take exception to something so innocuous in my story that was otherwise so balanced and neutral?

The answer lay in the tense, heated atmosphere that preceded the 1987 Assembly elections in West Bengal, thanks to Rajiv Gandhi's whirlwind tours, raising expectations of a battle royal between the Left Front and the Congress. Even Jyoti Basu felt the heat, his nerves too were on the edge.

During my field trips I realized very soon that the ABP was being consciously partisan towards the Congress in its election coverage. I refused to join the bandwagon and reported what I saw and felt on the ground. I categorically predicted Congress's rout in Priya Ranjan Dasmunsi's home district, West Dinajpur, blaming the PCC president, and at that point the face of the Opposition, for the impending catastrophe. My copy surprised Aveek Babu as I had personal relations with Dasmunsi, often earning the dubious distinction of being his 'chamcha' (yes-man). My report saw the light of day on the day of the polling, after gathering dust on the news editor's table for almost a fortnight. The story did not even appear on the front page.

Aghast, I confronted Aveek Babu, and asked him agitatedly why my copy could not be carried earlier. He smiled and then confessed, 'Your copy was brilliant but I chose to wait as I thought it may damage Congress's prospects in the state.' The ABP, however, could do nothing to alter what was inevitable. Dasmunsi came a cropper in his home district and the Congress failed so miserably that Rajiv Gandhi never came back to the state as long as he was the prime minister. Out of 294 Assembly seats, Congress bagged a mere 42. Leading from the front, Basu became the chief minister for the third time.

I had only a casual acquaintance with Basu as I covered his party in the country's capital. He was a frequent visitor, routinely attended the party's Polit Bureau meetings, but would never say a word to the waiting journalists. During an informal chat many years later, he explained his silence, 'For us communists, the most important mantra is discipline. I am not authorized to speak to the media on party matters, so why would I talk?'

He did break such a self-imposed discipline only once when, in 1996, Basu's party denied him the opportunity to become India's first-ever communist prime minister. In an interview with M.J. Akbar soon thereafter, he openly denounced CPI(M)'s decision as a 'Himalayan blunder'. The party, however, chose to remain silent. His comrades understood the old man's anguish allowing him to clear his chest. Basu never changed his position on the issue.

For me, as also my paper, it turned out to be an emotive issue as we saw it from the narrow regional prism, considering it a great betrayal by the CPI(M)'s southern clique led by Prakash Karat. We roared in protest just as our predecessors did when the 'Gandhian clique' forced another Bose (Subhas Chandra) out of the Congress, denying him his legitimate recognition. We targeted for attack particularly those Trojan horses who opposed Basu despite being Bengalis. Only two stood out as exceptions, Somnath Chatterjee and Buddhadeb Bhattacharjee.

As Bengalis, we nourish a deep psychological wound over the historical injustice meted out to us in 1947 that gradually led to our increasing marginalization in national politics in independent India. A united Bengal would have sent more number of MPs to Indian Parliament than UP has traditionally done, establishing thereby our undisputed preponderance in Lutyens' Delhi. We were denied the opportunity the moment the state was partitioned to accommodate the Muslim League's demand ignoring the explicit wishes of a majority of other Bengali leaders to the contrary. Thus, when Jyoti Basu's name cropped up as a prime ministerial candidate, the Bongs found a rare occasion to celebrate forgetting all divides for the moment.

But that was not to be as the majority in CPI(M)'s Central Committee, that had to be convened twice on two consecutive days to decide on the issue, turned down the proposal. With just about sixty odd Lok Sabha MPs in a house of 544, the party thought the idea ludicrous, throwing the ball back in the court of quarrelling non-Congress Opposition parties to form a government. Eventually, H.D. Deve Gowda, former Karnataka chief minister, emerged as the consensus candidate. Basu took an active part in reconciling conflicting interests and ambitions of the sundry Opposition outfits.

What prompted Basu to publicly criticize his party's decision? Was he not aware of the ground realities? Did he become greedy and overtly ambitious that blinded his pragmatic vision? Was he not aware he was breaking the cardinal principle of party discipline by openly criticizing the decision? In short, what was wrong with Jyoti Basu in the winter of his political life?

Four years later, in 2000, I had the occasion to ask him all these questions during a long interview in his hotel room in Jerusalem where he went virtually defying his party ideologues before demitting office as the longest serving chief minister of West Bengal. He admitted his criticism of the party decision might be construed as violation of discipline while adding, 'I did not challenge or oppose my party's stand, I just aired my personal views. In our party, all contentious decisions are taken on the basis of majority and once a decision is taken even the dissenters have to fall in line. That's the way a communist party works. That's the way I have been all my life. Here too, I was a minority and went by what the majority wanted.'

Basu admitted he would have faced an unenviable job as prime minister of a miniscule party as the pulls and pressures from all sides would have been truly irksome. But he was confident of carrying even a ramshackle coalition at least for a period of two years. As he said, 'My age standing as also my experience of successfully running a coalition in my home state would all have gone in my favour. I am quite adept at managing contradictions, notwithstanding ideological differences of coalition partners.'

What would he have achieved in case the party obliged him?

'I had two objectives in mind. First, my assuming prime ministerial responsibilities would surely have bolstered the dying Left movement in places where we were once quite strong and powerful. That way the Left would have regained some of its lost grounds and political relevance. Second, I would have got the first real chance to change the face of Bengal in a meaningful way by accelerating all-round economic developments. As chief minister I have only partially succeeded, as, in our country, all the real powers are vested with the Centre.'

I was a bit surprised to see Basu explaining his stand with such candour and honesty in a recorded interview. He was of course pretty relaxed in his silk lungi and bush shirt, having already downed a couple of pegs of premium Scotch. Although quite spartan in his lifestyle otherwise, he was known for his weakness for good food and Scotch.

Once I teased him for accepting a dinner invitation at my boss's house, clearly a no-go for a communist leader. 'Rakhi, your boss's wife is a great cook. I just could not resist the temptation,' Basu had quipped.

Although a proud Bengali, Basu, like many in his generation, was a pukka sahib in his attitude and temperament. He could read Bengali but hardly write it. For long, he did not even know how to sign his name in Bengali; it had caused him great embarrassment in the 1950s when a group of women admirers requested him for an autograph in Bengali. Basu was neither an ideologue nor a scholarly person like many communist leaders of his time. He preferred English pulp fiction when he had leisure time to read, either at home or during long flights. He hardly spoke in ideological hyperboles and deeply believed in the parliamentary form of democracy. He got attracted to communism in London when, as a student immediately before the Second World War, Basu came under the spell of the Communist Party of Great Britain (CPGB). His legislative career began in 1946 as an Opposition member losing his Assembly seat just only once in 1972, in a heavily rigged election.

London was his favourite city after Kolkata where he went to study law but came back a communist convert. Every summer, he would pay an official visit to London to cool his heels during his long stint as chief minister. He was criticized in the media for such annual pilgrimage wasting money from the state exchequer but Basu remained characteristically unfazed. There was frequent murmur in his party circles but none had the gumption of raising the matter in any party forum. As the undisputed leader, he was allowed this annual liberty every year during summer.

Basu was known most for his common sense and pragmatism and these characteristics set him apart from his party hardliners. As a result, all his working life he had to confront ideological roadblocks within the party conceding defeat on most occasions. When, soon after assuming state power in West Bengal in 1977, the CPI(M) decided to banish English language from primary level school education, on Ashok Mitra's recommendation, Basu firmly opposed the move though without any success. When in the mid-1980s, militant trade unionists owing allegiance to various Left parties were opposing introduction of computers in public sector banks and offices, Basu had welcomed the technological transformation as being inevitable. He wrote a long letter to the party's Polit Bureau criticizing the disruptive movements of the Left trade unions. I scooped the story for ABP from Delhi after getting hold of a copy of Basu's secret letter. My mole in the party was quickly identified after I got similar access to many secret, sensitive party documents and reported them in my paper. While my equity as a reporter rose, the axe fell on my source who lost his job. Till date, I nourish a sense of guilt for my friend's dismissal.

There were a few occasions though when on some issues he would stick to his guns, paying scant regard to objections in the party. One such issue was the state's industrial policy that needed a thorough relook in the context of large-scale economic reforms introduced by the P.V. Narasimha Rao government at the Centre. After deliberations at the state party level and without taking the matter to the Central Committee, Basu, in 1994, introduced his investment-friendly new industrial policy with a view to herald a new era of speedy economic growth and rapid industrialization. Buddhadeb Bhattacharjee, who succeeded Basu, took up the initiative in right earnest before floundering in the face of Singur and Nandigram mass movements many years later.

In this new initiative, Basu found his mate in Somnath Chatterjee who was made chairman of the West Bengal Industrial Development Corporation. A well-known barrister and parliamentarian, Somnath, a lightweight in the party hierarchy, considered Basu his guru, shared his pragmatism and plunged headlong to successfully carry out his new mandate. For the next six years, till the time Basu decided to declare his glorious innings, the Jyoti–Somnath duo led the movement for regeneration of Bengal's economy and change the negative perception of the state as an economic laggard that remained mired in the Stalinist past. 'Come to Bengal, give us a chance,' became their new mantra.

A year after the introduction of the state's new industrial policy, Basu and Chatterjee decided to head for the US to seek investment for the state, marking a complete shift from their earlier anti-capitalist policies. Even as Basu avoided visiting the US as a communist leader, his father, however, had gone there to study homeopathy and earn his medical degree.

I accompanied them in that trip to watch the fun of two communist stalwarts, moving from door to door in the United States with a begging bowl in hand. I was sure their visit would make much colourful copy that my readers would lap up.

For his unassailable stature as a politician, Basu was however a poor communicator and an uninspiring public speaker. Even in the US, he delivered his routine domestic political speeches that invariably targeted New Delhi for its stepmotherly attitude towards West Bengal.

Aghast, I confronted Basu with an uncomfortable question during a luncheon hosted in his honour by Merrill Lynch in New York. 'What you are saying may prove counter-productive and may not help matters. After hearing you none would feel motivated to come to Bengal.'

Basu answered with a deadpan expression, 'No, people should know the truth. I am only explaining the historical and factual context of why we find it difficult to progress with a hostile central government.'

What Basu lacked was however more than made up by Chatterjee who delivered passionate speeches, explaining in detail Bengal's comparative advantages over the rest of India, pleading prospective investors almost with folded hands. During the trip, Chatterjee also signed a good number of memorandum of understanding (MoU) with a host of business houses. Thereafter, he was nicknamed 'MOU Dada' as most of the assurances did not fructify causing him a great deal of embarrassment later.

The most interesting side show of Basu's stay in New York was his visit to the *Forbes* headquarters in the city's posh Greenwich Village. For me, the visit was of symbolic significance as the magazine was a vociferous proponent of unfettered capitalism and called itself a 'capitalist tool'. The editors gave Basu a tutorial on the magazine's history and heritage, along with a guided tour of its museum. As he was coming out, Basu was given a green tie by way of a memento that carried the insignia of the 'capitalist tool'. Flabbergasted, Basu promptly handed it over to his son Chandan, who was accompanying him and who has always been a known capitalist.

Siddhartha Shankar Ray was then the Indian Ambassador in Washington with whom I had close personal relations. My wife Kasturi and I were his first guests soon after he went to the US capital at the behest of P.V. Narasimha Rao. His official residence was huge, almost palatial, where most of the rooms remained locked. Ray, I could make out, was thoroughly enjoying the challenge of his new ambassadorial assignment in the world's most important capital at a time when India's economic liberalization coupled with the end of the Cold War opened a chapter of closer and more meaningful Indo-US relations. Through painstaking work and networking among the US bipartisan leadership, Ray prepared the groundwork for improved bilateral relations. In those days, the Indian Ambassador to Washington used to be given a paltry $500 by way of entertainment allowances, clearly a throwback of the Cold War era when Moscow ranked higher than Washington for the Indian Foreign Office. As Ray quipped, 'With 500 dollars in my pocket I am taking on the profligate Pakistanis, by far the most challenging job of my life.'

I stepped into Ray's official residence for the second time as a member of Basu's media entourage. These two gentlemen were sworn political adversaries. Yet, at a personal level they were the best of friends, enjoyed each other's company and shared a few secrets. Between the two, Ray as C.R. Das's grandson had nobler pedigree and was far more charismatic. Unlike Basu, who remained mostly a briefless barrister upon his return from London, Ray, a few years junior, was a successful lawyer all his life. Yet, in the realm of politics, Basu far outshined his friend to emerge as a far more credible, respectable and successful leader.

What followed that evening in the chief minister's official reception was an unbelievable spectacle of two friends openly praising each other sky-high in utter disregard of age-old, bitter political rivalry. Basu complimented Ray for shunning opportunistic politics all his life as also his unimpeachable personal honesty and integrity. Ray returned the favour by calling his friend the most credible and respectable figure of contemporary Indian politics.

Both Basu and Ray stood out as representatives of a fading era when arch-rivals in politics could also be close friends. Not many are aware that before going underground during the Emergency, Basu was sheltered by Ray, the then Congress chief minister, in his house.

In Washington, we stayed at the famous Watergate Hotel. Every evening, Basu would routinely enquire about my well-being or whether I needed any help. I could make out that behind Basu's stern exterior lay the mind and heart of an affectionate father. The revelation drew me closer to the grand old man.

In November 1996, I travelled with Basu to Dhaka, where he went as the country's goodwill ambassador before the renewal of the Farakka agreement over sharing of Ganga waters between India and Bangladesh. Deve Gowda's government at the Centre courted Basu's support, West Bengal being the most important stakeholder in this bilateral arrangement. For Basu too, the issue was politically sensitive as it had a direct bearing on the Kolkata port and its navigability, particularly during the dry months. Basu rose to the occasion as a national statesman, and his active help and cooperation cleared the way for the two countries to conclude a rather thorny deal amicably.

Dhaka laid a red carpet for Basu, gave him a rousing reception, normally preserved for heads of state when on a state visit. Basu reciprocated the warmth wherever he went. He had his ancestral home at a place called Baradi in Narayanganj, not far from Dhaka, where his father had built a two-storeyed mansion very close to Baba Loknath's ashram. As a communist, Basu was an atheist, but his god-fearing parents were disciples of the famous monk.

Prime Minister Sheikh Hasina Wajed made special arrangements for Basu's visit to his ancestral home and deputed her foreign minister to accompany him during the journey. Basu felt uncharacteristically nostalgic as the steamer negotiated the mighty Padma River on its way to Narayanganj. 'I used to come here during school holidays. The journey then was pretty arduous as it involved first a steamer, then a country boat and finally a long walk. For me the biggest attraction was, however, the delicious meat curry that was served on the steamer during lunch. That was the best meat curry I have ever had in life.'

Buddhadeb Bhattacharjee and Asim Dasgupta, two important ministerial colleagues accompanied Basu on his Dhaka trip. So did Gautam Ghosh, an acclaimed film-maker who was then shooting a documentary on him. Sitting in the first-floor drawing room of his ancestral home that had been given a fresh coat of paint, Basu went down the memory lane before the camera describing in detail his childhood experiences in Baradi. He spoke reverentially of Baba Loknath and the monk's influence on his family members. Basu remembered, he too visited the nearby ashram in the company of his father to seek the Baba's blessings.

After an hour-long stay at his ancestral home, Basu visited the Baba's ashram before addressing the local crowd who gathered in large numbers to have a glimpse of their 'ghorer polapan' (son of the soil). Amidst thunderous applause and constant showering of flower petals, even Basu sounded emotional as he thanked the locals for receiving him with such warmth and enthusiasm. He said that he would have been happier if his wife Kamal, a great devotee of Baba Loknath, was with him for the occasion. While his two other communist colleagues stayed away from the ashram, Basu had no qualms entering the inner sanctorum barefoot and offering flowers before a bronze bust of the Baba.

That was quintessential Jyoti Basu, never a hypocrite.

As I said before, his chief ministerial innings drew to a close and Basu, in open defiance of party ideologues, decided to pay an official visit to Israel in the summer of 2000. While there were ostensible signs of unease in the Left circles, Atal Bihari Vajpayee's government welcomed Basu's pragmatic decision.

Basu, as he told me during the journey, refused to stay in a state of denial about Israel and its existence. 'Does it really matter if I turn a blind eye to a historical reality? Also, at a personal level I have a great deal of curiosity for this country that has always remained unknown. I wanted to visit South Africa and I did. Israel is my last destination.'

In Jerusalem, Jyoti Babu was lodged at the famous King David Hotel where Bill Clinton also stayed when he came there a few months before. For the first three days he had no official engagement as Jaswant Singh, India's foreign minister, was visiting Israel during the same time. This gave me the rare opportunity to watch Basu in the avatar of a tourist. Of course I knew its tremendous worth as a copy.

A visit to the Western Wall, also known as the Wailing Wall, in the older and historic part of Jerusalem was first on the agenda. It is arguably the holiest of Jewish sites as it stands as a remnant of the holy Second Temple that stood there before being destroyed by the Romans in 70 CE. It is called the Wailing Wall since the faithful congregate from the world over come here essentially to wish and lament. The mystical aura associated with the wall is also found in a popular Israeli song that says, 'There are people with hearts of stone and stones with hearts of people.' For a faithful, this is no ordinary wall as it has ears.

The sprawling courtyard leading to the wall was swarming with visitors as Basu's limousine reached the entrance. We could also see the golden dome of the al-Aqsa Mosque, the most important Muslim holy site after Mecca and Medina, glittering in the afternoon sun. Two separate entrances led to these two sacred sites of two faiths.

As is common in a gurdwara or a mosque, here too, one cannot step into the precincts with the head uncovered. Without any fuss, Basu too put on a skull cap, made of paper, before striding steadily towards the site. For women visitors there was a separate enclosure, a fact that in those days greatly agitated Israeli feminists who demanded parity in all places of worship. Rabbis with flowing beards in their traditional black robes were either reading scriptures or wailing violently in front of the wall.

Those who wanted to make a wish were being asked to write it on a small piece of paper to be placed in one of the innumerable holes in the wall. Basu's chauffeur, a pleasant middle-aged gentleman who was doubling as our tour guide, informed us, 'A Jew, wherever he might be, would offer his prayers only in the direction of this wall. We believe the holy presence has never left the site.'

The tutorial over, the gentleman took out a small notebook from his pocket, forwarded it to Basu requesting him to scribble his wish on it. Basu smilingly snubbed his chauffeur, 'Do you think a man of my age would still have an unfulfilled wish?'

Basu also got down to see the Church of Holy Sepulchre where the Christians believe Jesus was both crucified and buried. A flight of steps from the Muslim quarter of the ancient town brought us down to a busy, winding cobbled road that covered at least four stations of the Via Dolorosa, representing the final episodes of Jesus's last journey. The stations came in chronological order beginning with the place where Jesus was stripped and ending at a tomb where he was believed to have been laid to rest. Basu maintained a stoic silence lending his ears to the tour guide's passionate narration of events that brought tears to my eyes.

On the way back, Basu felt tired and held my hand as we

started climbing the steps, steep and too many in number for a man of 86. We took our time stopping at every step for a few seconds. At the end of the journey, smile returned to his face as Basu quipped, 'I hope your God will bless me, now that I have visited three holy sites of three great world religions. I wonder how all of them were born in almost the same place, so close to each other.'

Dead Sea, a natural endorheic waterbody at the lowest point of the Earth, was our destination next morning. The northern tip to the Dead Sea was at best an hour's journey from Jerusalem via the West Bank. The highway going up and downhill had hardly any scenic beauty as we could only spot a few tired camels wandering lazily in the sizzling summer heat.

Tourists flock to the spot for sunbathing and natural phototherapy, a mystical cure for many human ailments. The weaker sunlight caused by the lower altitude of the area and extra atmosphere bring large number of Westerners here for sunbathing. The tourism industry flourishes here, with all kinds of sea-extracts and various naturopathy treatments being peddled to gullible tourists at exorbitant costs.

Soon after lunch, almost all members of the delegation disappeared, leaving Basu with his glass of gin and tonic in the hotel lobby. I stayed back to give him company. That for me was more rewarding than floating in the acutely salty seawater.

Before we left Jerusalem, news arrived from Kolkata that Mamata Banerjee's Trinamool Congress had wrested the prestigious Calcutta Corporation from the Left. I could notice a tinge of sadness in Basu's face, as I asked for his comments on this unexpected political development.

'Does it have something to do with your impending retirement? A Left Front without Basu at the helm may not be a good idea for your party's future in the state.'

Basu felt a bit flattered, saying, 'The inevitable has to happen.

I am old, sick and tired. I cannot say like Tennyson that, "Men may come and men may go, but I go on forever."'

Did Basu care for how he would be judged by posterity? Or how he would like to be remembered?

The grand old man snapped. 'Does posterity remember anyone? Do you remember Akbar the Great?'

Prophetic, I told myself many years later when, in 2014, the birth centenary of West Bengal's last political grandmaster came and went as quietly as death itself.

11

Pranab Da: The Comeback Hero

26 April 1986 was a Sunday. One of those Sundays that I shall never forget—among many other things—nor will Pranab Mukherjee, the former president of India. It was on this day that Mukherjee was expelled from the Congress by Rajiv Gandhi. For many politicians that would have meant either the end of their political career or switching over to another party. Not for Pranab Da. His story is that of a rare spectacular comeback, and that too within the same party.

The wound that Jyoti Basu's comrades had inflicted on Bengali hearts in 1996, by denying him the opportunity to be the nation's first Bengali prime minister, was healed to an extent in 2012, when Pranab Mukherjee became India's first Bengali president.

Luckily, I have had the opportunity to know this remarkable man up close and personal over the past three decades. My association with Pranab Da goes back to the mid-1980s, when he was weathering the worst political hailstorm in his life. But he was well known to my father much before that, in the 1950s, when he was my dad's student at Siuri's Vidyasagar College. He spoke about Pranab Da as a shy, serious student of history, who would ask probing questions about the Tudors and Stuarts of England. There were no sign yet that he would eventually blossom into the most successful and powerful politician from Bengal in the country's capital.

Pranab Da has a great deal of admiration for my father as a teacher, which helped me build a strong rapport with him over a remarkably short period of time. When Pranab Mukherjee was expelled from the Congress, I was posted in Delhi as the ABP's correspondent. It was during this difficult period in Pranab Da's political career that I started meeting him almost every afternoon and talked to him for hours. I came back wiser after every such meeting. Talking to him, I have found over the years, has always been a rewarding experience. That way he was my guru in Delhi on whom I relied over and over again for either a fact-check or a valuable perspective on every conceivable issue concerning history, politics or economics. A stickler to rules, Pranab Da would never divulge a secret nor yield to any provocation. But he would shower you with detailed information and in-depth analysis should you have an interesting question and have the abilities to engage him in a freewheeling discussion.

He would often say, 'I hate talking to uninformed and uneducated journalists who would ask stupid questions.'

26 April of 1986 was also one of those rare Sundays when Priya Ranjan Dasmunsi chose to stay back in the capital to attend to some pressing ministerial and party responsibilities. He had invited me for lunch at 16 Janpath, his official bungalow. Lunch over, we were engrossed in the Bengalis' favourite pastime when in full stomach—PNPC, *para-ninda-para-charcha*: in plain English, bitching about others. The RAX phone (secure phone lines then given to ministers and top bureaucrats for their exclusive use among themselves) rang. Arun Nehru, Rajiv Gandhi's cousin, was the caller. He was then the Union home minister, the most powerful member of the prime minister's kitchen cabinet as also his most trusted troubleshooter.

He told Priya, 'We are expelling Pranab from the Congress. On behalf of West Bengal PCC, you are expected to issue an official statement welcoming the decision.' Priya Da sat on his chair stunned. It took him quite a while to digest this piece of information.

In a way, Pranab Da himself was responsible for the catastrophe. There was no dearth of signals indicating his quick marginalization both within the government and the party. Following Rajiv's historic victory in the 1984 Lok Sabha elections, Pranab Da was promptly dropped from the cabinet as Vishwanath Pratap Singh, the Raja of Manda, succeeded him as the country's new finance minister.

Pranab Da failed to digest the insult meted out to him and he walked straight into Arun Nehru's traps. Instead of lying low and biding patiently for the tide to turn, he soon became the rallying point for disgruntled and disgraced Congressmen, occasionally airing his differences and grievances publicly. When, at the party's centenary session, Rajiv talked of launching a crusade against the 'power brokers', everyone knew who were his targets. Pranab Da retaliated in an explosive interview to *The Illustrated Weekly*. Soon he gathered around himself a group of Congress heavyweights who felt as marginalized as him—R. Gundu Rao, former chief minister of Karnataka, Jagannath Misra, former chief minister of Bihar and Sripat Misra, former chief minister of UP. The 'Gang of Four' shot into prominence when Kamalapati Tripathi, the veteran Congress leader from UP joined the rebels as their leader.

Panditji, as Tripathi was known to all, was a close associate of the Nehru–Gandhi family for generations. He lived in a sprawling bungalow on Janpath, bang opposite Lal Bahadur Shastri's erstwhile official residence, which was also very close to the AICC's official headquarters on 24 Akbar Road. An astute and cunning politician, Panditji, however, had the air of a god-fearing, pious, octogenarian Brahmin completely impervious to worldly problems and intricacies. Every afternoon I used to go to his bungalow after attending the regular and boring press briefings at the AICC headquarters. Panditji enjoyed his new-found importance, indicated by the presence of an ever-increasing number of journalists fishing for his rebellious quotes. He listened to all the questions patiently with a smiling face but refused any direct answer, speaking mostly in philosophical niceties.

Rajiv did not take the occasional raving and ranting by the rebel leaders very seriously. The situation took a dramatic turn when a confidential letter written to the prime minister by Tripathi got leaked to the press, creating a flutter in the capital's political circles and a great deal of embarrassment for Rajiv Gandhi himself. The letter was a scathing indictment of the new prime minister and his policies almost blaming him for destroying the party and subverting its vital interests. The content of the letter made headlines in every newspaper all over the country, forcing the establishment to quickly formulate a damage-control mechanism. As Panditji was far too important politically, the axe fell on the comparatively lesser and lighter 'evil'—Pranab Mukherjee.

More than three years later, when Pranab Da eventually returned to the Congress, much water had flown down the Yamuna. Yet, in their first meeting before the formal revocation of the expulsion order, Rajiv raised the long-forgotten issue of Panditji's letter and said, 'The moment I finished reading the letter I had understood who could be its real author. In the Congress party today I can't think of anyone else quoting Shakespeare, Tagore, Milton so poignantly.'

Why Rajiv hated his mother's closest and most trusted lieutenant has remained an unsolved political riddle. The widespread rumour is that he reminded Rajiv of the time-honoured tradition of nominating the senior-most cabinet minister to interim prime ministership in the event of the sudden demise of the prime minister. A.B.A. Ghani Khan Choudhury, union minister of Railways in Indira's cabinet and Pranab Da's bête noire in West Bengal politics, was the architect of the rumour that had many takers in those uncertain days in the gossip capital of India. Among them the most prominent was Arun Nehru, who was always keen to clip Pranab Da's wings.

Pranab Da was not a fool who did not know his limitations when pitted against the obvious and the unanimous heir apparent. *'Dara Singher sange keu kusti lore?'* (Does a sensible person invite Dara Singh for a bout of wrestling?) He had chided me in Bengali when on one occasion I tried to dig out the truth.

After his readmission into the party, Pranab Da spent every afternoon at the AICC office in a small room allotted normally to a joint secretary. Hardly anyone came to visit him and he spent his time mostly reading newspapers. Shortly thereafter, Rajiv was tragically assassinated while campaigning for the party in Tamil Nadu. He watched everything from a distance and maintained a low profile. He did not know then that a few years later, he would serve Rajiv's widow and regain his proverbial number two position. Nor did he know then that in 2012 the same Congress party would nominate him as the presidential candidate and send him to Raisina Hills as India's first Bengali president.

∽

Pranab Mukherjee's rise to the highest echelons of power in Lutyens' Delhi and his long innings at the top is a saga unmatched and unparalleled in the political history of post-Independence Bengal. Bidhan Chandra Roy, the architect of modern Bengal, had been one of the most venerable political figures in India during his days. He was a close friend of Motilal Nehru and called Jawaharlal Nehru by his first name. Jyoti Basu, the Marxist patriarch and the architect of India's longest and most successful coalition experiment, remained, all his life, one of the nation's most respected and adorable political luminaries. But none of them went outside the confines of their state to take a plunge into national politics. Siddhartha Shankar Ray, the flamboyant Bengal Congress leader and former chief minister, was a friend of Indira Gandhi and enjoyed her confidence in the 1970s. Yet he was gloriously inconsistent in his political behaviour, intermittently disappearing from the horizon to practice law.

Pranab Da's political success, in a way, also baffles the pundits and defies conventional political wisdom about leadership. Unlike Bidhan Chandra Roy, Jyoti Basu or Siddhartha Shankar Ray, he was not born with a silver spoon, coming as he does from a nondescript village in the backward district of Birbhum. Even after becoming the president, Pranab Da has not discontinued the practice of returning to his village every year during the four days of Durga Puja to perform the rites himself. While earlier he sat before the idols in full public view, as the president, he had to do it in private, behind closed doors. As he explained to me, 'I am supposed to be the protector of the country's Constitution and as such I cannot offer Puja publicly. As a private citizen, however, I am within my rights to pursue my own religious beliefs.'

At a time when political leadership within the Congress belonged largely to the urban, Anglophile aristocrats, Pranab Da truly represented rural India. He went to a village school and then graduated from a district college. During his childhood he had to walk several kilometres to reach the nearby primary school, a healthy habit that has stayed with the man till date. Every morning, he walks briskly for forty-five minutes in his jogging suit. The telltale signs of Pranab Da's rural background and upbringing and his ordinary education stayed with him even as he continued to scale newer heights in his party and in the central government. Despite his four-decade-long Delhi life and intimate association with North Indians, his Hindi remains atrocious and his English pronunciation, with a thick Bengali accent, evokes muted laughter in any congregation of the well-bred, English-educated elite.

Early in his ministerial career, Indira Gandhi took a caring note of it and suggested to him that he retain an English tutor to brush up his pronunciations. She even volunteered to find him one who would do this job discreetly. But Pranab Da politely refused, saying, 'Madam there is no point trying to square a circle. What has been done cannot be undone. I have to carry the baggage of my background wherever I go.' Pranab Da is critically aware of his limitations and often laughs at himself at this handicap.

In my long association with the man, I have seen almost all the shades of his personality and character from very close quarters. A quintessential 'addabaj' (a typical Bengali trait of chatting with friends and family for hours on every subject under the sun), Bengali bhadralok, he loves to talk about his village and his mother. In every sense of the term Pranab Da was his mother's child who taught and brought him up with utmost care and guidance. As a boy, he was known for all conceivable mischief for which he got regular whacking from his mother. As Pranab Da says, 'I could climb any tall mango tree just like a monkey and was perceived as a threat by anyone in the neighbourhood who had a garden. I would eat a dozen mangoes in no time sitting under the same tree I had plucked the fruits from. Everyone complained to my mother as I waited for the evening with bated breath. She was merciless in enforcing discipline and equally sweet when I slept next to her.'

Pranab Da left Bengal's shores to join national politics in the late 1960s and always remained, with intermittent breaks, a Rajya Sabha member, till he first tasted victory in Lok Sabha elections in 2004. For a long period of time, he was thus ridiculed as a 'rootless wanderer' who survived on Indira's 'misplaced trust and confidence'. Was he a sycophant like Dev Kanta Barua who once equated India with Indira? Pranab Da denies the charge emphatically, recalling from his elephantine memory several occasions when he fought with her over various political and governmental issues. Often, he claims, Indira changed or modified her decisions having found merit in Pranab Da's arguments. When she did not, Indira would just say, 'Okay Professor, I have heard you long enough. Now do exactly what I tell you.' The verdict pronounced, Pranab Da would follow the instruction in letter and spirit. Pranab Da was a loyalist indeed, but hardly a sycophant.

Much of these doubts and allegations were laid to rest when, in 2004, he was declared a winner from the Jangipur Lok Sabha constituency in Murshidabad, a well-known and for long an impregnable Left bastion. For once, he shed his well-crafted serious image to become publicly ecstatic and emotional. On that tour I travelled with him as he went from one public meeting to another to say, 'From now on, no one will call me a rootless wanderer, an alien in his homeland. For me this is a dream come true, a dream I have cherished and nourished ever since I entered politics.' Tears of joy rolled down his eyes as he spoke in a high-pitched voice visibly choked with emotions. I believe, in Pranab Mukherjee's long political career, that was his happiest hour.

Five years later, in 2009, he won again with a wider margin. By then his rapport with the poorest of the poor in the Muslim-dominated backward district had been firmly established. As an MP he did exactly what everyone else does, showering on his constituency largesse and patronage to the extent possible and permissible.

However, by 2004, Pranab Da had already resigned himself to what he grudgingly understood to be his fait accompli. Not for him the cherry on the cake. Thus, when Sonia Gandhi did a Mahatma and declared Manmohan Singh as her choice, Pranab Da was hardly surprised. He accepted the announcement with perfect equanimity. Two decades ago, when Pranab Da was the country's finance minister, he made Manmohan the Reserve Bank governor. He might have bled internally to see his subordinate being catapulted to that coveted position but, externally, he showed exemplary grace and restraint.

Like P.V. Narasimha Rao, Pranab Da also has high regards for Manmohan Singh at a personal level. He admires his honesty and integrity as also his brilliance as an economist. In the eight years under Manmohan's stewardship, the duo never fought with each other in public. That did not mean, however, that they did not have differences or major disagreements over various issues. Pranab Da felt flattered and beholden when, after a road accident, Manmohan sent a special aircraft to expeditiously carry him back to Delhi. He was pleasantly surprised to see the prime minister waiting to receive him at the airport. Breaking earlier protocols, Pranab Da was then advised by Manmohan to travel by a special aircraft on his official tours, a gesture he fondly remembers.

Only once the relation soured and almost came to a breaking point when a confidential note of the Finance Ministry, implicating in a roundabout manner P. Chidambaram's complicity in the 2G scam, got mysteriously leaked to the press. The resultant wild media speculations holding him responsible for the leak infuriated Pranab Da. The speculation seemed credible in the light of the known estrangement between Pranab Da and Chidambaram.

By way of strange coincidence, both the prime minister and the finance minister were in the US then, but for different reasons. While Manmohan was in New York to attend the annual session of the UN General Assembly, Pranab Da was in Washington for his official engagements with the World Bank and International Monetary Fund. The media controversy over the leakage infuriated Pranab Da so much that he hurriedly cancelled his pending appointments in Washington and rushed to New York to settle scores with the prime minister. Pranab Da, known, feared and ridiculed for his mercurial temperament, often losing his cool at the slightest of provocations, was this time determined to give the prime minister a piece of his mind, fully prepared for a showdown. Pranab Da told Manmohan that enough was indeed enough. He would catch the next flight home and put in his papers.

It took Manmohan a long time to assuage Pranab Da's frayed tempers even after the prime minister conceded the fact that the finance minister was not responsible for the leakage. It was during the animated discussion that Pranab Da let out a secret to Manmohan. 'Mrs Gandhi gave me a very important advice. She told me not to keep any copy of an official paper that was being sent to the PMO. Till now I have never deviated from the practice. But now I will give it a second thought.'

With Sonia Gandhi, however, Pranab Da's relation has always been warm and cordial based upon mutual respect and understanding. There are certain traits in Sonia's character and leadership that he admired unhesitatingly, not failing to point out at the same time why and where the daughter-in-law overshadowed Indira. The first thing is her manifest honesty and direct approach towards life. He told me umpteen times, 'Sonia is not a habitual liar; she will tell you an unpalatable truth to your face. You know where she stands on every given issue.' Second, as he further pointed out, in matters of party politics she does not play favourites and does not believe in divide and rule. Third, she is a patient listener and values everyone's views and judgement. More often than not she goes by consensus and generally refrains from imposing her will or decision on the party and government. As Pranab Da repeatedly emphasized, he found himself fully comfortable in such a transparent atmosphere.

A voracious reader since childhood, he cannot sit idle without reading something, even if it's rubbish. It could be the official files; a hardbound serious book on history, politics, economics or diplomacy, a biography or a memoir; a newspaper or a periodical; or even a Bengali 'panjika', an almanac, if nothing else was available at hand. This habit backed by an enviable, elephantine memory and a rare capacity to slog twenty hours a day, distinguished him in a crowd of fortune seekers bereft of either education or insight. As a result, till he went to the Rashtrapati Bhavan, he was sought after for every little problem, thanks to his deep reservoir of experience.

Paradoxically, Pranab Da's so-called indispensability had been his major handicap in pursuing another dream that he cherished as he entered the winter of his political life: to retire from public life as India's president. In 2007, when the president's post fell vacant and the Congress was looking for a suitable candidate, Pranab Da discreetly expressed his desire to move to Rashtrapati Bhavan. The Left leaders with whom Pranab Da enjoyed unique rapport and were then supporting UPA-I took up the campaign on his behalf and persuaded Sonia to accept his candidature.

One night Sonia broached the matter with characteristic dignity and candour. She lost no time to convince the aspirant that she was not opposed to his candidature. Then, after a pause she asked Pranab Da the most baffling of all questions he had faced in life: 'You have to do me a favour. Just tell me who can replace you in the cabinet and perform your role. Give me a name and you will be our candidate.' Pranab Da sat dumbfounded for a while and then broke into laughter. Sonia joined too.

In 2012, Pranab Da was initially convinced for the same set of reasons his name would not be considered yet again. He was wrong. Luckily for him, Pranab Da emerged as the consensus choice for almost every other party except the BJP after Sonia proposed his name and Manmohan endorsed it. What turned the dice in his favour or why his so-called indispensability was no longer taken into account remains to be unravelled. It could be that Manmohan found in it an honourable exit route for a man he no longer wanted in his cabinet as the finance minister.

On the day Pranab Da emerged as the UPA's presidential candidate, I was in Thailand holidaying with my family. I called him late at night to congratulate. In my long association with him I can't recall another occasion when I found him so happy and ecstatic. Then he shared with me what Sonia Gandhi told him this time.

'Pranabji, this is in recognition of your lifetime contribution to the Congress party.'

Pranab Da believes this was nothing other than divine justice.

At a personal level, the former finance minister is no less discreet when it comes to spending money. Just consider this. On a late evening, Pranab Da came to Kolkata primarily to attend the wedding ceremony of a junior party colleague. By the time he landed, all the shops were closed and he was not carrying any gift. An accompanying political colleague sitting in the front seat of his car came to his rescue suggesting he could find some fine sarees for the bride from his wife's boutique nearby. Upon enquiry, he found the price varied from one thousand to twenty thousand rupees and solicited the finance minister's advice. Pat came the reply: Go for a ₹1000 one.

12
In the Tigers' Den

'Kali Da!' I cried out. Notwithstanding the cliché at that moment I could compare the man I was shouting for as the proverbial straw, myself being the drowning man! All my persuasive skills had proven unproductive and had failed to convince my interrogators. Kali Da was therefore my last hope.

One of the most unforgettable assignments that I was sent on during my stint in Delhi as the ABP correspondent had landed me in that part of Sri Lanka where few journalists dared set foot in the 1980s. Yet, there I was in Jaffna in 1987.

Three young men were ruthlessly grilling me at the small and dimly lit restaurant at Jaffna's Gnanams Hotel. One of their assault rifles lay idly on the table with the barrel pointing at me. I knew they were important members of the Liberation Tigers of Tamil Eelam (LTTE) but did not know their names. I told them my name, showed my calling card as also the Government of India's Press Information Bureau (PIB) ID. They, however, simply refused to be convinced even after an hour-long nerve-racking interrogation. They took me for a spy, either from Colombo or New Delhi, and tried relentlessly to dig out which of the two I really was.

Did I look like a Sinhala? According to unsubstantiated historical accounts, Bengalis in pre-historic times had substantial contacts with the island nation now named Sri Lanka. It was also claimed that Vijay Singha, a Bengali king, once conquered the place following which large-scale migration took place to Bengal. Satyendra Nath Dutta, a Bengali poet, took note of it in a poem that we were taught in school.

My editor, Aveek Sarkar, had instructed me to do a story on this possible connection between Bengal and Sri Lanka, just before I left for Colombo in early July 1987. I did speak to a few Sinhala historians and archaeologists but to no avail. They virtually dismissed the idea calling it a figment of a poet's imagination. I, therefore, had nothing to file on this.

I could not blame the LTTE cadres for being so suspicious of my presence in Jaffna at a time when the town remained out of bounds for journalists. India had violated the Sri Lankan air space on 4 June 1987. An Indian ship carrying relief material and a few journalists reached the Kankesanthurai harbour on 26 June. None of the journalists was allowed to step out by the Sri Lankan authorities. Also, as a general rule, journalists, mostly Indian and Western, who came there, did so after getting in touch with the militants and always with their explicit approval. It was, therefore, very difficult for them to believe and digest the story I told them regarding my arrival.

Yet facts can often indeed be stranger than fiction.

When I landed at the Palali airbase in a Sri Lankan Air Force plane with a batch of Sinhala soldiers, I did not even dream of visiting Jaffna. I went on a conducted tour, given regularly to foreign correspondents by the Sri Lankan Army in those days, merely as a public relations exercise. The drill went exactly like this: At Palali you would board a helicopter gunship guarded zealously by machine gun toting commandoes for a short and quick aerial survey of the Vadamarachi region, the worst affected area in the war between the LTTE and the Sri Lankan forces. At the airbase you would be given a briefing by a senior Sri Lankan

Army official over lunch and then brought back to Colombo in the afternoon. The purpose of the exercise was to dispel the widely held notion, particularly in India, that the Sri Lankan forces committed excesses against its own people in the offensive they launched against the LTTE in the region. That was just a few days after India intervened in Sri Lanka's internecine warfare and violated their air space to drop relief material for the trapped Tamil population in the Jaffna peninsula. Indian journalists who rushed to Colombo in the wake of the intervention were, for obvious reasons, given precedence by the Sri Lankan authorities for the conducted tour in the war-affected region.

The land route from Colombo to the Jaffna peninsula via the Elephant Pass fell into virtual disabuse as a consequence of the civil war. It was a long, arduous and hazardous journey no one undertook for fear of mines, booby traps and sudden ambushes by the militants. The Sri Lankan forces therefore took the aerial route for safety as the Tigers did not, yet, have anti-aircraft missiles. In the Jaffna peninsula they used the biggest and only airbase at Palali, not far from Jaffna town, for launching operations in the region. In times of peace preceding the outbreak of the civil war, Palali was also a regular airport for commercial passenger traffic. The airbase lay very close to Kankesanthurai, a regular navy harbour. An Indian ship laden with relief material had reached the harbour a day before I went to Palali.

The tour in the gunship was exciting but quite futile for reporting purposes. The helicopter flew at a fairly high altitude, making it impossible to gauge the extent of war damages a few thousand feet below. The pilots gave a casual running commentary of the region and what happened during the war in a language hardly comprehensible. It was predictably a one-sided version of the story that blamed only the Tigers for aggravating the situation. The tour was simply hogwash and I felt frustrated and dejected as the chopper came back to the airport amid violent flutters of surrounding trees.

And then Kali Da appeared on the scene almost as a godsend, virtually from the blues, to dramatically alter the course of my journey on that fateful afternoon. My spirits lifted in no time and I felt ecstatic.

The middle-aged army officer deputed to look after me was a soft-spoken, friendly Muslim gentleman and had a detached, almost philosophical view about a war that involved Sinhala Buddhists and Hindu Tamils. Over a quiet and simple working lunch he talked more about the Eastern Province, his home, where the situation was drifting from bad to worse. Before coming to Palali I had toured the Eastern regions extensively, staying both at Batticaloa and Trincomalee. He gave me a very patient and anxious hearing as I narrated my experiences there in graphic details. Suddenly, we heard noises, emanating from the courtyard a few yards away from the army canteen. Our conversation was abruptly broken as the officer rushed outside, with me hot on his heels.

It was a small crowd, at best twenty in number—all Indians. They were members of the Indian Red Cross and had come from Delhi to conduct and oversee relief operations in the war-ravaged peninsula. Two of them came to the Muslim officer's cubicle and handed over a list of the members. After they were gone I took the list from the officer out of sheer curiosity and found a Bengali name right at the top. Kali Sarkar. I stormed out of the room. My reporter's nose was itching violently.

Kali Da was a tall, middle-aged, mild-mannered gentleman who was equally surprised to see a fellow Bengali in the unlikeliest of places. As it turned out, at some point in his youth he had also worked for ABP as a stringer from Darjeeling and was aware of my name. He readily agreed to take me with them if I could obtain permission from the army authorities. I hatched a plot quickly and dragged Kali Da to the officer's chamber to introduce him as my cousin. Over a cup of tea I sought his permission to travel with them and the officer agreed without any fuss. It was agreed that I would return to the airbase the following afternoon to board a return flight to Colombo. I ran to board the Red Cross minibus heading towards Jaffna after visiting the war-affected areas of Vadamarachi.

What I missed from the air started unfolding before my eyes, the horror and the nature of devastation and destruction caused by the Sri Lankan air offensive that prompted Indian intervention. We saw an old church reduced to rubble amid a neighbourhood bombed and battered indiscriminately. Several villages looked deserted and at some, villagers came rushing when they spotted a group of Indians. Their version of the war, narrated in graphic and chilling details, ran contrary to the version I had heard just a while ago from the perpetrators. The village elders were fluent in English, a living example of the educated and progressive culture of the Jaffna Tamils. The Sri Lankan Army men acting as navigators, felt shaky and nervous as homeless and hopeless locals started raining choicest abuses on them. I found the situation amusing while taking verbatim notes of their narration and complaints.

One major target of the attack was Velvettithurai, LTTE leader Prabhakaran's village, and more specifically his ancestral house where his parents stayed before the attack. The bombing achieved nothing except damaging the house extensively as none of his family members was there at the time of the attack. The house resembled one normally inhabited by a middle-class family and we found several old black-and-white family photographs of the family in the rubble. The neighbours affectionately referred to the Tiger chieftain as 'Thambi' (younger brother) and spoke about his bravery, honesty and commitment to the cause of the Eelam. An elderly neighbour remembered him as a shy, book-loving, introvert child who showed no signs of a rebel. His father was a devout Gandhian and mother, a god-fearing Hindu. Prabhakaran got attracted to militancy much later under the influence of a schoolteacher who called upon his students to take up arms to fight against the discriminations heaped upon the Tamils. In 1975, he shot into sudden prominence after killing the Jaffna mayor from a point-blank range. His ties with his village snapped after the incident as Prabhakaran fled to the jungles and rarely came home to be with his family. Yet Thambi, despite his detachment, still elicited a rare shine in the eyes of his neighbours, young and old, male or female.

The accompanying Sri Lankan soldiers started feeling restive as the evening was drawing close and they were obliged to navigate the Red Cross van up to the no man's land between the areas controlled by them and the Tigers. Even though the intensity of the war had subsided following New Delhi's interference, there was no complete cessation of hostilities on either side. A Tiger suicide bomber had driven and rammed an explosive-laden truck into a Sri Lankan Army camp in the same area just about seventy-two hours before our arrival. The tense atmosphere was fraught with all-round fear, suspicion and anxiety.

Jaffna town was only a few kilometres away but our journey took a couple of hours after the Tigers took charge of our reception. It seemed bizarre and surreal that there could be two zones of actual control in the same country between two sets of warring citizens. Jaffna town and its neighbourhood still remained under the complete control of the Tiger guerillas and were still out of bounds for the Sri Lankan soldiers. India's intervention thus foiled Colombo's plans of capturing the real seat of Tamil militancy.

The boys who came to greet us as we crossed the no man's land after bidding farewell to the Sri Lankan Army men could hardly be described as soldiers, at least from their physical appearances. Most of them were in their teens and looked like school students.

A few also looked rickety, their ribs protruding from their lean chests. Yet all of them had guns slinging from their shoulders, cyanide capsules around their necks and all looked spectacularly cheerful. I noticed there was no girl or woman in their group.

Two of the boys first entered our minibus to garland each one of us, the first tentative signs of their warmth and hospitality. In a while, dozens of motorcyclists appeared from nowhere to form a quick procession in front of our bus. The formation was swift, meticulous as if rehearsed. Suddenly we turned into VIPs in an alien land living under the shadow of a bloody civil war.

The bike brigade moved at a snail's pace on a road dotted with potholes. The empty agricultural lands on both sides looked barren as if there were no harvests that season. As we moved closer to the town, houses began to appear on the horizon and we could spot hundreds of people waiting on the road to greet us. Most of them were ordinary-looking women in traditional sarees. We had to come out of the bus at least a dozen times as flower petals were showered on us and the women blew conch shells. Some raised slogans hailing India and Rajiv Gandhi. As a hack, I felt awkward as I knew none of this was meant for me. Yet at the same time I felt proud as an Indian and was deeply touched by their emotional gestures. The bike riders leading us up to Jaffna town disappeared as suddenly as they had come and our minibus stopped at its final destination—Gnanams Hotel, right at the heart of the town.

In the darkness, the small hotel looked just like a haunted house, certainly not in regular business. There was no boarder other than the Red Cross team. I checked into a room with Kali Da and together we cleaned it to make it somewhat habitable. Before coming to our room, we ordered rice and fish curry for dinner, as the restaurant owner pleaded his inability to cook and arrange for anything else. After about half an hour, there was a tap on our door and I saw three young men standing outside. 'We want to have a word with you,' one of them said very politely. As I put on my slippers I could guess something had gone wrong. Before stepping out I shouted to inform Kali Da, who was having a shower, that I was going to the restaurant with three strangers. I spoke in Bengali so that my visitors could not understand a word of it.

These three young men had nothing in common with the guerillas we met during our journey to Jaffna although they too belonged to the same organization. They were seniors, well dressed, well-mannered, holding higher and more responsible positions in the outfit. One of them with glasses looked the brightest. Without much ado he came straight to the point and asked me point-blank what I was doing in Jaffna.

I was aghast since no one was supposed to know my real identity and Kali Da too had introduced me as his cousin to his team. During the entire journey from Palali to Jaffna I had spoken with no one except the villagers in Vadamarachi. All along I was wearing a Red Cross hat and waved its flag when greeted by the crowd. Flummoxed, I asked a counter question, 'Why are you asking me this?'

'We know you are not from the Red Cross. We have our own Intelligence. Just tell us who you are.'

Compelled, I divulged my identity and narrated truthfully the circumstances in which I had landed in Jaffna. I also told them in brief the experiences of my visit to Colombo and other places. They listened to me carefully, ordered tea more than once, but would not accept me at face value. They would shake their heads vigorously in disagreement and go on repeating a veiled threat over and over again. 'If you are from the RAW, we will treat you differently. We will kill you if you are found to be a Sinhala agent.' Every time I heard it, I was unable to conceal my smile and laughter. The more I laughed the more obstinate and unreasonable they became. 'I carry just one card given to me by the Press Information Bureau of the Indian government. I have told you the truth. Now it is up to you to do what you think is best.' And then I shouted and called Kali Da to bail me out.

He came and narrated the same story while I sat in silence looking the other way. Then he came out with the clincher. 'He will leave Jaffna tomorrow but I will stay put for at least a month. You find out about him from your sources in Delhi and Kolkata. Take me hostage in case you find I lied to you.' The ice melted, all three of them apologized for their rude behaviour and truth triumphed. The young man with glasses who did all the questioning now extended his hand to introduce himself. 'I am Yogi. I look after the political division of the LTTE. Welcome to Jaffna.'

'*Satyameva Jayate*,' I quipped.

Till a minute ago the intermittent sound of canon fire coming from the nearby Jaffna fort—the only place in the vicinity under Sri Lankan Army control—felt lighter than the pounding of my heart. Commenting on the fort, Yogi said, 'A section of the Sri Lankan soldiers have been holed up there for a very long time. This is how they tell us they are alive. We call it the "fort-bell".'

As we warmed up to each other talking shop and sharing our perspectives about New Delhi and its future actions I sought from Yogi what any scribe would ask for in the land of the Tigers—an appointment with Velupillai Prabhakaran. 'He would be leaving for Delhi soon. Let me see what I can do for you.'

Yogi's half-hearted pro forma assurance did not sound very convincing and I chose not to bother him with repeated requests. After such a long and eventful day and nerve-shattering interrogation, I was dying to have a shower, eat rice and fish curry and crash on my bed. The cold shower rejuvenated me a little but the dinner was a disaster. What came as fish curry on the table was a piece of rotten fish lost in a small bowl of red chili paste. None of us could bear it after a gulp. I ran to the tap to wash my mouth.

Yogi reappeared on a motorcycle around midnight and ordered me to sit on the pillion. 'The boss has agreed to see you. But it would just be a courtesy call and no interview. Okay?' At that hour of the night, the town predictably wore a dark, deserted and sleepy look. For centuries the ancient town had been under the occupation of successive colonial rulers—the Portuguese, the Dutch and finally the British. As Yogi sped along, he also gave a commentary of places, pointing to a historical church here or a big public library there. Suddenly, he stopped the bike and took out a black cloth from his trouser pocket. 'From here, you will have to go blindfold. That is the rule.'

Prabhakaran sat all by himself in a small, ordinary room, in his civilian attire. His portly figure as also his squeaky voice disappointed me a great deal as I sat down on a cane chair in front of him. He looked tired, tense and lost in deep thoughts. Our meeting did not last for more than five minutes and instead of talking about anything else he paid rich tributes to Subhas Chandra Bose and called Netaji and Bhagat Singh—his two idols. I told him that I had translated Bose's autobiography, *An Indian Pilgrim*, from English to Bengali. I suspected that Prabhakaran had agreed to see me only because I was a Bengali. Yogi smiled in agreement as we came back via a different route seeing a few more landmarks of the town.

Next morning I took a passenger bus from Jaffna to return to Palali at the appointed hour suggested by Yogi. Kali Da gave me a letter of introduction on the Red Cross letterhead, in case I was harassed by the Sri Lankans en route. In the bus, I was offered the front seat, treated again as a VIP as Yogi came to see me off. I became the centre of everyone's attention as if I had all the answers for their legitimate queries. For a few minutes I became the official spokesman of the Indian government, impressing my fellow passengers with my limited knowledge and information of Delhi's possible moves. The friendly driver even allowed me to

With Sachin Tendulkar at Centurion Park Stadium, Gauteng, South Africa

With former West Bengal Chief Minister Jyoti Basu, near the Wailing Wall in Jerusalem, Israel

With former West Bengal Chief Minister Buddhadeb Bhattacharjee in Milan, Italy

Suman Chattopadhyay (third from left) with former Prime Minister Rajiv Gandhi in the PM's special aircraft

With the Sarkar brothers, Arup and Aveek (centre), at the Salt Lake Stadium, Kolkata

With Mamata Banerjee, when she was the Railway Minister in the Atal Bihari Vajpayee government

Sharing a musical moment with renowned Tagore scholar Kazuo Azuma at the latter's residence in Tokyo, Japan

With Pranab Mukherjee at the launch of the author's book on the former President of India

smoke inside the bus.

The happy and carefree atmosphere inside the bus changed dramatically as we crossed into the Sri Lankan controlled territory. The discussion stopped, laughter subsided and everyone sat stiff on his or her seat. In a stretch of 7 to 8 kms, I counted twelve check posts manned by the young conscripts of the Sri Lankan Army. At every stop, the passengers had to disembark from the front gate and re-enter through the rear gate after invasive frisking. No one talked, no one asked any question, and the young soldiers hardly smiled.

Armed with Kali Da's letter in my pocket, I decided to play a prank on the young soldiers at the first check post. I came out first and tersely commanded the soldier to salute. Taken aback, he obliged without asking a question. I introduced myself as an Indian Red Cross member and commanded him yet again to pass on the information via wireless to his colleagues stationed at all the check posts. I also took the name of my Muslim officer friend based in Palali to further rattle and intimidate him. It worked like magic and I was treated as a VIP also by the other side everywhere the bus stopped. I returned to Palali in one piece to board the Sri Lankan aircraft headed towards Colombo.

Two years later, I was to visit another city as part of my assignment which was as war-tense as Colombo. It was Kabul. In Kabul, locals remained under the perpetual fear of Mujahideen missile attacks from all sides. In Colombo, the city reeled under the threat of LTTE bombers who could detonate explosives anytime anywhere—in a bus stand, in a hotel lobby, in crowded bazaars. As a result, downtown Colombo, facing the Bay of Bengal, had check points after every few metres and all the vital installations, including government buildings and banks, had armed guards manning them round the clock. The central telegraph office, where I went to transmit my copies to Kolkata, looked virtually like a fortress. The tourist inflow came down to a trickle and the occupancy rate in the swanky five-star hotels plummeted to abysmal depths. Everyone hurried back home before sunset, even the sprawling beach looked virtually empty in the evenings. I got a suite to myself at the Oberoi Hotel for just $35 per night.

If the Tigers were feared, Indians were hated and treated contemptuously by one and all in Colombo back then. At the airport's immigration counter, the Sinhala officer in charge made snide remarks at me the moment he saw my passport. The taxi driver who drove me from the airport to the hotel bombarded me with uncomfortable questions about India's 'dadagiri'. Ranasinghe Premadasa, the second in command after President J.R. Jayawardene, went about spreading venom and vitriol against India. The Buddhist monks, the most influential section in the Sinhala society, were equally critical of Colombo and New Delhi. The newspapers were full of anti-Indian stories castigating in harshest words India's attitude towards a smaller neighbour. The stories of the resurgence of the JVP (Janatha Vimukthi Peramuna), a Sinhala militant outfit, rented the air, already thick with gloomy forebodings. The Indian High Commission, also heavily guarded, was then the only place in Colombo where an Indian journalist was welcome and felt comfortable.

J.N. Dixit, better known as Mani Dixit, the Indian high commissioner, was the second most important person in Colombo after the Sri Lankan president. He was haughty, had an air about himself and was a constant pipe-smoker. He had direct access to the Sri Lankan president and acted as Rajiv Gandhi's personal envoy in all his official engagements with the Sri Lankan establishment. For him, what India did was a geopolitical necessity, an action to safeguard the country's strategic interests in a volatile atmosphere. The Indian mission fed regular stories suggesting that Sri Lanka was getting closer to Pakistan and Israel in its effort to combat Tamil militancy in the northern and eastern parts of the island nation. It was also said that Mossad was being roped in for training the soldiers. The strategic importance of Trincomalee harbour was touted again and again to drive home the point that forces inimical to India's interests could not be allowed to take control of the location. The rationale, however, had no takers in the Sri Lankan capital.

Mani Dixit remained busy with his secret parleys and preparations and did not interact much with journalists. It was Hardeep Puri, a flamboyant Sikh foreign service officer, who held the fort as the political secretary and engaged himself extensively with visiting journalists. His beautiful wife Laxmi was also posted there in the same mission. Like Dixit, Puri was also a fierce nationalist and supported Delhi's actions unequivocally. He was a warm, hospitable and extremely articulate young man who gave both sides of the story. I struck an immediate rapport and friendship with Hardeep and invited him once for dinner to my hotel. He refused to come to Oberoi because its officials opposed the Indian action. I took him to Taj Samudra, another beautiful hotel nearby, where we drank and ate till the early hours of the morning. I shared with him my experiences of visiting the eastern parts.

On the afternoon I returned from Jaffna, I went straight to meet Hardeep to triumphantly tell him the story of my exploits. He took me straight into the high commissioner's room, my first entry during a fortnight-long stay in the country. Dixit heard me out patiently before giving me a golden piece of advice, 'Just listen to me. There is a late night flight to Madras. Board it and leave this country immediately. People here should not know you went to Jaffna.'

13

Of Bibi and Others

The man from behind the counter thundered, '*Sharabi ka naam?*' (What is the drinker's name?) I was so rattled that I could not make out at the first instance that the shopkeeper was addressing me. After I understood and obliged, he came back with the ultimate shocker, '*Sharabi ke baap ka naam?*' (Name of the drinker's father?)

My father, particularly being the kind of ruthless disciplinarian he was, couldn't have imagined in his most loathsome nightmares that his son would have to evoke his name to purchase a bottle of booze. That too in a foreign land!

In Pakistan, prohibition was imposed by Zulfikar Ali Bhutto in the 1970s and not by Zia-ul-Haq, his executioner who transformed it into an Islamic state during his eleven year-long martial rule. Thankfully, foreigners and non-Muslim residents were kept out of the moral disciplining. A temporary permit could be obtained from the local excise department that entitled one to two bottles of alcohol per week. The permits were also available in the grey market for a premium. I obtained one partly for medicinal purposes, to use it as an antidote for both cold and exhaustion! When I obtained the permit I didn't know that I would be asked to give an oral testimony of my identity and family history to a humourless vendor in a decrepit liquor shop in Lahore.

That was in the winter of 1989, my second trip to Pakistan.

Prohibition as a state act proves counterproductive and helps only the bootleggers, particularly in a land dominated almost completely by the Punjabis. Lahore, after all, was no Jeddah and a large section of the city's liberal, Westernized and uninhibited elite openly preferred a happy-go-lucky Punjabi lifestyle to the one dictated by a handful of obscurantist mullahs. The sharia laws imposed by the army general were thrown in the wind by the Lahori men and women. As a result, just as in Amritsar or Chandigarh, expensive alcohol flew like water in weekend parties behind heavy curtains in the city's plush enclaves or in the five-star hotel rooms. Unlike the Sikh or Hindu Punjabi women, many of their counterparts in Lahore smoked openly in blatant defiance of the rulers. Begum Abida Hussain, popularly known as Chandi Bibi, a minister in the interim federal government smoked while addressing media conferences sitting in her office. She came from Multan and represented an influential land-owning family. For all its trials and tribulations and intermittent stand-offs both with the jackboots and fundamentalism, Lahore with its parks and wide boulevards, historical monuments and architecture, food streets and nautch girls, ghazals and cricket, ultra conservatives and ultra-liberals, booze and smacks, remained the most enchanting, warm and hospitable city in the subcontinent. It is a city that grew on you even if you were a non-Muslim, non-believer and a stranger from the land of an estranged neighbour.

Zia-ul-Haq's sudden and mysterious death in an air crash near Bahawalpur in Pakistan's Punjab, which had also claimed the lives of the US ambassador and dozens of army officers, had brought me to Pakistan for the first time in August 1988. The massive turnout at his burial, running into millions, at the Shah Faisal mosque compounds in Islamabad, clearly demonstrated his enviable popularity despite being a military ruler.

What struck me in the mourning multitude was the presence

of a sizeable section of physically challenged young men and women who came to pay their last respects in wheelchairs. As it turned out, the general had particular fondness for them for a very personal reason. Among his children, Zia's favourite was a daughter who was a paraplegic.

When Indira Gandhi was assassinated, Zia had come to Delhi for her funeral. But Rajiv Gandhi did not return the gesture and sent President R. Venkatraman to represent India. In the sprawling enclave earmarked for foreign dignitaries, I spotted, for the first time, a young lanky Afghan in a Pathani suit, looking pensive and crestfallen—Gulbuddin Hekmatyar. Of all the Mujahideen leaders fighting the 'Soviet infidels' in Afghanistan from Pakistani territories, Gulbuddin was arguably the most ruthless, diabolical and unpredictable, but closest to the departed general who patronized the rebel leader with tonnes of dollars and armaments. Gulbuddin conceded, he felt orphaned and apprehensive with the sudden turn of events and prayed for the continuation of Zia's Afghan policy by his successors.

In the diplomatic game of one-upmanship with Delhi, Zia outwitted Rajiv virtually on every occasion. In the first four years of Rajiv's rule he came to India four times, once to see an India–Pakistan cricket match at Jaipur amidst heightening tensions between the two countries over massive Indian Army deployment on the border. His public relations exercises impressed many in India, including several Bollywood stars and my editor, Aveek Sarkar, who went to Rawalpindi on the general's invitation to play 18 holes on the plush Army Golf Course. I went from Delhi to Wagah border in Amritsar to receive Aveek Babu as he took the land route on his return journey. His long and easy-going interview with the general was a treat to read.

Notwithstanding the regime changes, one thing, however, remains constant for an Indian scribe visiting Pakistan, the constant shadowing by gun-toting security men. Their surveillance was bizarre and noticeable for its unbelievable crudity, lacking finesse and sophistication. During my first trip in August 1988, I felt a little intimidated finding two hefty gentlemen in Pathani suits following me everywhere in a police motorcycle. During my subsequent visits, I got used to it, learnt how to befriend my stalkers, innocently doing their assigned duties. I enjoyed playing cat and mouse with them and on occasions even shared my alcoholic treasures kept in my hotel rooms. Once I also helped an ailing man with all the details of my calls so that he did not have to strain himself chasing me all around the city. He accepted my information without raising a question as he, too, understood I was nothing more than an 'akhbar ki numayinde,' a harmless 'mehman', also on a thankless duty.

Akbar Zaidi, a young scholar and historian friend, was picked up by my stalkers and taken to the nearby police station in Karachi in 1990 after he had dinner with me at a Chinese restaurant. He had to face a barrage of questions during his hour-long detention all pertaining to me and our relationship. A frightened Akbar called me at my hotel room from his residence well past midnight to narrate his harrowing experience. Unfazed, I asked, 'Did they want to know what all we ate at the restaurant?' Akbar was least impressed with my humour and cautioned me—'Be careful'—before hanging up.

That same afternoon I had heard from Ashok Sharma, Indian deputy consul general in Karachi, stories of his own plight and members of his family and saw for myself the kind of harassment he was being subjected to by the Pakistani forces. A Student Federation of India (the student wing of the CPI[M]) member in his college days, Ashok was fairly well conversant with Bengal and the state's communist leaders, particularly Buddhadeb Bhattacharjee. As an Indian Foreign Service probationer he had also spent a few months at Jhargram. In no time we were engrossed into an animated discussion on the future of communism in India while driving to his residence from the Deputy High Commission for high tea. Suddenly, he went silent and asked me to look into the rear-view mirror. Four men in civilian clothes were following us in an open jeep with a mounted machine gun pointing at the car. Ashok said they were men from Pakistani military Intelligence deputed to maintain round-the-clock vigilance on him and his movements. Two other groups followed his wife and children daily, even to the local bazaars and schools. Anyone who spoke to them, even the shopkeepers in the market, were regularly asked the same questions and harassed. All these, as Ashok said, were being done with one singular objective: He should quit Pakistan immediately.

'Why?' I asked.

'Because they believe I am a RAW agent. The chaps do not know what it takes to become an Indian Foreign Service officer.'

Serving in the Indian mission in Pakistan has always been the ultimate test of grit, nerve and endurance for an Indian. I presume it will be the same for a Pakistani in New Delhi.

The only time I found the Pakistanis quite impervious towards the Indian scribes was immediately before the 1988 winter elections when the whole nation seemed gripped in a euphoric, celebratory mood at the prospect of restoration of democracy after the longest spell of military rule. As a practice, Indian journalists were allowed to visit only three cities—Lahore, Islamabad and Karachi—and stay within city limits under all circumstances. But I slipped into a newly bought Pathani suit and rode on a bus from Lahore to reach Peshawar without anyone even taking note of it. Or even if they did, no one made a fuss about it and I was not hauled up. My beard, for a change, came in very handy during that illicit journey to see Khyber Pass and meet Khan Abdul Wali Khan, the leader of Awami National Party (ANP) and the son of Khan Abdur Ghaffar Khan, known in India as Frontier Gandhi.

The real takeaway from that meeting, which I recall to this day, was the amazing candour and friendliness of Wali Khan. I met him in his drawing room, which also served as his election campaign headquarters. The tall, lanky, handsome Pathan gentleman was busy talking to election strategists of his party. Was he surprised at the sudden appearance of an Indian journalist virtually from nowhere, without an iota of prior intimation? Well, even if he was, he didn't show it. Instead, he gave me a true Pathan hug, and made no effort to hide his happiness at meeting a friend from India. Indeed, Wali Khan had always been a target of the Pakistani political class as a 'friend of India'. The vibes that I received from him, right through the brief meeting, told me that his detractors did have a point there.

Of course right at the beginning he told me that the meeting had to be brief, not more than thirty-forty minutes, because he would soon have to leave for the election campaign. This was an epoch-making moment in Pakistan's history. The sudden death of President Muhammad Zia-ul-Haq had brought the long military dictatorship to an abrupt end. Slain former Pakistani premier Zulfikar Ali Bhutto's wife Nusrat and their daughter Benazir had galvanized the whole nation into a movement for the restoration of democracy. And in this extremely important National Assembly polls, Wali Khan's ANP had struck an alliance with the Pakistan Peoples Party (PPP), which had raised many eyebrows. I was no less intrigued myself, because Zulfikar Ali and Wali Khan were sworn enemies. The latter had alleged on the floor of the National Assembly itself that Prime Minister Bhutto was conspiring to assassinate him. During those years, Wali Khan had survived four attempts on his life. My first question to him was therefore obvious: why this alliance with the PPP? The Pathan leader was candid and simple: Children should not be made to bear their father's sins, he said. But more importantly, according to Wali Khan this was too precious an opportunity to put Pakistan firmly back on the track of democracy to be wasted because of personal rancour. All pro-democratic forces, he was convinced, must come together behind Nusrat and Benazir.

We talked a little more of politics before the discussion meandered to his younger days, when he was actually a member of the Indian National Congress. He recalled his meetings with the Mahatma and Jawaharlal Nehru with great fondness and nostalgia. Soon it was time for us to part, as he started off to an election rally. As I left Peshawar, so far away from the mainstream political hubbub of Karachi, Islamabad, Pindi or Lahore, I left with the thought that the overwhelming goodwill which Benazir commanded at that historic moment could hardly be matched in the history of Pakistan. Today as I look back, I can't but rue: what an opportunity lost!

Benazir Bhutto—who returned to Pakistan in 1986, two years before Zia's death—was clearly the front runner, way ahead of her rivals in the Pakistan Muslim League (PML). She disbanded the MRD (Movement for Restoration of Democracy), a motley group of political outfits led by the PPP, which fought incessantly for the return of democracy during Zia's military rule. Zulfikar Ali Bhutto's Iranian widow, Nusrat, led MRD when Benazir lived for years in exile. Her decision alienated and antagonized some of her old allies who openly criticized her for courting erstwhile supporters of the martial law regime, many of whom were either rich businessmen or landowners. In doing so, she was actually following in the footsteps of her slain father who also gave nomination to the rich and powerful, brushing aside the claims of party loyalists. Like Zulfikar in 1977, Benazir too set her eyes firmly on the prime minister's chair, enlisting the support of those in the Pakistani 'establishment' who would help her achieve her goal.

Her gamble paid off only partially. She became the first woman prime minister of an Islamic state but her party could not secure simple majority in the national parliament, sowing the seeds of acrimony and destruction right from the beginning. But that was to happen nineteen months later. In the winter of 1988, preceding the polls, Benazir, still recovering from her first delivery, took the country by the storm.

I first saw Benazir on 14 November 1988, two days before the elections, when she came to Lahore leading a historic procession not witnessed in Pakistan since the Partition. She started from Gujranwala in Punjab, some 40 kms from Lahore late in the morning and reached the state capital well after sunset. Thousands patiently waited for her for hours, all jubilant and enthusiastic to have a glimpse of 'Bibi'. After crossing the bridge over Ravi River on the outskirts of Lahore, she alighted from her jeep to mount a specially decorated truck painted with PPP's colours. She was looking cheerful in a green salwar–kameez and red and black dupatta, her eyes hid behind odd-sized sunglasses, which she did not remove even after dark. The hysteric crowd, that included a large number of poor, went berserk breaking the security cordon created around her by party volunteers. The spontaneous madness soon gave away to shouting slogans in Punjabi—'*Todde nara Benazir/Mere nara Benazir/Raj karegi Benazir/Wazir-e-Azam Benazir*'. (Your slogan: Benazir/My slogan: Benazir/Benazir will rule/Benazir will be the Prime Minister.)

In the night-long procession, a few kilometres long, Benazir hardly spoke. Standing atop her truck she only smiled and waved her hands towards cheering crowds on both sides of the road, occasionally throwing garlands at them. Standing in the same truck with her was Sarfraz Nawaz, former Pakistani fast bowler and PPP's candidate from one of the seats in Lahore. I also noticed, particularly, the response of frenzied women for whom Benazir brought hopes of liberty and emancipation from the excesses of Islamic rule. It appeared that women constituted her core constituency.

In that election, Benazir contested from a number of constituencies including one in old Lahore that had the city's largest share of poor population. Predictably, she spent a long time there stopping over and over again to satisfy her electorate. The unruly procession, sloganeering and dancing, suddenly stopped and went silent in front of Khawaja Ali Zaveri's Mazar. Benazir alighted from the truck to offer her prayers there. This time round, she truly needed divine blessings to fulfil her dreams.

The atmosphere changed dramatically once the procession entered Nawaz Sharif's constituency. For so long Benazir saw only human waves greeting and following her spontaneously. Here she met, for the first time, some resistance from a sizeable section of Nawaz's supporters who came out bravely to wave their party flags. In the charged atmosphere, Benazir took control of the situation herself ordering her supporters to stay calm and not fall into any trap. Still, some of the enthusiasts kept raising slogans personally attacking the Punjab chief minister—'*Na maa sharif na baap sharif/ yeh hay kaun Nawaz Sharif?*' (Sharif means 'noble', so the slogan goes: Neither is his mother noble, nor is his father noble/Who is this Nawaz Sharif?)

Nawaz's rebuff in more slanderous language came the next day, the last day of campaigning, when he organized a fairly well-attended rally at Lahore's Regal Chowk, after entering the city heading a day-long procession. The Punjab chief minister made caustic remarks about Benazir's mother questioning her chastity and stopping just short of calling her a whore. He showed a picture of Nusrat dancing intimately with US President Gerald Ford when he had visited Pakistan many years ago. The picture was distributed in the rally. Another picture showed Bhutto kissing a white woman on the cheeks. Calling the mother and daughter '*besharam aurat*' (shameless women), Nawaz exhorted the audience to throw the Bhutto family into the Arabian Sea. Immediately thereafter, a huge bunting carrying Bhutto's picture was brought down from an adjacent tall building and set on fire. It became clear that a nervous and jittery Nawaz had conceded the game to the 'Daughter of the East' even before it began.

The mud-slinging did not remain confined only at the level of top leadership. It was a no-holds-barred campaign in which the opponents took potshots at each other using four-letter words at will. In one street corner, I counted, as a PML candidate calling his opponent '*behen-chod*' (sister-fucker) at least twenty times. Unaccustomed to such unrestrained abusive campaigning I felt somewhat uncomfortable in the beginning. Gradually, it dawned on me that I was witnessing a typical Punjabi battle conducted and executed in a freewheeling, casual and happy-go-lucky Punjabi style.

∽

In less than two years, Bibi messed it all up—lost power as also the reservoir of love, affection and goodwill of her countrymen. I reached Karachi a week after her dismissal in August 1990 to find the city reeling under sectarian and political violence between the Muhajirs of Muttahida Quami Movement (MQM) and the Sindhi supporters of the PPP. On 14 August, Pakistan's Independence Day, a violent clash took place at Jinnah's burial ground killing two dozen people, sending reverberations throughout Karachi and spoiling the festivities under heavy security cover. I went to Bilawal House (named after Benazir's son), to look for the deposed prime minister. In November 1988, I had seen the place teeming with people, supporters and favour-seekers. On 14 August 1990, the huge mansion in Karachi's Clifton area wore a completely deserted look as Benazir was away in Larkana, her ancestral home, historically famous for the ancient Mohenjo-Daro civilization.

In November 1988, I had met Altaf Hussain, the charismatic young leader of the MQM, a party that held near complete sway over Karachi—the capital of Sindh province. The party was born a few years ago to agitate against the plight and discrimination of the thousands of Muslim refugees who came from India following the Partition. Most of them came from various parts of Bihar and UP to find the status of unwanted refugees in a country that was supposed to be a dreamland for them and created by their forefathers. Their anger, frustration and despondency found political expression in the MQM. Benazir wooed the MQM to her side when she failed to acquire absolute majority in the elections. The marriage of convenience did not last as the Muhajirs of Karachi saw no end to their misery even with a friendly government in Islamabad. The alliance broke and Karachi lapsed into chaos and frequent blood-baths, prompting President Ghulam Ishaq Khan to dismiss Benazir's government.

I felt as if I was in Lucknow or some Muslim areas of Mumbai when, before the elections, I visited the Muhajir mohallas in Karachi. In Pakistani Punjab, an Indian, however welcome, still felt like a stranger but not so in Karachi because of its cosmopolitan culture and close affinity to Muhajirs. Everywhere, in every home, I was treated not like a 'mehman', but a brother from the land of their ancestors. Many of them, mostly elders, fondly remembered their happier days in Delhi or Lucknow or Kanpur prior to the Partition, often giving graphic details of their erstwhile habitats and surrounding neighbourhoods. I realized many of them knew and loved Delhi more than I ever cared to do. As I also belonged to an uprooted refugee family from erstwhile East Bengal, I could easily empathize with the bleeding hearts, understood their nostalgia for the days gone by as also their profound sense of loss. On every face of the older generation I found a reflection of my father's.

In ordinary circumstances, the prime minister's dismissal

would have evoked countrywide protests and anger but I could not find anyone in Karachi who blamed the president for an arbitrary act. Everyone agreed it was Benazir's own doing, a unique case of squandering a historic opportunity in such a short span of time. As Razia Bhatti, an eminent Pakistani editor, wrote in *Newsline* magazine, 'After waging an eleven year struggle for democracy marked by remarkable courage and endurance Benazir Bhutto took less than twenty months to throw it all away. It was not that she had tried and failed; the tragedy was that she seemed not to have tried at all.'

Benazir's arrogance, haughtiness and 'could not care less' style antagonized and alienated a sizeable section of senior party loyalists some of whom were her father's close lieutenants. Ghulam Mustafa Khar in Punjab and Jam Sadiq Ali in Sindh, both PPP stalwarts left the party in disgust. She failed miserably to carry on with her political partners on whose support she depended for her own survival. The MQM in Karachi declared war against the PPP. Even Khan Abdul Wali Khan of the moderate and liberal Awami National Party of the frontier province swore to teach her a lesson. In less than twenty months, Benazir exposed all the chinks in her armour that brought her downfall. Even Rajiv Gandhi took longer than her to discredit himself in India.

To cap it all, there were the two Zardaris, father and son, Hakim Ali and Asif Ali, who turned out to be the worst crooks Pakistanis had seen in their post-Partition history. In their inexplicable haste to make quick bucks, Benazir's father-in-law and husband involved themselves brazenly in all kinds of shady deals—from allotment of government plots to purchase of aircraft for Pakistan Airlines. Everyone I visited during the tour gave me a new story of their financial misdeeds. The newspapers and magazines, then enjoying a new bout of freedom went hammer and tongs against the Zardaris exposing corruption scandals, one after the other, almost every day. Asif Ali was dubbed 'Mr Thirty

Percent'. That rate, so went the joke in Islamabad, had to be paid to him to secure any government contract, no matter how small or big the contract might have been!

The Bofors scandal rocking India before causing Rajiv's downfall seemed like a child's play in front of the mega scandals of the Zardaris. But unlike in India, Pakistan still did not have a V.P. Singh who could galvanize the nation. Yet the writing on the wall was quite clear, Bibi had no chance of returning to power in the next round of elections slated for October 1990.

Ardeshir Cowasjee, a Parsee gentleman and distinguished industrialist of Karachi, took the Zardaris to court and filed a writ petition against them seeking punishment for their corruption. At the drawing room of his old-style bungalow, he gave me a detailed account of charges against the Zardaris and said finally in his chaste, heavily accentuated English, said, 'You would pay them compliments if you call them only plunderers. They are much worse than that.'

Benazir remained nonchalant and put up a brave face pleading innocence, at least publicly. I saw her at a press conference in Islamabad a few days later at a private home of a senior PPP functionary. She was at her combative best, pooh-poohed all the charges brought against her husband and father-in-law and levelled counter-allegations of corruption against her detractors. For her, it was a case of the Satan chanting scriptures. She vowed not to leave the country and claimed her husband would do the same.

It was not the same Benazir Bhutto I had seen in Lahore in the winter of 1988, when I saw her next year, in 1989, during Rajiv Gandhi's day-long visit to Islamabad on his way back from Moscow and Paris. Her poise looked dented as she was asked to answer difficult and tricky questions involving her acts of omission and commission during her tenure. Her efforts to put up a carefree appearance lacked conviction despite her impeccable dress and loud make-up. Two years ago, Pakistan accepted her as the logical heir apparent, the daughter of a martyr who fought relentlessly for restoration of democracy. Her desperate efforts to project herself as a woman victim in a male-dominated polity, a victim of conspiracy and machinations, had very few takers. Pakistan wrote her off well before the bell rang for the next round of polls.

∽

A few months before Benazir was ousted, I had a chance meeting with her sister, Sanam, when she came to Delhi on a private and confidential visit. She came with three of her very close friends, two of them were also friends of mine—Sugata Bose and Ayesha Jalal—both historians based in the US. Sugata had been a close friend from my college days and I got to know his Pakistani girlfriend, Ayesha, during my occasional visits to Boston. One of the brightest Pakistani historians of her generation, Ayesha shot to fame with her maiden and path-breaking book on Mohammad Ali Jinnah titled, *The Sole Spokesman*.

Benazir was not initially in favour of Sanam's visit to India primarily for political reasons. Kashmir became a flashpoint in India-Pakistan relations yet again and the initial bonhomie between Rajiv and Benazir had ended by the time Sanam planned her visit. Benazir apprehended that her sister's visit at this juncture would be misinterpreted by her Pakistani detractors, compounding the troubles. But Benazir yielded after exacting a promise from her sister that during her stay in India, she would do nothing to invite public glare.

Sanam, as Benazir wrote in her autobiography[4], had never been political. She had always chosen to keep her circle of friends small, disliking the attention she got as a Bhutto and the constant

---

[4]Benazir Bhutto. 1988. *Daughter of Destiny: An Autobiography*. London: Simon & Schuster.

questions about her father. She has lived up to that description till date in her life, living a divorced life in seclusion with her two children. All attempts to bring her to politics following Benazir's tragic assassination in 2007 failed as Sanam remained unwavering in her resolve.

Yet the veil of secrecy around her private visit almost got punctured when the PIA flight carrying Sanam and her friends landed at Delhi International Airport in the afternoon. Abdul Sattar, former Pakistani envoy to New Delhi and a close confidant of Benazir, was in the same flight. He was coming to Delhi as his prime minister's personal envoy to meet Rajiv Gandhi and concerned members of the Indian Foreign Service establishment to sort out problems regarding Kashmir. Sattar could not recognize Sanam and mistook her for a television star. But S.K. Singh, the then foreign secretary and a former Indian envoy to Islamabad who was waiting to receive Sattar, did not fail to spot Sanam. Sattar and Singh, both consummate veteran diplomats, however, readily agreed to honour and respect her privacy. Even I wrote a feature about her visit many months after she had left. That was the deal between Sugata and me when he invited me to join their group.

Sanam, ('Mani' to her close friends and family members) was the third child and second daughter of the Bhuttos after Benazir and Murtaza. Shah Nawaz was their youngest brother. Benazir and Sanam, very close to each other by age and relation, went to the same convent school in Islamabad and then to Harvard University for higher studies. Zulfikar's hanging dragged Benazir and their mother into politics, but Sanam kept aloof and chose to be a private person. In the November 1988 national elections, Benazir tried to persuade her sister to contest from Lyari a pocket borough of the PPP in Karachi. She refused.

As we drove from Delhi to Agra to see the Taj, all five of us huddled in the same car hired from the hotel, I asked Sanam why and how she remained so apolitical, a few minutes before we stopped at a nondescript dhaba to have tea. My question, it seemed, spoilt her mood as she shot back, 'Why the hell should I be in politics? My father got hanged. One of my brothers got killed mysteriously in a restaurant in Paris. Another brother lives in exile as he cannot come back home. This is what politics has given me. I hate it from the core of my heart.'

The two sisters looked alike, the younger more like her mother. Yet they stood on two different poles in their attitude towards life and their assessment of it. Sanam told me that even Benazir had no political ambition till her father was imprisoned. That way she was partly forced by the circumstances to step into her father's shoes. 'But I have always found the four walls of my home a better place than the political battlefield. I am happy that way, with what I am and where I am.'

Sanam married before her elder sister, a love marriage, not very common in Sindhi feudal families. Even Benazir had many suitors, some of whom loved her dearly. Yet as a political animal, she was circumscribed more by the prevailing customs and prejudices, not being able to shake off the burden of a Bhutto lineage. As a result, Benazir's marriage turned out to be a week-long extravaganza of national importance when hundreds of invitees and celebrities from all over the world descended at Karachi. (Aveek Sarkar was also invited; his gift to Benazir was a painting especially drawn by M.F. Hussain on Bhutto's hanging. Sanam told me her family was more shocked than amused to see it.) Sanam, on the other hand married Nassir Hussain in a small gathering of friends and chosen relatives. The occasion was so informal that she asked for her mother's permission to wear jeans instead of a saree on her wedding night.

At Agra, Sanam was behaving just a like a school kid out on an excursion with friends. At the outer gate of the Taj Mahal, she felt nervous when she was asked to deposit her handbag with the security men. The moment we came out after spending an hour she went to a corner to open her bag and count her dollar bills. I enquired from the locals where the dollar would fetch the highest return. Sanam promptly went to the shop in an adjacent lane to exchange money. I found the experience amusing, seeing the sister of a neighbouring state's prime minister looking for a few more rupees in the grey market.

At the Agra Fort we hired a local guide for ₹15 at Sanam's insistence. She lapped up in all seriousness every word the young guide spoke, fact and fiction, as we walked from Begum Mahal to the small jail where Shah Jahan had remained incarcerated and could have a full view of his late wife's memorial. When the guide indicated to a badly bruised wall that was once diamond studded, Sanam, like a kindergarten girl, asked him, 'Where have all the diamonds gone?'

'To Pakistan,' I replied to put the baffled guide at ease.

Back in the Delhi hotel, we had dinner at a restaurant famous for its Mughlai cuisine. Sanam discarded the fork and knife immediately after the tandoori roti was served and started to eat with her hands. That was the only time when she came out of her shell to tell us family anecdotes involving moments, both happy and sad. She abhorred politics but did not ever fail in her duties to stand by family members in times of tragedy and distress. Immediately after Bhutto's execution, she left Harvard to join her mother and sister in Pakistan. She took upon herself the task of looking after the family when Zia put both Nusrat and Benazir behind bars. She accompanied Benazir to Paris to bring the dead body of his slain younger brother to Larkana where he was buried in the family graveyard. What Sanam meant was that in a family like hers, one family member was needed to stay away from limelight and play the role of a sheet anchor for everyone else. 'I have performed the role.'

14

Kabuli Pulao

That afternoon, the Ariana Afghan Airlines Boeing had only three passengers—Appan Menon, then with *The Hindu*, a talkative Sikh youth who kept us thoroughly entertained during the short journey, and me. Other than the pilot and his assistant in the cockpit, there was no other crew member, male or female, to take care of the empty flight. No security instructions, no beverages, hot or cold, hard or soft. Our destination: Kabul.

As a Bengali and a Kolkatan I had a special fascination for Kabul, immortalized in our literature, first by Rabindranath Tagore in his short story 'Kabuliwala' and then by Syed Mujtaba Ali in his travelogue, *Deshe Bideshe*. I knew a few Afghans who lived in a ghetto very close to ABP's Kolkata office. Some of them could be spotted regularly in the adjoining lane, waiting patiently, either on a motorcycle or under a tree, for hours together to collect their monthly installment of interests, prohibitively high, from the borrowers. They hardly spoke with anyone as they waited, intermittently sipping tea from clay cups bought from the nearby tea stall, all the time keeping a close vigil on the office exit gates. Lending cash to habitual borrowers and peddling hashish to the addicts had been their only known profession.

Hamdi Bey used to borrow money regularly from a hugely built Pathan with intimidating looks. On a few occasions I had to visit him in his mohalla, on Hamdi's behalf, to plead for an extension of the deadline for repayment. Once, he stormed into Hamdi's house early one morning after the latter's repeated failure to pay back the loan. Borrowing money from the Kabuliwalas carried a stigma among middle-class Bengalis and the lenders, when necessary, exploited it to the hilt. The strategy employed by them was to humiliate the recalcitrant borrower either publicly or in front of his family members so that he obliged in utter desperation. In a way, Kolkata's Kabuliwalas were loved and feared, and lived an isolated existence without disturbing anyone. But they could turn ruthless and violent on truant defaulters. For some inexplicable reasons they always remained insulated from the law of the land; even the police hardly bothered them.

The plane cruising well above 20,000 feet, suddenly took a steep unnerving descent and then regained height. This sudden loosing of height and then shooting up continued for quite some time. After breaking the cloud cover it went into a spiral precipitation inside the mountains before taxing down on to the runway. Our Sikh companion seemed unfazed and continued talking even as I cursed myself for accepting the assignment.

I was told later that Afghan pilots had perfected the art of this highly risky descent to escape guerilla attacks from adjoining mountains. As the plane came directly over the airport it corkscrewed downward carefully keeping as close to the airport grounds as possible, throwing flares to divert the US-supplied portable missiles, called Stingers, that went after heat. The flares plummeted to earth at a temperature of more than 5000 degrees. Hundreds, including many children, used to be burnt by showers of scorching magnesium or by picking the flares up after they landed. The last time a domestic Afghan airliner was shot down by a guerilla Stinger was on 3 September 1985 near Kandahar, killing all the fifty-two people on board. With the Soviet soldiers back home and the Afghan capital virtually under siege on all sides by the rebel Mujahideen, nothing, predictably, could be left to chance. We arrived in Kabul on 14 March 1989, nine days after a fierce battle began for the control of Jalalabad near Peshawar.

The international airport wore a deserted look and the baggage area was empty. As we disembarked and proceeded to collect our baggage, a slew of Mi-24 Hind helicopters flew past in low formation heading for an unknown destination. No one checked our baggage, no one was available at the customs counter. At the exit gate, a security man with a Kalashnikov smiled at us when we disclosed our identity. In Najibullah's Kabul, Indians were welcome guests.

At first sight, Kabul looked like a city in monochrome where grim public buildings seemed to have taken on the hue of the mud-plastered homes that stretched across a wide plain, ringed by snow-capped peaks of the Hindu Kush. Broad, tree-lined avenues and crumbling neoclassical villas in the centre, however, reminded one of a grand past. The bitter snowy winter was almost over and the sunbathed city and its trees heralded the welcoming onset of the spring. After a harrowing, stomach-churning descent, my spirits lifted as the dusty, vintage taxi sped along the roads of a city that looked busy and perfectly normal in the early afternoon of a working day.

We checked into Hotel Kabul, a depressing old-style, three-storeyed structure in the heart of the city, very close to all the government buildings. The hotel, too, was nearly empty. The round clocks on the wall behind the reception desk, put up to show times in various international cities, stood silent and the middle-aged male receptionist was lost in deep slumber on a worn-out couch nearby. The lone telephone at the reception was meant only for local calls and there was no guarantee that international trunk calls would ever materialize. An old telex machine that had no assigned operator sat on a table in a corner. (It would come back to life only for an hour any time past midnight. I operated the machine myself and kept a perforated tape ready and handy so that not a minute was wasted when the connection came.) The cheap carpet on the floor exuded a pungent odour as the broken vacuum cleaner waited to be replaced. There was another bigger and more comfortable hotel overlooking the hills on the outskirts where all the 'firanghee' journalists stayed. But that was beyond our means. We resigned ourselves to our poor man's fate in Hotel Kabul for the next fortnight.

Adolph Dubs, the US ambassador to Afghanistan, was assassinated in the same hotel in February 1979. Posing as policemen, a group of militants kidnapped him, brought him to the hotel and demanded the release of their leader. The negotiation got botched up and the ambassador died in crossfire. Washington did not send his successor to Kabul for ten years and the fortress-like US mission closed down shortly after the Soviet withdrawal. Dubs had been holed up in Room 117 and Appan insisted that I take the same room. In the land of uncertainties where there would be long power cuts at night, I refused to be further bothered by an American ghost in that haunted mansion.

∽

Immediately after checking in, Appan and I went to a bank bang opposite our hotel. The woman, who didn't wear any burqa, at the teller counter verified our US dollar traveller's cheques carefully before disappearing somewhere. Together we had asked for a thousand US dollars to be exchanged. After an extremely anxious wait for about an hour she resurfaced with a male colleague and politely asked us to go inside through a backdoor. Wads of green notes, all in the denomination of 5 Afghani waited for us on a huge wooden table. The woman apologized for not being able to give us currency notes of higher denominations as both of us stood there dumbfounded for a while unable to comprehend how on earth we would be handling the stockpile. We came back to our hotel rooms, emptied our suitcases and went back to the bank. We must have looked like bank robbers straight out of a Bollywood thriller!

Later, when, after a few days, we found out an open, thriving currency market not far from our hotel we realized, we got short-changed at the bank that gave us an unfavourable exchange rate. Shekhar Gupta, then with *India Today*, was also in Kabul at that time. Gupta, always smarter than anyone of us, took the unofficial route to get a better deal.

The money market was a spectacle. Known as the Prince's Market, on the banks of River Kabul, it operated in a courtyard that could be accessed through a dark alley. In the adjoining buildings, established money changers operated out of their pigeonholes while the freelancers, hundreds in numbers, with wads of foreign currency notes in their hands, roamed around the courtyard quoting the ongoing exchange rates at the top of their voices. The volume of transaction in one single market, we were told, was a few times higher than all the Kabul banks put together and the entire operation was legal and authorized. We found many Indians and Pakistanis doing brisk business along with the Pashtuns, Tajiks and Hazaras in a 3,000-year-old historical city that still embraced every 'mehman' who came, settled and regaled in a vibrant cosmopolitan culture.

In March 1989, the world was led to believe, thanks mainly to the US official propaganda, that Najibullah's PDPA (People's Democratic Party of Afghanistan) regime ruling Afghanistan would crumble like a house of cards. The process would start with Mujahideen victory at Jalalabad that would in turn facilitate large-scale defection from the Afghan Army, leading finally to Kabul's fall. It would be a matter of weeks, the US officials predicted as Gulbuddin Hekmatyar's guerillas, backed by both Washington and Islamabad, had launched an attack on Jalalabad. I landed in

Kabul to witness the anticipated new phase of history unfolding at the Afghan capital, to greet the advancing rebel columns of Hekmatyar and Co at the entry point of Kabul.

The reality on the ground, however, presented quite an anticlimax and I for one really felt disappointed. Najibullah, nicknamed Ox, because of his physical built, was not merely in full control of the situation in Kabul, but his army, backed by superior air power and long-range Scud missiles, also held its ground in Jalalabad. Among others, it surprised and shocked the Western journalists most of whom were camping there in droves hoping to see the tragic end of the Soviet-backed regime. In my daily dispatches sent every night, after a great deal of perseverance and trepidation, I wrote faithfully of what I saw and heard which greatly antagonized my editor. After about a week he sent me a stinker that questioned my audacity to go against the prevailing Western wisdom. 'How can you write such crap,' the message read, 'when the whole world says otherwise? Every US newspaper says the days of Kabul regime are numbered.' I felt sad and disappointed but at the same time appreciated my editor's difficulties. In those early days after the Soviet withdrawal it was difficult to convince anyone outside that Kabul, contrary to Western perception, was not falling after all.

It did not. Not only were the Mujahideen forced to beat a humiliating retreat from Jalalabad suffering heavy casualties and embarrassing their masters, Najibullah's regime merrily survived in power for another three years, till 1992. More than the rebels, always at each other's throats, it was the disintegration of the USSR and the rise of Boris Yeltsin that sealed Najibullah's fate, paving the way for mayhem, anarchy and mass slaughter in Kabul following the Mujahideen takeover. In 1989, no one in the Afghan capital had heard the name of a breed called the Taliban.

That, in a way, made our days in Kabul somewhat boring and quite predictable. It was not that the city didn't feel any reverberations of the ongoing war or was lying completely immune from it. Kabul remained very much under siege and foreign journalists were not allowed to step out of the city limits in any direction. The fabled Salang Pass, the lifeline between Kabul and the Soviet border on the north, was under the control of Ahmed Shah Massoud, the Lion of Panjshir, and arguably the best of the Mujahideen leaders. On the other side, the road leading to the Khyber Pass was also out of bounds because of the ongoing war in Jalalabad. The war coverage, therefore, meant lapping up a one-sided version of the government's spokesperson who routinely told us half-truths and usual lies. Kabul, never a stranger to intrigues anyway, was a war zone of propaganda and rumours spread by all stakeholders.

The withdrawal of the Soviet masters did not impact the protégé's regime so much because large-scale military and economic assistance continued unabated under the supervision of a few hundred of Moscow's military experts. They left behind literally all their material except for the vehicles needed to transport the Soviet soldiers back over the border. Even the weaponry deployed by Moscow in East European countries was transferred to Afghanistan. According to one estimate, we learnt that in Kabul, Najibullah's armoury had no less than 1,300 Scud-B missiles, hundreds of short-range Frogs, several hundred tanks and innumerable trucks. Not since the Britain-and-France-mounted Berlin airlift in 1948 had there been a comparable effort to keep a beleaguered outpost supplied. Except when the airport remained closed because of rebel attacks, between twenty-five and forty IL-76 aircraft had been flying into the Afghan capital carrying arms and supplies. Appan and I used to go to the Bagram airport every day to see the flight movements to find out, first-hand, the nature and intensity of the Soviet help and encouragement.

The city's de facto boss was therefore Yuliy Vorontsov, the new Soviet proconsul who came to Kabul partly to assure

Najibullah that Moscow was not about to abandon him. On the day he arrived, we were told, Najibullah's elite troops lined the entire route from the airport to the Soviet Embassy to ensure his safe passage. Vorontsov was a big gun in Mikhail Gorbachev's foreign ministry and accordingly threw his weight around in a city where all the Western embassies had already closed down their missions fearing anarchy and bloodshed. After a couple of guerilla missiles hit the Soviet Embassy compound, Vorontsov held a press conference to condemn the US-Pakistan axis for supporting the Mujahideen and not responding to the call for peace and reconciliation. What he said was completely predictable, but our visit to the Soviet Embassy was surely an experience. It was like a fortress. Just getting our vehicle near the embassy required that we pass through several check points, delta barriers and hairpin turns, many of which were barely possible to negotiate except at a very low speed. On the compound a missile was kept as an exhibit, an American Stinger, according to the embassy staff. But an American journalist, ostensibly an expert in military hardware, emphatically denied it to be a Stinger. He claimed it was a Sidewinder air-to-air expended missile that was last used in the Vietnam War. The Russians, however, remained unfazed even after their bluff was called.

∽

Occasional missile attacks targeting either the airport or the Soviet Embassy or the business district where we lived, kept on reminding us that we were in the midst of a full-blown war. Throughout the day we would also hear the thud of a Scud directed towards Jalalabad and fired from an adjacent military base. The missile attacks, when misdirected, claimed innocent lives including those of children. The madness of the rebels antagonized the civilians who were not otherwise favourably disposed towards the regime of the infidels. Yet the ordinary Kabuliwala, long used to war and violence, accepted these incidents with a sense of equanimity and resignation, as if living in perpetual insecurity was very much an integral part of their normal lives.

Afghan soldiers, armed with anti-aircraft artillery and missiles guarded the airport and their counterparts patrolled the city in Soviet tanks and trucks. The city was dotted with solid new bunkers manned by the elite commando units of the army. Night-long curfew became the order when only stray dogs kept company of the patrolling sarandoi (police). Throughout the day one or the other helicopter clattered overhead leisurely emanating familiar noise. But hardly anyone paid any attention and it was business as usual underneath, on the streets, in the bazaars and offices. When the unusual becomes the usual it is destined to lose its charm.

The impact of the war was felt bitterly in the markets when the frequent siege of the passes by the rebels led to soaring prices of all essential commodities, aggravating the misery of the people. In our hotel, we were served half-cooked beef during every lunch and dinner as nothing else was available. That, too, was frighteningly expensive. City folks queued in front of tandoors to buy nan that cost 20 Afghanis each, thrice more than the usual price. However, the sabzi mandi was always full with vegetables and dry fruits. Even Pakistani oranges, smuggled through some unknown routes, found their way on the shelves. Outside the information ministry a bookshop was doing brisk business selling books by Russian authors. The spectre of Mujahideen storming into Kabul and taking over the city appeared as remote as Islamabad.

For us, it was difficult to gauge the public mood about the regime for two reasons: the language barrier and the constant company of a KHAD (state Intelligence agency) member foisted on us by the foreign ministry on the second day of our arrival. His name was Nur Mohammad, a KGB-trained spy who spent several years in Moscow and Budapest. He was tall, middle-aged, unusually thin for a Pathan, and had a heart-warming smile. Unlike his masters, he was not irreligious and disappeared routinely for his namaz. He wore the same suit every day and was mighty proud of his bush-like grey moustache. He was affable, friendly, talkative, but shadowed us everywhere we went. He was more curious about India than about the rebels' preparedness for the ongoing Jalalabad battle. Outwardly at least, he appeared quite a misfit for a spy network known, hated and feared for its notoriety and ruthlessness.

Nur Mohammad was at his best when, after downing a couple of tall pegs of Scotch during our late evening chit-chats in our hotel rooms, he would give us a lecture on the characteristic traits of innumerable tribes and sub-clans in Afghanistan, cracking jokes about his own tribe—the Pashtuns. Like a suave quizmaster, he would occasionally ask us questions to test our general knowledge about the Pathans. 'If you ask a Pathan whether he has an enemy, what would be his reply?' Nur would ask with a glint of mischievous smile in his eyes and then answer himself after a brief pause. 'The Pathan would say, yes, I have a cousin.' Then he would burst out in laughter.

But the happy-go-lucky man would withdraw into his sulking, reticent mood if we asked him probing questions about either the KHAD or the regime. Like many other ordinary Kabuliwalas, Nur too was convinced that Najibullah was there for a long haul and that the Mujahideen were no more than a bunch of bloodthirsty, bickering scoundrels, no match for a trained, disciplined and organized army. He believed that the departure of the Soviets had deprived the rebels of the raison d'être of their existence. The country was now free from foreign occupation and was no longer being ruled by the infidels.

The regime survived solely on the support provided by Moscow, but the ordinary Kabuliwala held the Russians in utter contempt—a natural consequence of a long and brutal occupation.

Almost everyone we spoke with had a harrowing tale of some kind of Russian brutality and thuggish behaviour. The most vocal were the owners of the small shops in the main market area who complained of widespread extortion by the patrolling Russian soldiers. They picked up from the shops whatever they liked and refused to pay for them. An American journalist roaming alone at night had to run for cover when a small crowd of agitated Kabuliwalas mistook him for a Russian and chased after him. The next thing he learnt was a Pashto sentence that meant, 'I am not a Russian.'

The afternoon official briefing on the ongoing civil war over Jalalabad in the Afghan foreign office, a few hundred yards from our hotel, was the most boring part of our daily chores. Mr Amin, the spokesman, was a frail gentleman in suit whose only job was to read out a brief written statement in English in a monotonous droll. He looked stern and serious, almost like a school headmaster and refused to answer any question from any of the attending journalists, overwhelmingly American. The only time the briefing became lively was when, instead of reading out anything, Mr Amin produced two haggard-looking youths in Pathani suits and introduced them as Pakistani spies captured on the battlefront. They narrated their stories in rustic Punjabi that none in the press conference understood. Not even Mr Amin. When pressed for an English translation of their narration, he shrugged his shoulders before hurriedly leaving the venue.

Appan and I were, therefore, surprised when Nur requested us to visit Mr Amin at his residence for lunch. At home we saw a completely different person: warm, hospitable and talkative. He confessed that in his official avatar he behaved differently mainly to avoid the Western journalists. With us, Indians, he was his normal self and answered all our queries elaborately. He even cracked a few jokes about the country's president. He introduced his only son, in his teens, but his wife and daughter never stepped out to greet us. Yet she cooked the best pulao I have had in my life. Tired with the half-cooked beef, I devoured the home-made food almost like a famished refugee and asked for more and more. Appan chided me mildly for throwing all sense of decency out of the windows. He did not know what it meant to be a starving Bengali Brahmin!

Almost every other day during our stay, we heard stories of rebel missiles falling on civilians in various parts of the city, killing innocents including women and children. The ebullient Sikh youth we met on our flight to Kabul came rushing to our hotel one afternoon requesting us to visit his mohalla that was hit by missiles a while ago. As a history student I knew Ranjit Singh had turned Kabul into the capital of his empire. Yet I did not have the slightest idea that so many Sikh families still stayed in the city. Two kids had died from a missile attack while playing in a nearby field in the locality which seemed like a little piece of Ludhiana or Jalandhar. The wailing of the two young mothers over the bodies of their beloved rented the air as the male members were making preparations for their last rites before sunset. Yet the Sikh community seemed determined to stay on in a city that was becoming increasingly unsafe for all, particularly for the people of Indian origin. They would rather die in Kabul, their homeland for generations, than seek shelter in Indian Punjab as refugees.

On our way back we decided to walk down the streets to have a glimpse of the city and its dwellers. Always an enthusiastic guide, Nur gave us a running commentary as we crossed the alleys and thoroughfares and stopped at the bustling bazaars to buy knick-knacks. Most of the houses made of grey mud bricks looked grim, dusty and unstable, reflecting the poor standard of living of most of the Kabuliwalas. The city also had gated communities built by the Soviets for their own use and their Afghan cronies. Those houses, thousands in numbers, had round-the-clock electricity, running water and heating facilities for the winter. Now that the occupiers had left, the houses had been taken over by Najibullah's ministers and high officials. Although an occupying force, hated by one and all in the city, the Soviets did not remain totally impervious to the necessity of upgrading Kabul's civic amenities. They introduced modern trolleybuses, built a few factories and set up cultural centres. Most important of all, women in Kabul felt safe as long as the Russian armoured vehicles roamed the streets. Najibullah's strongest constituency, as I soon found out, had been the women who, till then, chose not to hide themselves behind burqa or veils but wore jeans, tight T-shirts, even stilettos. The most vocal supporters of the regime, some of them even joined the army to hold the conservative clerics and rebels at bay. Nur recollected the bygone era under the exiled King Zahir Shah when on Kabul streets girls used to be spotted in miniskirts, openly courting their fiancées. Kabul was once a liberal, tolerant and irreverent place much like any European city. The Kabuliwalas, besides being warm and hospitable to all kinds of mehmans, were known for their sharp wit that faded gradually with the Soviet occupation and the country plunging into endless fratricidal wars.

As we came near the banks of the Kabul River, not very far from our hotel, we saw a gathering of loud and cheering all-male crowd, all looking at something in the middle. It was a fierce battle between two well-grown dogs, each supported by a team standing on opposite sides. Both the dogs were bleeding profusely having been hit by the opponent's blade firmly tied to one of the front legs. Nur said the battle would not stop unless one of the dogs gave in to its injuries. The spectacle was as much frightening as sickening. I felt a sudden churning in my stomach and quickly left the crowd to regain my composure.

The luncheon meeting at Amin's house over delectable pulao and mutton kebabs brought us a rich and unexpected dividend. The same evening Nur came to our hotel to jubilantly announce that we would be taken to Mazar-i-Sharif next morning to see the Nauroz festival. It would be a trip meant only for the three visiting Indian hacks including Shekhar Gupta. Immediately, Appan got into a generous mode and started offering Nur tall Patiala pegs of Scotch bought from the Indian Embassy. 'Long live India-Afghan friendship,' we said loudly as our glasses clinked.

∽

The mountainous road from Kabul to Mazar-i-Sharif could have been a desirable option in normal circumstances. The breathtaking scenes of the Panjshir Valley surrounded by the snow-capped Hindu Kush drew a large number of tourists on this road before Ahmed Shah Massoud raised his well-trained and well-armed anti-Soviet militia and took control of the Salang Pass. We were therefore taken by a small Soviet-made Afghan Air Force plane. For some inexplicable reasons, we were treated like VIPs and were offered lavish breakfast during our hour-long journey. Nur, despite constant prodding and pestering, refused to divulge what awaited us in the holy northern city bordering Uzbekistan.

Nauroz means New Year's Day, in Afghanistan's context, the first day of spring and the beginning of the year in the solar Hijri calendar. According to experts, 'It is celebrated on the day of the astronomical equinox. The moment at which the Sun crosses the celestial equator and equalizes night and day is calculated exactly every year.'

'Happy Nauroz,' I greeted Nur as we disembarked from the aircraft to get into an official car waiting for us at the tarmac.

We were driven straight to the fabled Blue Mosque, a holy shrine and an architectural marvel in the centre of the city. Mazar-i-Sharif drew its name from the noble shrine. It was widely believed that Ali ibn Abi Talib, cousin and son-in-law of the Prophet, was finally buried here. It was a huge and beautifully laid out complex with sprawling parks and a series of buildings. In the car, Nur had announced that we would witness a rare spectacle there, the Jahenda Bala festival, to be attended by the country's political and military bigwigs. It would be presided over by Abdul Rashid Dostum, a trusted ally of the president and the undisputed master of the Balkh province including Mazar-i-Sharif.

The ceremony itself was nothing spectacular whose high point was the raising of a special banner with a colour combination resembling Derafsh Kaviani, the royal standard of the Sasanid rulers of Persia. But the gathering was massive, their reaction loud, spontaneous and tumultuous. It was a veritable sea of humanity that reminded me of the Dussehra celebrations at Delhi's Ramlila grounds. Dostum's popularity was also on display as the cheering crowd rose in thunderous applause when he stood up to greet the audience before hoisting the colourful banner. On the floors of the Blue Mosque and the adjacent buildings we saw thousands of colourful pigeons fluttering about. It is a widely held belief that some of them change their colour while resting in the holy precincts for a few days.

A leader of the Uzbeks, Dostum was a controversial and maverick character. Early in his life he was a small-time trade union leader. After the invasion of the Soviets he raised a 20,000 strong militia and supported the foreign infidels. When the Soviets left installing their puppet Najibullah in Kabul, Dostum quickly swore allegiance to the president to retain his control over the northern provinces. While the rest of Afghanistan seemed war-ravaged, Dostum's territories remained an oasis of peace, prosperity and tranquility. In 1989, Mazar-i-Sharif was arguably the safest city in entire Afghanistan. After staying for almost two weeks in besieged Kabul, it seemed, we had crossed over to a new and different country that bore no resemblance with any other part of Afghanistan.

We left the car at the parking lot of the mosque and decided to walk the distance to the state guest house where we would stay for the night. It seemed as if the whole city had come out on the streets to take part in the celebrations and revelry. In Kabul, the Pashtuns were the most visible tribe. But Mazar-i-Sharif seemed like a melting pot of all the tribes—Uzbeks, Hazaras, Turkmen, Tajiks and also Pashtuns. We saw colourful makeshift stalls on both sides of the main thoroughfare doing brisk business in all kinds of merchandise including expensive carpets and shawls. The food stalls exuded a tempting aroma of tandoor dishes and pulao and I felt suddenly very hungry. Nur vetoed my suggestion of eating in one of those stalls, promising better and more stimulating stuff at the guest house. He kept his word as we were served delicious nan, meat, pulao and dessert, all made especially for the special visitors on the special occasion of Nauroz.

At the guest house, Nur introduced us to a gentleman called Ismail who from then on would be our local guide and mentor. He was a Tajik who crossed over to Dostum's side after battling with the Mujahideen for many years. He was a charming young man in his late thirties, wore a Pathani suit, and carried an assault rifle on his shoulders. Two armed bodyguards carrying guns accompanied him all the time. Even before lunch he looked visibly intoxicated, and over lunch in his broken English gave us a lecture on the city including its Hellenic past. In his company, I felt somewhat uncomfortable.

In the afternoon, we were driven to a nearby stadium to witness another signature event of the Nauroz festivities—a Buzkashi match being played between two groups of local horsemen. The field was dusty, rugged and without a blade of grass. It was virtually an open field with a small section of broken cement gallery in one corner. Ismail virtually bulldozed his way through the surging crowd to get us seats in the front row. It was obvious he was some kind of a local heavyweight who commanded fear and obedience. No woman could be spotted in the crowd as the game was forbidden for them. However, every male spectator, young and old, was carrying a gun as if they had come not to see a sporting event but to a battlefield. Even the tiny tots on the elders' laps had toy guns in their possession.

Buzkashi, Ismail explained, was a composite word found in the Tajik language. Buz meant goat, Kashi was grab and run. But the corpse that lay at the centre of the pit in the middle was that of a calf, not a goat. The rule of the game was very simple though the way it was being played looked bizarre and funny. Each team of horsemen had almost a hundred members and there was no way one could identify who was playing for which team. For there was no jersey, no referee, no linesman. Every member of the two teams had just one goal in mind: to snatch the corpse, take it around the two poles on two sides and put it back in the pit from where it was taken. Every such successful attempt earned the team a point. What really ensued following the start looked like unmitigated madness, almost like rugby on horses. Soon the field as well as our gallery was covered with dust blurring our vision almost completely. Ismail remained cheerful and nonchalant but we promptly decided to walk back to our guest house to have a bath.

At night, Ismail, our generous host, virtually went for the jugular. At his instance, the guest house drawing room was spruced and decked up for a mehfil. Carpets were laid out on the floor, covered with spotless white linen. Flower vases full of fresh tulips were kept on all corners of the room including in the centre. All for a dance recital by a beautiful woman who kept entertaining us till the wee hours of the morning. Ismail invited a few local officials who soon turned the room into a noisy, vibrant tavern. Russian vodka flew like water, we smoked hookah, some others took opium. Dead drunk, I fell asleep on the floor and was then carried to my bed by Ismail's bodyguards on their shoulders.

Our return flight was in the afternoon. In the morning, I went out to the street and bought a beautiful red velvet jacket for my daughter, Tupur, who was then barely 3 years old. I thought she would look just like the Red Riding Hood and kiss me for such a beautiful gift.

But what happened three days later when I returned home to New Delhi was just the opposite and remains etched in my mind even now. The door opened, Tupur came running and threw herself up on my lap. I opened the handbag, took out the red jacket and gave it to her. Without casting a glance, she threw it on the floor and asked me, *'Baba, ebar theke tumi amader barite thakbe to?'* (Dad, will you be living with us from now on?)

I sat dumbfounded and after a while wrote a short story in Bengali based upon the experience.

—◆—

15

Moscow: Watching the Curtain Lift

I sweat profusely. With every step taking me closer to the counter, I could hear my heart beat louder and louder until it felt like a veritable din as I slipped my passport across the glass window. I was inside the Moscow airport. The young Russian immigration officer sitting on a high stool on the other side of the thick glass pane was in military fatigues and looked like a no-nonsense soul. I expected the officer to look straight into my eyes and call the bluff. Any moment now, I was convinced, I would be asked to step aside, whisked away in a few minutes for a long and gruelling interrogation before being boarded on a return flight. With luck running out, I might also land up in the nearest police lock-up.

That's exactly how a police officer at the Mumbai airport had predicted my future, when after one and a half hours of persuasion and cajoling he let me board the flight as the last passenger, barely a few seconds before the captain ordered the closure of the gates. 'Rest assured,' he had said with a degree of finality, 'you would be sent back by the next flight. The Russians won't let you in.'

As it happened, I was travelling to Moscow without a valid passport. Well, I was not completely at fault. My passport carried two expiry dates on two pages. I took the later date as the final one, without ever bothering to see that the page was cancelled by the issuing officer who had made that mistake. The cancellation stamp was barely visible. The actual date was long over. Even the Soviet Embassy in Delhi had not detected it and had issued me a visa. Unlike most of the countries, the Soviets did not endorse visas on passports and issued a separate sheet to accompany the document. As I learnt later, the practice was being followed by the communist country to keep the visitor's identity a closely guarded secret, to save him from possible harassment in his home country. In the colonial era, many Indian communists secretly visited Moscow to seek guidance and help from their comrades in the Communist Party of the Soviet Union (CPSU). Israel, too, I found out several years later, follows the same procedure.

It escaped the attention of the Mumbai immigration officer too, who happily stamped my passport. A middle-aged police officer in mufti chanced upon it while randomly checking passengers' passports. It was this officer who had reluctantly allowed me to board the flight, albeit with those ominous predictions.

As no flight was available from Delhi, my office bought me a business class ticket on a British Airways flight that was to go to Moscow via London from Mumbai. It was August 1991. That was the first time I was travelling business class, but my anxiety had spoilt the whole fun of it. Immediately after I landed at Heathrow, I rushed to the money exchanger for some coins and called Gouri Chatterjee, my news editor, then holidaying in England. I beseeched her to speak with the Indian Embassy folks in Moscow about my predicament. Gouri Di started laughing and said, 'Any intervention by them will be counterproductive. Take your chance.'

So I did. The young man did not even look at my passport. He tore down one page of the visa sheet and stapled the other one. 'Spasiba,' I thanked him loudly, and rushed out of the airport after collecting my luggage. In my belly, I had this bizarre feeling of escaping the Gulag hoodwinking the KGB![5]

I was the first Indian journalist to land in Moscow after the coup against Mikhail Gorbachev failed and saw the public wrath against the communists raging in the city like a tornado. Perhaps I am also the only Indian to have officially walked into what was still considered by the world as the 'land behind Iron Curtain' without a valid passport!

From the airport I drove straight to the Indian Embassy to renew my passport. In the stretch between the Indian Embassy and Hotel Rossiya I did not miss the serpentine queue in front of the McDonald's. But that was an old story and I had seen a larger queue in a newspaper photograph quite some time back. Everything in and around the hotel looked the same—as it were two years ago in 1989 when I stayed here as a member of the media delegation accompanying Prime Minister Rajiv Gandhi.

Hotel Rossiya was opened in 1967, during the Khrushchev era. Sprawling across 30 acres, and located close to the Red Square, it was the largest one in entire Europe and remained so till being bulldozed in 2006 to pave the way for a glitzy mall. It was notorious for gruff service, baffling bureaucracy, sinister food and bizarre Soviet touches such as radios that could only pick up one station and could only be turned off by being unplugged. The bed was not really a bed, but a slab of wood like a wooden shelf. Equally spartan were the rules that governed the entry and exit of guests. It took a special card to enter the hotel and each of the hotel's long corridors was watched over by a surly 'dezhumaya', a matron who collected room keys from guests whenever they went out. Those who came back late at night got a mouthful from the sleepy hall monitor as she retrieved their keys. The harshest restrictions, though, were on meetings between foreign guests

---

[5]Gulag was a system of labour camps maintained in the Soviet Union during 1930–55; KGB was the state security police of the former Soviet Union

and Soviet citizens. Even innocuous encounters were considered suspect.

Yeltsin and his rebellious followers had sent the tank-mounted soldiers packing, but the hotel, even during my second visit, retained all the paraphernalia of the communist era. I had to deposit my passport with the grumpy and unfriendly receptionist who kept me waiting for close to an hour before giving me a receipt. I had the same eerie feeling as I confronted a fat middle-aged matron on my floor. The small soap cake in the toilet was worse than what one could get at a Kolkata grocer's and the toilet paper frighteningly coarse in texture. Standing in the hotel lobby one could hardly believe the world had already turned upside down just outside.

I experienced the first noticeable change well past midnight when my bedside telephone suddenly went alive. The caller was a man whose broken English in Russian accent was hardly comprehensible. 'Hundred dollars,' that was all I could make out in the first instance. Then the brief conversation went like this:

'Who are you? Why are you calling me at this hour to ask for hundred dollars?' I asked, bewildered and angry.

'Good girls. Sixteen, seventeen, eighteen…Very, very good.'

The pimp sounded confident when I asked how he would be able to smuggle in girls escaping the round-the-clock hotel vigilance. 'No problem,' he replied, and I could almost see the chuckle on his lips, as he continued, 'I am hotel staff.'

'No, thank you,' I hung up. The phone rang again within minutes.

'Ok, fifty dollars…forty?'

'No, not interested.'

'All right, thirty. Last price.' I broke into a laughter before bidding him goodnight.

The next day, Shekhar Bhatia of *The Telegraph*, who was staying at another hotel, narrated a more harrowing experience.

He was almost mobbed at the hotel lobby by a group of beautiful and desperate teenaged girls who took the elevator with him and virtually chased him up to his room before a hotel employee came to his rescue. In a flash, Arthur Koestler came to my mind, who, in his masterpiece, *Darkness at Noon*, wrote about a similar incident of nubile girls offering cheap sex as he crisscrossed the country on a train. Open prostitution came to Moscow even before the Soviet Union formally dismembered and Gorbachev threw in his hat.

∽

By Kolkata standards, the assembled crowd in front of the Russian parliament building, also known as the White House, was nothing spectacular. Nor was the number of the dead. During the siege from August 19 to August 21, only three young people died under one of the advancing armoured tanks. The army, after vacillating for two days, finally switched sides and the seventy-two-hour-long coup virtually ended in a whimper. The three boys, however, became martyrs overnight and a memorial was built in their names at the same spot where they were crushed. In non-communist Russia it soon became a tourist attraction like the Vietnam memorial in Washington D.C.

In the immediate aftermath of the dramatic putsch and its more dramatic failure, Moscow became a city of gossip and wild speculations. Even though 'Gorby' was back in the capital from his Crimean dacha (country house) and Boris Yeltsin looked firmly in control of the transition issuing one decree after another, people were still worried and nervous. They could not simply digest the fact that the CPSU and the KGB, two invincible institutions of the post-Revolution era, could just wither away into oblivion. Many felt the coup would be re-enacted to be followed by widespread state repression and retribution. They found it difficult to come to terms with the unfolding reality that seemed like a fairy tale. It was the twentieth century's biggest political earthquake without the accompanying tremor and collateral damage.

On Moscow streets, Gandhi won over Lenin. I found the prevailing atmosphere bizarre and surreal. The incredible failure of the coup leaders, their glaring mistakes, non-adherence to the time-honoured coup manual in the communist regimes evoked—for the next few days—heart-warming laughter among the otherwise pensive Muscovites. They wondered why Yeltsin, the rallying point of people's resistance was not arrested in the first place in a midnight swoop or why the lines of communication, including telephone and electronic transmission, were not snapped automatically. The consensus was that the plotters led by KGB Chief Vladimir Kryuchkov were not brave hearts. They simply could not master courage needed critically during such a cataclysmic occasion. A Russian journalist told me he had seen Soviet Vice President Gennady Yanayev's nicotine-stained fingers trembling as he addressed the press to declare Gorbachev's dethronement.

Two days before my arrival, the statue of Feliks Dzerzhinsky, founder of the Soviet secret police[6], was, brought down from its pedestal in front of the KGB headquarters by an angry crowd aided officially by the city's municipal authorities. On the same day, a decree was issued banning communist party activities in Moscow.

With Dzerzhinsky gone, people started debating what would be the next obvious target. 'Lenin, who else?' Someone from the Indian Embassy told me in a hush-hush tone and advised me to visit his mausoleum without any further delay. During those days the Indian Embassy officials kept a low profile following the faux pas of the Narasimha Rao government that supported

---

[6]The All-Russian Extraordinary Commission for Combating Counterrevolution and Sabotage (Cheka), which later became the secret police and preceded the KGB.

the coup based on Intelligence gathered from Moscow. India, a time-tested ally of the USSR, looked almost like a pariah in the immediate aftermath of Yeltsin's historic victory.

I rushed to revisit Lenin lying in an embalmed state in a dimly lit glass case. Suddenly a growing number of people from Moscow and afar were coming to see the granite edifice fearing that Lenin's body would be taken away to be finally buried near his mother in St Petersburg. I stood behind a few hundred people who had already gathered there early in the morning to pay homage to their leader despite the death of communism a few days earlier. Most of them were elderly Russians who rejoiced the arrival of democracy, yet their love and respect for Lenin remained intact. As the queue moved slowly in a disciplined manner to the winding steps down into the crypt, reminiscent of the tomb of some Egyptian pharaoh, I asked the man just in front of me to explain this continuing respect for Lenin. 'He was a good man. He was the best man. Under him we lived well. We have come to see him off with tears,' was the gentleman's simple reply.

On the same morning, a larger crowd, comprising mostly young men in T-shirts and jeans, gathered in front of the White House to mourn the death of the three martyrs. The barricade put up by the agitating crowd to thwart the moving army tanks remained untouched for a week after the coup's announcement. The area surrounding the Russian parliament building wore a festive look, almost matching the colours of the sky. Floral wreaths were placed in front of the makeshift martyrs' columns, as silent onlookers walked past, some of them carrying printed photographs of Jesus Christ in their hands. Romanov, my Russian interpreter who charged me a bomb to exploit my ignorance of his mother tongue, quipped, 'These boys are the new heroes of the second Russian revolution.' Only then it truly sunk into me that I was indeed becoming witness to one of the most important historic moments of the twentieth century.

In the heat of victory, the Yeltsin government lost no time in pursuing a policy of punishment and retribution. Among other institutions, the axe also fell on *Pravda*, a 79-year-old newspaper started by Lenin that, over time, became synonymous with the CPSU and Kremlin. Five other communist newspapers were also banned. As had been its tradition, *Pravda* toed the official party line handed over by the coup leaders, completely miscalculating the popular mood of defiant resistance. Quickly thereafter, the paper took an about-turn, writing in a front-page article, 'The materials published in this newspaper, were again, like many times before, biased and indecisive. We must openly state that one of the reasons for that is the newspaper's long time dependence on orders from above.' The volte face cut no ice as the Russian government promptly issued a decree and stopped its publication. It appeared to many that the Russian president was being vindictive, acting in the same manner as his communist adversaries by settling personal scores. Even though *Pravda* extended full-throated support to Gorbachev and his various reformist agenda, it was not very favourably disposed towards Yeltsin. During the Russian president's official tour to the US many months before the coup, *Pravda* translated a story from an Italian paper that ridiculed Yeltsin for being a 'drunkard' and a 'spendthrift'. His alcoholism and erratic drunken behaviour was, however, the staple of Moscow's gossip everywhere. Even Sonia Gandhi, I learnt from one of her close associates, detested the Russian president for being an alcoholic.

When I reached the *Pravda* office in northwestern Moscow, the long dingy corridors were nearly empty, an occasional figure strode past in the gloom. Half-finished page proofs of the paper's last issue hung on the walls in the conference hall, and a small bust of Lenin appeared to look pensively at the remnants of what he had founded on 5 May 1912. As a Kolkatan and also as a student of history I felt an inexplicable sense of emptiness. I stood there for a while gazing at what was then looking like a haunted mansion. Once an unabashed beacon of the communist world, its desolate surroundings, with shuttered offices, reflected the state of the party.

On the ninth floor, a small group of the paper's editorial staff was meeting to do a job that was, till the other day, an exclusive preserve of the party top brass—choosing a new editor. They were a bunch of greying middle-aged departmental editors, trying their best to come to terms with the changing realities. They looked nervous, yet their spirits were high. They denounced Yeltsin in one voice and called his move to ban newspapers undemocratic. They were not sure when the paper would resume its publication but had already decided to bring about certain necessary changes. It would no longer be the organ of the central committee of the CPSU and would not carry the masthead slogan: 'Workers of the World Unite'. The picture of Vladimir Ilich Lenin would also be pulled from its place on the front page to announce, in no uncertain terms, *Pravda*'s break with its own history. Quite an ending for the publication once described by the *Great Soviet Encyclopedia* as 'the largest and most popular Soviet newspaper, which together with the party has followed a major historical course in the struggle for the victory of the socialist revolution and the building of socialism.'

∽

However, no one was much bothered about Yeltsin's excesses and his thuggish treatment of political opponents or the media. As I found out, Yeltsin enjoyed a special rapport with the people in Moscow who looked up to him not merely as a rallying point of the rebellion but as someone who always sided with them against the privileged communist apparatchik[7]. Many of them

---

[7]Communist Party members

fondly remembered those days when as the communist party chief of the city unit—a post he owed to Gorbachev—he led a spartan life refusing all the privileges of public office—a country dacha, a limousine, the special sops and the insularities of a cosy and cloistered life. Unlike his party comrades, Yeltsin stayed in a simple flat and went to work frequently by bus or the subway. His popularity soared when he was spotted in government shops often talking to commoners about their difficulties. Yeltsin continued his crusade against the party bosses and their privileged lifestyle even after he became a member of the Polit Bureau, a move that finally cost him his party membership. Undaunted, Yeltsin staged a comeback based upon the people's unstinted support in his usual truculent manner, winning a seat from Moscow in 1989. Two years later he became Russia's first elected president. The cherry on the cake came when he defied the coup plotters and mounted an army tank in August 1991 exhorting the uniformed soldiers to desist from helping those who wanted to bring back dictatorship and the eternal night. In the aftermath of his victory, everyone in Moscow, including Gorbachev, was dancing to Yeltsin's tunes; no one was prepared to shed a tear for the *Pravda* hacks.

I also learnt that Raisa Gorbachev had disappeared completely from the public glare after her return to Moscow with her husband from Crimea. The city was agog with rumours that she suffered a minor stroke, unable to grapple with the dramatic change in their fortunes. Yet I found no one in the city who was even slightly concerned with the first lady's health conditions. The most intriguing remark about the issue came from a young girl selling matryoshka dolls in front of a subway station. 'Americans should be worried about her, not us,' she told me.

Her sarcasm summed up the hatred an average Muscovite felt towards Gorbachev's wife. While the Western media pampered Raisa, finding in her a reflection of an American first lady, at home, she was despised precisely for the same reasons. Many Muscovites I met thought she was either a Tartar or a Jew who had also slept with Leonid Brezhnev[8] in an effort to smoothen her husband's future prospects in the party. In a nation where ordinary women stood in queues for hours to get substandard goods, Raisa Gorbachev was more of an anachronism, a fashionable lady from another planet, wielding petticoat influence upon a fawning husband.

Yeltsin himself echoed the popular sentiment on a number of occasions both within the party and outside of it. As *Le Monde* reported, in his speech before being sacked from the Communist Party, Yeltsin castigated Gorbachev's wife thus, 'I must ask the Polit Bureau to spare me the petty guidance of Raisa Maksimovna and her almost daily telephone calls and admonitions.' He criticized Gorbachev's dependence on his wife even on matters related to statecraft and proudly proclaimed, 'In our house I am the boss.' When asked during a TV interview what he would do if the Gorbachevs called on him at his residence, Yeltsin replied, 'I will ask Gorby to take his seat next to me in our drawing room and ask Raisa to join my wife in the kitchen.' Naina, Yeltsin's wife, who preferred to remain in the shadows following the tradition of other Soviet leaders' wives, became adorable overnight, simply by contrast. To an average Russian, Naina was just another one of them, a sweetheart babushka (grandmother or older woman).

But Mr and Mrs Yeltsin would have found things quite different if the KGB had agreed to do a Tiananmen[9] in front of the Russian parliament. The organization, long used to blindly following the party diktat, saw an unprecedented split, with the majority,

---

[8]Tartars and Jews were generally looked down upon in Soviet Russia. Leonid Brezhnev was probably Russia's last super-powerful political president of the Cold War days.
[9]From mid-April to early June 1989, China erupted in popular protest demanding democratic reforms. Beijing's Tiananmen's Square being one of the main centres of demonstration. The Chinese government put down the rebellion promptly through a massive military operation killing hundreds of protesters.

including the Alpha Unit in charge of operations, refusing to fire at their own people, storm the parliament building or kill Yeltsin. But the involvement of their boss, Vladimir Kryuchkov, otherwise known as a Gorbachev faithful, badly sullied the organization's image and reputation. No one in the KGB had the courage to face the rampaging mob that gathered right in front of their office at Lubyanka Square to uproot the huge statue of their founding father from its pedestal. One of the first things Gorbachev did upon his return was to dismantle and reorganize KGB beyond recognition and appoint Vadim Bakatin, who looked more like a Hollywood romantic hero and a known liberal, as the 'traitor's' successor.

The KGB, feared and hated in its own country as a state instrument of terror and repression, had actually gone into a major public relations exercise to change the organization's public image in the months preceding the coup. Ironically, Kryuchkov now imprisoned as a plotter, gave his full support and encouragement to the initiative. A few days before the coup, its Moscow district office even staged a Miss KGB contest! Oleg Tsarev, deputy head of press services for the organization, told me this as I sat down in front of his huge wooden desk at the KGB headquarters. He was somewhat critical of the public rage against the KGB and found it incomprehensible even after its role in foiling the coup. 'Yes, Kryuchkov is guilty. But the KGB, as an institution, was never involved in the coup, nor did it conspire against the Gorbachev regime,' Tsarev said, still unable to digest why their leader chose a suicidal path. 'For all I know, Kryuchkov supported glasnost[10]. We started talking to people in a well-planned and coordinated confidence-building exercise. Now with his own hands he has destroyed what he himself had built.'

---

[10] A Russian word meaning any process of justice or governance being conducted in the open. In 1986, Mikhail Gorbachev turned it into a slogan for transparent governance.

Tsarev's office on the first floor was unusually quiet when I went there without a prior appointment. As I walked through the wood panelled halls, the place looked quite prosperous by Moscow standards. Downstairs, two young soldiers stood guard in front of two closed black doors. They reminded me of their compatriots in front of Lenin's mausoleum who could be mistaken as statues unless one went very close to them to see their eyelids blinking almost invisibly. Down below, lay the notorious basement prisons. Those too were empty.

The friendly public relations officer then gave me a guided tour of Yuri Andropov's room, the former KGB chief who succeeded Brezhnev as the Soviet president. It seemed the rooms used by Andropov were kept as some kind of a museum for public viewing. His meeting room and the inner room both had marble fireplaces and the adjoining bedroom had a single bed, refrigerator and a table. He then showed me pictures of captured CIA agents and some clever eyeglasses. A captured spy would remove the glasses and nonchalantly chew the end to inject poison into his mouth. 'When you are caught,' my guide elaborated, 'they let you keep your glasses. The glasses are a CIA invention.'

I expressed my interest in going to the basement to see the dreaded prisons. The press officer, so far warm and friendly, suddenly went stiff and told my interpreter in Russian that our time was over. The same afternoon I met a group of elderly people who had formed a small organization called Union of Victims of Unjustified Repression, which was clamouring for the KGB files of the Stalinist era to be thrown open. All the members of the organization had a story to tell about how the KGB tortured or killed on grounds of unsubstantiated suspicion. Now that the communists had been thrown into the Volga, they wanted to know all the details of the perpetrators, not so much in a spirit of revenge but out of an undying sense of curiosity. One of them was sent to the Gulag at the age of 16 for being 'the son of an enemy of the people.' He wanted to know why his father was shot and why he had to spend the best years of his life in prison.

∽

Moscow, in August 1991, was still a city where the middle class and the poor pervaded the dreary government apartments. The rich were part of the communist oligarchy, happily ensconced behind the curtains with their own lifestyles. Vladimir Putin was still a nobody and the Moscow of his times with its glitzy downtown was still a far cry.

The fall of the communist regime sent shockwaves among the poor. The middle-aged portly woman who came to my hotel room every morning for house cleaning felt that she, along with her husband, would now face penury with rouble becoming more and more unstable every passing day. 'We have saved a few thousand from our salaries over thirty years. The savings should have seen us through in our old age. No longer. In one stroke our lives have become uncertain, our future totally bleak,' she kept on telling me in her broken English, a language she had assiduously cultivated over the years to endear herself to foreign tourists. Even my cab driver whom I hired for the entire duration of my stay, was not very hopeful about the future. He was an amazing person, read four newspapers carefully every day and was a chain-smoker. He was not unhappy that the communists were gone but had a very poor opinion about Yeltsin's abilities to preside over the destiny of such a huge nation at the time of the critical transition. He proved prophetic as Russia, and Moscow, slid into chaos and crony capitalism soon thereafter.

The change of guard generated a mixed reaction from the poor average Russians. But for the elderly Bengali communists who were still in Moscow in August 1991, the news came as a nightmare. I hunted out two of them—Nani Bhowmick and Gopen Chakraborty.

Gopen came to Moscow seven years after the Revolution in the disguise of a sailor and stopped at Berlin to meet Manabendra Nath Roy, a firebrand Bengali communist of that era and a close friend of Lenin. A member of the erstwhile Anushilan Samiti, an extremist nationalist outfit, Gopen was still sceptic about the communists. 'Roy told me to visit the USSR to see for myself what the Bolsheviks were doing. I took his suggestion and came to Moscow. It is here that I turned into a communist,' Gopen said, reminiscing about his days in the Russian capital.

Nani, like many other Bengalis working on the cultural front of the undivided Communist Party of India, came to Moscow in the late 1950s to work in the Bengali department of Progress Publishers that used to print books and periodicals in twelve Indian languages. Most of his colleagues who came for the same work returned to India. But Nani stayed back, married a Russian girl and led a happy family life with his wife and only son.

A fortnight had passed after the coup. Nani, then in his eighties and mourning the sudden death of his son, was still unaware of the earth-shattering events sweeping his city. When I told him the truth he refused to believe it and dismissed me contemptuously. For verification he then asked my interpreter. When he endorsed what I had said, the old man called for his wife working in the kitchen. I cursed myself for shattering the make-believe world of a benign octogenarian for whom communism was still the be all and end all of his life. As he heard his wife telling the same story, Nani tried to hide his face behind both his hands, panting breathlessly like an asthma patient. 'I knew he would be devastated to hear all this. As it is we are finding it difficult to bear with the loss of our son. That is why I chose to spare him,' Mrs Bhowmick said in broken Bengali with tears rolling down her cheeks.

16
Ayodhya, 6 December 1992

7 a.m. Faizabad

Founded around 1722 by Saadat Ali Khan, an important feudatory chief during the dying days of the Mughal Empire, as the capital of Awadh, it is now a nondescript district headquarters-town in Uttar Pradesh, some 600 kms from New Delhi. We left our hotel and boarded our car, mentally calculating that it would not take us more than 20 minutes to reach Ayodhya, about 7 kms away.

We could hardly believe what we saw: a deluge of saffron. Flags, festoons, signboards, people's dresses, headbands. Any count could at best be a hazardous guess, but they looked to be in millions. In Sangh Parivar's parlance, they were karsevaks, Hindu religious volunteers. And they had congregated on the streets of Faizabad from all over India. Then there were thousands more, who stood on the pavements on both sides of the road to express solidarity with the karsevaks. Bajrangbali, our driver, had the unenviable task to wade through this and was understandably terrified. Like us, the ocean of karsevaks was also heading towards Ayodhya.

Believed by many Hindus to be the birthplace of Rama, the great hero of the epic Ramayana, Ayodhya holds a very special place in many hearts, and is dotted with around 6,000 temples. The exact date of the town's establishment is a point of great contention. Between Hindu mythological tradition and more conventional history, the date varies from the Treta Yuga (i.e. some 900,000 years ago) to circa 700 BCE. What is more important, however, is that the town is also considered holy by many Muslims because, according to one tradition, Shea, the grandson of Adam, is buried here in a cemetery on the banks of Sarayu River.

But by no means is Ayodhya the only place in India which is considered holy by both Hindus and Muslims. According to most records, things in this town took a nasty turn after Hafizullah, an official of the Faizabad law court, claimed in 1822 that a mosque founded by Emperor Babur in Ayodhya was situated at the birthplace of Rama. Ever since, members of the two communities have clashed over the possession of a small piece of land, the first one being recorded in 1853. Matters worsened after Hafizullah's claim slipped into official colonial records, such as P. Carnegy's historical sketch of Faizabad (1870), H.R. Nevill's *Faizabad District Gazetteer* and as a footnote in Mrs A.S. Beveridge's English translation of *Babur-nama: Babur's Memoirs* (1922). Finally, when idols were suddenly found inside the dilapidated mosque, with the Hindus claiming that it was a miracle and the Muslims insisting that they were smuggled in, at the dead of night on 22 December 1949, the building was closed to both Muslims and Hindus by a government administrative order.

Despite long and complicated litigations over the issue, things lay low for years until, following an order of the district and sessions judge, the padlocks were removed and Hindu priests were allowed to enter the structure on 1 February 1986. Rajiv Gandhi was the prime minister then. Severely mauled by the nationwide criticism of giving in before Muslim fundamentalists in the Shah Bano case, perhaps he calculated that it would be a balancing act if his government did not challenge the verdict in a higher court and allow the Hindu priests to have their day. Capitulating further to the Hindu demand, three years down the line, just before the 1989 parliamentary polls, the Rajiv Gandhi regime allowed the Vishva Hindu Parishad (VHP) to organize the shilanyas (laying of the foundation stone) for the planned Rama temple at the site on 9 November 1989. This action boosted the VHP-BJP-RSS[11] combine to advance its Ram Janmabhoomi (Rama's birthplace) campaign across the nation.

Since then, the call for karseva, i.e. congregations of volunteers to 'build the Rama temple', was given thrice—first in the autumn of 1990, then again, exactly a year later in 1991, followed by another one in July 1992.

But on this day it clearly appeared to be a different ballgame. Never before was the congregation of karsevaks so huge. Thousands had already assembled in Faizabad before the break of dawn, chanting *'Jai Shri Ram'* in unison and marching towards Ayodhya. The air was heavy with a curious mixture of melodious bhajans and thundering slogans vowing to build the temple at any cost: *'bachcha bachcha Ram ka/mandir ka hai kam ka* (Every child of Lord Rama/Will work to build the temple).

I started covering the Ram Janmabhoomi movement from 1986, soon after the BJP adopted it in its party programme at Palampur, Himachal Pradesh. The very sight of young Rama fanatics, wearing saffron headbands, wielding sticks and flexing their muscles, used to send shivers down my spine. Over time, I got used to them. Not only that, whenever in Ayodhya, we scribes used to unwind in our hotel rooms by making fun out of these slogans. The one that compulsively did rounds among those waiting at the telegraph office to send their copies was, *'bachcha bachcha Rum ka, kya prabandh hai shaam ka?'* (O children of Rum, what alcoholic provision have you made for the evening?).

---

[11]VHP-BJP-RSS: Vishva Hindu Parishad-Bharatiya Janata Party-Rashtriya Swayamsevak Sangh

When our stocks ran out, we ran to the nearby army barracks, where one would get unlimited supplies of military rum at a high premium after midnight. Incidentally, the wittiest explanation of our gods' association with the various kinds of elixirs of life was told to me by a veteran BJP leader: 'Brandy pe Brahma base, Rum pe base Rama, Whisky pe Vishnu base, Desi pe Hanumaana'. (Brandy's for Brahma and Rum for Lord Rama, Whisky for Vishnu and country liquor for Hanuman).

The Ram Janmabhoomi movement had turned Ayodhya into a mini-Varanasi, with small shops having sprung up in large numbers in every lane and bylane of the town, selling flowers, incense, sweets and every other conceivable ingredient required for a puja. An equally large number of shops were selling souvenirs like saffron headbands, cassettes of Rama bhajans by Sadhvi Rithambara and trishuls of various sizes. When one of our compatriot scribes, Swapan Dasgupta, had got us a few such bands the day before, we chided him for being a fanatic.

As we left the hotel for Ayodhya that morning, it was beyond our wildest nightmares that those headbands would be our saviours on that fateful day. The 150 odd journalists who had assembled in Ayodhya from across the globe had sent routine copies to their publications the night before, and the overwhelmingly common tone was that this time around too, the karseva would be a damp squib.

The central Margdarshak Mandal, which was the central committee of the Ram Janmabhoomi movement, had decided in a meeting on the morning of 5 December that it will only be a symbolic karseva with sand from River Sarayu. The meeting was attended by 110 of the 160 members who were unanimous about the symbolic karseva. In the afternoon, Acharya Bamdev, Paramhans Ramchandra Das and Ashok Singhal addressed a press conference to brief the media on the details of the proposed karseva.

Bamdev was the most venerated of all the sadhus who were involved in the movement. Chairman of the Ram Janmabhoomi Salvation Committee and convener of the All India Sant Committee, Bamdev was known as the 'Acharya of Acharyas'. An itinerant sadhu, he had no ashram of his own and loved to introduce himself as a teacher. On the other hand, Paramhans Ramchandra Das, head of the Digambar Akhara of Ayodhya and chief of the Ram Janmabhoomi Nyas, stood as a veritable contrast to Bamdev. The octogenarian sadhu, frail, with an unruly tuft of hair and flowing beard had a stentorian voice good enough to address a few thousand devotees without using an amplifier. A compulsive talker at a high pitch, Das had a major role in the 1949 movement when the small idol of Rama was installed inside the Babri Masjid. It was but obvious that he would be part of the movement that aimed to build a temple around the idol.

Das ensured that he did not allow either Bamdev or Singhal to say much at the press meet. What we could gather was that at the break of dawn, all karsevaks would be taken to the huge Ramlila Ground on the banks of the Sarayu. They would then be divided into batches of thousand and these batches would enter the karseva venue through the eastern gate with sand from the Sarayu banks. After performing karseva, which would mean filling the concrete structure built in July, they would exit through the western gate in a file and reassemble at the Ramlila Ground. Sadhus and leaders of the movement would palliate their toil with day-long religious discourses.

The VHP took the help of five specialists for the construction of the temple. They were: architect Chandrakant Sompura; Vinod Mehta, an engineer from Ahmedabad; Anand Swarup Arya of Roorkee, Krishna Dutta, a professor from Dehradun; and Braja Mohon Seth, a civil engineer and a former brigadier of the Indian Army. Sompura had made a design of the temple that was preserved as a well-kept secret with the Sangh leaders. However, some of us had the good fortune to have a look at it in July 1992.

8.30 a.m. Ramlila Ground, Ayodhya

When we reached the banks of the Sarayu, we were surprised to see a crowd of not more than ten thousand, most of whom were filling polythene bags with hands full of sand from the riverbank. Where were the two hundred thousand karsevaks that we were expecting? We smelt a rat. Was the press meeting hogwash then? Did the leaders have other plans up their sleeves?

Upon reflection, I have felt that the Babri Masjid would have stayed intact if the plans were not changed at the eleventh hour. While the mosque was being destroyed and was falling like the wall of Jericho, we heard that it was Vinay Katiyar who pressurized the leaders of the movement against a symbolic karseva. He argued that repeated tokenism in the name of karseva would not go down well with the devotees who had been clamouring for action for a long time. Katiyar was the chief of Bajrang Dal. He had won the Faizabad Lok Sabha seat on a BJP ticket in the 1991 general elections. He is a belligerent man, who does not mince words. When during the karseva in October 1991, a few young men scaled the dome of the Masjid, Katiyar had to face the wrath of the karsevaks in trying to dissuade them. This time round, he wanted a more concrete action plan that would satisfy his supporters.

The karsevaks were in no mood to leave the Masjid premises and go to the banks of the Sarayu. When we reached the karseva venue, B.P. Toshniwal endorsed the changed plan. 'It has been decided at the last moment that the karsevaks would congregate at the Rama Katha Kunj ground, from where they would be sent in small batches to the venue,' he said. In other words, they would be spared the long walk. The decision seemed justified and never did we anticipate that the assembling two hundred thousand karsevaks near the venue could be part of a bigger agenda, until around an hour later, when the first signs of lawlessness became visible.

While we were talking to Toshniwal, the Rama Katha Kunj and its approach road were overflowing with karsevaks. RSS volunteers were manning the Rama Deewar with great alacrity. Ram Shankar Agnihotri, the loudmouth spokesman of the VHP, had informed us that a special arrangement for journalists had been made on the roof of Manas Bhavan, adjacent to the venue on its eastern side. But who would care for a seat in the stands when one could get a decidedly better view from the sidelines? I proudly displayed the pink press card given by the VHP and was promptly allowed by RSS volunteers inside the mosque premises.

When I had come to cover the karseva in July, I noticed that the BJP government of Uttar Pradesh led by Kalyan Singh had changed the very look of the mosque premises. It had acquired 2.77 acres of land next to the mosque and levelled it. There was no sign of the spot which was the centre of dispute owing to the laying of the foundation stone of the temple in 1989. Instead, the July karseva aimed at laying the foundation of the main entrance of the temple designed by Sompura. The gate would be 166 feet long and 80 feet wide. Throwing the court order to the wind, the July karseva ended after the foundation was laid. The December karseva was meant to 'cleanse' this foundation.

10 a.m. Karseva Site

A crowd of hardly 500 volunteers and sadhus greeted us at the site. A copper pot adorned with a vermilion swastika was shining in the morning sun, right in the middle of the site. All arrangements for an elaborate puja were complete, with the whole area decked up with mango leaves, garlands and flower petals. Acharya Bamdev was supposed to preside over the official karseva at quarter past twelve. That would mean that the sadhus would start the puja and cleansing of the platform while the karsevaks, in small batches, would fill the cavities with sand. Tej Shankar, the royally treated

Supreme Court observer, seemed happy with the proceedings. The evening before, he had faxed the apex court that all was well and in keeping with the court's directives. That is, no construction work was happening in the acquired land.

One of the first to arrive at the venue was Acharya Haricharan Das of the Vaishnava sect of Chitrakoot and with him a teenaged sadhu who was a sight to behold. Wearing a turmeric-coloured dhoti tied like a lungi, Raghunandan had covered his upper torso with a namavali printed with *'Hare Krishna Hare Rama'* (a namavali is a shawl with names of gods printed on it). Every part of his body, the shaven head downwards was covered with the red of the tilak. The first thing he did after taking his seat was to bring out two shovels from his bag. Dharamdas, the six-and-a-half-foot tall sadhu, who was nearby, promptly held him by his neck and threw him out of the premises. It seemed that Dharamdas, the pehalwan who shadowed Katiyar wherever he went, was there to ensure that the court directive was complied with in letter and spirit. Certainly a teenaged sadhu had no business to defy court orders under his nose.

Even as Raghunandan was trying to gather himself from the sudden assault, about 200 karsevaks were trying to elbow their way in. All of them were wielding trishuls. Many of the jawans of Provincial Arms Constabulary (PAC) had vermilion tilaks on their foreheads and even the RSS knew that they were hardly dependable. The RSS volunteers themselves formed the second line of defence behind these PAC jawans. One of them assured the police, 'Don't you worry. We'll handle this.' The PAC jawans were only too happy to have this assurance. The PAC, a paramilitary outfit, formed during the regime of Chief Minister Narayan Dutt Tiwari, had never remained neutral during communal riots in the state. Every time a karseva took place in Ayodhya, the PAC stood behind the karsevaks openly. It would have been impossible for the karsevaks to break the security cordon and reach Ayodhya during the karseva of 1990, if the PAC had firmly stood its ground. The karsevaks' happiness with the PAC was in equal measure of their unhappiness with the CRPF (Central Reserve Police Force).

The moment the PAC distanced itself from the scene, a scuffle ensued between the RSS volunteers and the karsevaks. A deluge of karsevaks kept lashing at the gate. Moments later, they were hounded away by the volunteers. The resistance lasted for not more than fifteen minutes. About 150 young men with trishuls and iron rods barged in at the site. The karsevaks went into a tizzy, gyrating with chants of *'Jai Shri Ram'*. This 'Rama dance' which was a mixture of tandava, breakdance and disco, was also a by-product of the Ram Janmabhoomi movement.

Maniram from Rajasthan was one of the revellers. His wafer-thin torso bore obvious signs of poverty, but that did not take away his zeal. He accosted me, looked into my eyes and my press card, and with a frightening frown yelled, *'Jai Shri Ram'*. I repeated the chant with him, something that I had learnt to do with experience. And then I asked, almost apologetically, 'What about the court orders?' Moments later, I was surrounded by ten other karsevaks, spitting venom at the court and telling me in no uncertain terms that a media person would be better off by staying away from the scene. An RSS volunteer came to my rescue and with folded hands asked me to move away. Arguing would be foolhardy, I thought and moved to a nearby hillock that till the previous year housed the police control room. I saw Shrish Chandra Dikshit, former DIG of UP police turned BJP MP from Varanasi and vice president of the VHP, in a saffron cap, sitting on a brick. Giving him company were Uma Shankar Bajpai, DIG of Faizabad division, along with the leader of the almost non-existent Panther Party of Kahsmir, Bhim Singh, with his journalist wife, Sheela.

10.30 a.m. Leaders Arrive

Amid the din and bustle, Ashok Singhal entered the site from the Hanumangarh Road, accompanying Shiv Sena MP Moreshwar Save. A huge cheer of *'Har Har Mahadev, Har Bhavani'* greeted them. Singhal showed him around, as though Save was a VVIP. In about ten minutes came L.K. Advani and Murli Manohar Joshi, both with grim faces. Joshi exchanged greetings with us and almost like a soliloquy said, 'Let's see what happens.' And then both the BJP leaders left, taking the approach road off Hanumangarh, to the roof of the VHP office in Rama Katha Kunj that was turned into a makeshift dais for the leaders after the crowd was shifted from the banks of the Sarayu.

All the while, the number of karsevaks at the Sankat Mochan gate was increasing like floodwater. The RSS volunteers were now clearly being outnumbered and many of them were injured during the scuffle. Next to the gate were three metal detectors leading into three narrow lanes. This was the official route for the devotees to enter the structure housing the 'Ramlala'. A few karsevaks chose to climb atop the metal detectors and were dangling their feet from above. Dharamdas was trying in vain to dissuade them. I suddenly found three journalist friends, Manimoy Dasgupta and Ashok Malik of *The Telegraph* and S.N.M. Abdi of *The Illustrated Weekly of India*, beside me. 'We have just surveyed the back of the mosque. A few hundred karsevaks with spades and shovels have assembled there. I have a fear that they will demolish the mosque today,' said a visibly frightened Abdi. 'Do not read much into those preparations. Even if someone scales the tombs of the mosque, they will raise a saffron flag there and nothing more. Similar things happened last year on 31 October, CRPF jawans pulled them down,' I assured Abdi.

Abdi's worst fears came true, but at least, at that point in time, I had confidence on the political will and the discipline of the RSS leaders. I was proved wrong.

11 a.m. The First Breech

I was smoking, a few too many cigarettes than I normally would. Shankar, a karsevak from Baramati in Maharashtra, the home turf of Sharad Pawar, came up and asked for a smoke. 'It's futile to lecture us on the court orders. Every time, we are being made pawns of a stupid political game. It's now or never,' he warned. Even as we spoke, I saw a group of young men in yellow headbands rushing through the approach road gate. They were members of RSS's Rapid Action Force. They pounced on the euphoric karsevaks and beat them out of the territory. A photo journalist, a foreigner, was trying to take snaps. 'No photo, no photo,' screamed a few members of the RSS's force. Some of them chased him. The poor man lost his balance and fell on some loose bricks. The RSS volunteers seemed teeming with confidence, having won this pitched battle. The battles went on for an hour. And the RSS volunteers were up against a formidable enemy, egged on by local leader Mahesh Narayan Singh. 'Those who are combating us are not disciples of Rama. And neither are they karsevaks. They are plants of V.P. Singh, Mulayam Singh and Narasimha Rao. Do not fall into their traps,' he kept thundering.

Dharamdas was at his job. He snatched a cane rod from a PAC jawan and started beating up the karsevaks mercilessly. Moments later, I saw him lying on the ground, with a few karsevaks sitting on him and beating him black and blue. Dharamdas was a wise man. He clearly saw this as a lost battle, somehow regained his foothold and ran away for dear life, clutching at his saffron dhoti. That was the final frontier that the karsevaks had to cross. With his exit, the floodgates were thrown open. Hundreds of karsevaks romped through the various entry points and, like a herd of wild bison, ran towards the mosque. I looked around and found no trace of Dixit or Bhim Singh or his wife. Geetha Siddharthan of the *Sunday Mail* was the only person other than me on the hillock. To my utter disbelief, I saw that two youths had scaled the middle tomb and were dancing away to glory.

Even a moment before this, the leaders of the Sangh Parivar had no inkling of the madness that was happening at the karseva site. Sitting pretty on the roof of the VHP office, they mistook the battle sounds for some street brawl. The top leaders of the Sangh Parivar, Rajmata Vijaya Raje Scindia, L.K. Advani, Murli Manohar Joshi, Ashok Singhal, H.V. Seshadri, K.S. Sudarshan, Vinay Katiyar, Uma Bharti and Sadhvi Rithambara were enjoying the December sun and cracking jokes among themselves. It was a picnic alright. Seshadri and Sudarshan, two very influential leaders of the RSS, had been camping in Ayodhya for a week now. They had visited every camp of the karsevaks and explained to them in great detail the court orders and how important it was to maintain discipline. These leaders were confident that no one from the Sangh Parivar would dare defy them. And they were there in person to ensure that everything went smoothly.

Although Advani reached the pinnacle of political success riding on the wave of the Ram Janmabhoomi movement, the BJP had done precious little for the cause before the summer of 1989. It was Ashok Singhal, the all-powerful general secretary of the VHP, who led the movement from the front. He got together sadhus from across the country and united them. Singhal nursed a grief within, as he was not so much in the limelight as an Advani or a Joshi was, but he was politically astute enough not to bring it out in the open. However, his attitude reflected his confidence and arrogance. He hated the so-called 'pseudo-secular press' with all the contempt at his command.

The two undisputed queen bees of the movement were Uma Bharti and Sadhvi Rithambara. Both were powerful orators and rabble-rousers who could address a captive audience for hours. In terms of popularity among the karsevaks, they were way ahead of Advani or Joshi. Uma reached Ayodhya a few days before December 6. Rithambara was seen on the spot only on that morning. Advani and Joshi came to Ayodhya from Lucknow where they addressed a rally along with Atal Bihari Vajpayee. Vajpayee, as was always his wont, did not participate in the karseva and went back to Delhi.

It was anyway a big day for journalists, just to have all the top leaders of the Sangh Parivar on the same dais in an open arena. Vinay Katiyar was the man in charge. Clad in an impeccably creased white dhoti-kurta, he started off the proceedings at the stroke of eleven. Yugpurush Paramanand, the guru of Rithambara, explained how the karseva would be conducted. Ashok Singhal warned the crowd not to fall prey to the provocative stories that the media was writing about the karseva and not to breach discipline. As it happened, the crowd did not give two hoots about Singhal's diktat on discipline but they certainly did take a cue from him on how to handle the press.

Murli Manohar Joshi, the then BJP president whose journey to Ayodhya from Delhi proved disastrous, was visibly moved to see an ocean of humanity in front of him. In a trembling voice, he delivered a speech, the high point of which was a comparison of Arjun Singh, the Union Human Resource Development minister with a eunuch. Rajmata Scindia was worse off. She could not hold back her tears of joy and could only say a small prayer that the temple be built. The Queen Mother of Gwalior, who had disowned her son Madhav Rao, had been a venerable figure in the Ram Janmabhoomi movement. In 1990, she tried to organize a large number of karsevaks to march to Ayodhya. Again in July 1992, when the sadhus were at a loss on how to react to the Supreme Court verdict against karseva, the Rajmata came to Ayodhya on behalf of the Sangh Parivar to appease them. Although she did manage to keep her daughter, Vasundhara Raje, in the BJP fold, the latter was not half as serious as her mother about the Ram temple. She was happy vacationing in Jaipur while the mother camped in Ayodhya.

12 p.m. The First Assault

Even as the Rajmata was speaking, the war cry from the karseva site broke the quiet of the Ram Katha Kunj. All those who were cordoned off by RSS volunteers and were listening to the leaders, stood up. Not that much could be seen from there. A number of them started bolting towards the Ram Deewar and a scuffle with the volunteers followed. Uma Bharti was immediately called upon to try and assuage the crowd, which was on the verge of a rampage. Even her razor-sharp voice got drowned in the din. Dumbfounded, she stood still, her half-finished lecture having cut no ice with the karsevaks. Seshadri, the second in command of the Sangh Parivar, whispered something into the ears of Singhal, who hastened down from the roof and, escorted by a dozen volunteers, walked out to the karseva site.

It was too late by then. Singhal tried to brave the deluge of karsevaks by standing on the platform with arms spread out but that did not deter even one among the advancing mob. On top of that, a stream of invective was hurled at him: 'Down with politics and hypocrisy'. The arrogant and undisputed leader stood helpless with a blank stare, with his dhoti almost coming off.

I ran with the karsevaks past the PAC and CRPF jawans and stood in a corner, after having entered the structure. At least a couple of hundred karsevaks were already atop the dome. A few thousands more were storming in like an army of ants. All of them were armed with sticks, rods or trishuls. At least a hundred were carrying sledgehammers and shovels. Both the dome and the outer walls were under attack. In about ten minutes, half of the outer wall was reduced to a gaping hole. 'Charge tear gas,' shouted D.B. Ray, the SP of Faizabad, and saw with a surprised look the PAC jawans, carrying tear gas shells, ambling away from the structure with an air of quiet resignation. The CRPF followed suit.

12.30 p.m. Attack on the Media

One of the CRPF jawans whispered a friendly advice, 'Out of this place. Quick, if you value your life.' Within moments brickbats started raining from atop the dome. A CRPF jawan tried to protect us with his cane shield, but even then, a flying brickbat whistled past me and hit one of my fingers. My notebook flew from my hand. I somehow managed to retrieve it and never brought it out again on that fateful day. Sensing more trouble, I put the press card too in the pocket and took out the '*Jai Shri Ram*' hairband gifted by Swapan the previous night. I tied it around my neck like a bow tie, but soon realized that it was not going to serve as any talisman for me in this hour of crisis. To my horror, I saw a karsevak with a long bamboo pole chasing me. Thankfully, I knew the place well enough to bolt my way into the Sita Rasoi Bhavan. I was not alone there. The house was full of journalists and photographers, some of whom had lost their cameras or film rolls or video cassettes. Ajay Singh, *Pioneer*'s photographer from the Lucknow bureau, was sitting with a sling around his right hand. He had for company our beloved Thapa from *Navbharat Times*, who was also injured. I went up to the roof. Debasis Bhattacharya of *Aajkaal* and Avijit Lahiri of *Bartaman* were already there and so was Mohan Sahay of *The Statesman*. All three were unscathed, even though a portly lady of the Durga Vahini was targeting Mohan with brickbats in both her hands. What did Mohan do to be singled out as her target could not be readily ascertained. Fortunately, all of us escaped the wrath of the lady unhurt, including Mohan.

1 p.m. Futile Appeals

A short distance from Sita Rasoi Bhavan, Ram Katha Kunj wore a deserted look, as the meeting was already over. L.K. Advani was sauntering on the roof with his head down and buried in his chest. Deepak Chopra, his personal secretary, and Pramod Mahajan, were standing with their hands on their heads, clearly displaying a sense of resignation. As Swapan approached Mahajan, he wailed, 'This is a disaster. If this madness can't be stopped right now, we are doomed.' In the meanwhile, all hell had broken loose inside the mosque. Spades, shovels and sledgehammers were raining on the dome. The blackish-green outer layer of the wall gave way to an earthen hue. Clouds of dust were billowing up and amidst the dust we saw many karsevaks, tumbling down the dome to the ground, like mangoes from the tree during a nor'wester.

As Singhal returned from the war ground, the leaders of the Sangh Parivar got into a huddle in one corner of the roof, cordoned by carbine-toting securitymen from the National Security Guard (NSG) in their unmistakable sky-blue uniform. They would not let anyone reach anywhere close to the leaders. I heard Singhal giving up. 'I have failed. Now you guys go and appeal,' he said. Hearing this, Seshadri, ran up to the stage and snatched the microphone from Acharya Dharmendra and started pleading with the masses. Advani and Mahajan went downstairs to listen to the 1 p.m. news bulletin of 'Akashvani', expecting to hear the news of the dismissal of the Kalyan Singh-led BJP government of Uttar Pradesh.

A series of pleas began. 'We do not have the Mulayam Singh government but our own government in UP. We must cooperate with them and the police. Those who have entered the structure do come out immediately and take part in a peaceful karseva,' appealed Seshadri. All the other leaders, like Sadhvi Rithambara, Uma Bharti, L.K. Advani and Murli Manohar Joshi, more or less repeated the plea in the same vein which went like this: 'You have accomplished what you wanted to do. Now, please listen to us and climb down the dome and ensure that no one, especially women, children and the old get hurt.' Only Vinay Katiyar was more aggressive. 'You have to listen to us and the sadhus. You have to climb down,' he thundered.

As we anticipated, every plea fell on deaf ears. A large section of the crowd that was listening to the leaders at Ram Katha Kunj now got up and marched towards the mosque. The RSS volunteers too, who were manning the walls from dawn, gave up their vigil. It was more important for them now to carry the injured karsevaks who fell from the tomb, to the first-aid room near the office. I suddenly found Prabhas Jain, chief photographer of *The Pioneer*, writhing in pain in a corner of the roof. He was among the many reporters and photographers who dared to be close to the mosque. We brought this up with the Sangh leaders, but no one was in a mood to even listen.

Even as scores of the injured were being brought in for treatment, the leaders again went into a huddle in front of the attic. Mahant Avaidyanath, the formidable MP from Gorakhpur, and a leading light of the Ram Janmabhoomi movement, was also there. 'All India Radio, in its 1 p.m. bulletin, has said that the karseva is going on peacefully,' announced Pramod Mahajan. The news here was that the troublemakers were from Maharashtra and South India, and therefore could not make head or tail of the appeals made in chaste Hindi by the leaders. A volunteer came gasping and said, 'Nothing can be heard there. Please go there and use the microphones,' he said.

Promptly began a second phase of appeals. The leaders took their turn. Seshadri spoke in all four South Indian languages while Advani raised his voice to rebuke the karsevaks. Ashok Singhal, having regained his poise, thundered, 'Can you hear me? This is Ashok Singhal.' The voices echoed on all the walls, but to no avail. After Singhal spoke, to my surprise, I saw a sadhu ranting his appeal in Bengali, my native tongue. 'You mean, even Bengalis are there?' I asked him. 'Of course there are. You had doubts?' the sadhu said with pride. So, I told myself, all this worry about the security of the mosque was a hogwash. These people were eminently proud at what the karsevaks were doing.

The leaders were speculating the identities of the karsevaks. 'The first man atop the dome was from the prime minister's constituency, Nandial,' said one. 'None of them are our men. They have been packed to Ayodhya from Mumbai by Bal Thackeray,' said another. 'Thackeray will take all the credit for today's incident; just check tomorrow's newspapers,' remarked Mahajan. The Rajmata clearly lost her patience. Grabbing the microphone, she shouted, 'Get these people by their necks and pull them down.' Advani, with a binocular, was trying to figure out what exactly was wrong. As he removed those, I asked, 'What did you see?' 'Nothing except that hundreds are getting hurt,' he said. Till now, the injured were being carried by hand. Now, there were a few ambulances in place, running to and fro with the injured.

2.45 p.m. The Reality Sinks in

All of a sudden, we saw that the two tombs that could be seen from the rooftop of Ram Katha Kunj had nobody atop them. Seshadri, who thought that the continuous appeals for three hours have had effect, suggested Advani that he should now congratulate the karsevaks. As Advani was coming down from the dais after his short vote of thanks, he confronted the horrible reality of the day.

A frail sadhu had climbed up to the roof with the small Ramlala idol wrapped in his dusty shawl. He was almost in a fit of convulsion, shuddering frenziedly, his body having scratch marks all over. He removed the drape and showed Advani the idol. 'Sir, one dome is being destroyed now. We could somehow save the Ramlala,' he gasped. The seasoned politician that Advani was, immediately realized that not only was the situation out of hand, but he was at his wits' end as to how to reclaim normalcy. Silent and defeated, he climbed down the stairs. We asked for his reaction. 'I have no information on the dismissal of the state government, but it seems a matter of time now. The central forces could be here any moment now,' he signed off.

A while earlier, we were speculating the same. If in fact the state government did get dismissed and central forces took charge of the mosque to rein in the unruly mob, they could resort to any measure that they deemed fit. The euphoric karsevaks would not take it lying down and a clear consequence would be many deaths, we shuddered to think. As a matter of fact, we had heard from the grapevine around an hour back that commandos of the Rapid Action Force of the CRPF wanted to take control of the situation and were on their way, but the district magistrate issued an edict to send them back to their barracks. The BJP government of UP was well in its constitutional rights to refuse the CRPF, and expectedly so, but if and when the government got dismissed, Delhi could give marching orders to the central forces. We all knew that the central government had a contingency plan in case of an eventuality like this. At least Home Minister S.R. Chavan kept saying so in the parliament for days in the run-up to this day. As such, twenty-eight battalions of CRPF jawans were already deployed at the Faizabad cantonment, notwithstanding vehement protests by Kalyan Singh. Of these, ten battalions comprised the RPF. We were confident that given the situation, the central government would not look by and bring these forces into action.

3 p.m. The Demolition

However, when not a single jawan of the central forces appeared in the distant horizon even as the clock struck three, which coincided with the news of the fall of the dome on our right, the leaders started breathing easy. Tapananda Brahmachari, the Bengali sadhu, lectured me. 'You live in ivory towers and live the lives of hedonists. How would you know the schemes of God Almighty? The fall of the mosque was inevitable.' Sadhvi Rithambara was brimming with pride, 'Whatever happens, happens for good, whether you want it or not.'

The leaders quietly accepted that the inevitable had happened and resigned themselves to their fate. Even as they went down to discuss the subsequent moves, the sadhus took centre stage. 'Block all roads that lead to Ayodhya. Go and sit on the highways. Make sure that the central forces are kept at bay,' they thundered on the microphone. 'Go to the temple and take your prasad,' was the continuous instruction that Swami Dharmendra kept blaring. Prasad, in this case was not any food, but broken bricks of the Babri Masjid. A long line of disciples carrying bricks was streaming downstairs, even as the two other domes were being demolished. Chandan Mitra, then the associate editor of the *Hindustan Times*, suggested that we visit the site before it got completely demolished. Mahajan's personal secretary assured us that he himself would take us down there and there was nothing to worry.

Not that there was no cause for fear. As we made our way through the crowd towards the mosque, the choicest of invective greeted us. Nonetheless, we braved them and approached the mosque. It was a grisly sight. The zeal and fervour with which the karsevaks were taking part in the demolition sent a chill down our spines. Those who had no tools to use were scratching away like mad with their fingernails on the domes. A few young men tied a noose around the domes and were trying to pull them down. Chandan and Ruchira Gupta, of *Business India*, climbed the hillock while the rest of us stayed down. Wherever we moved, a crowd encircled us. I looked in the front and saw an old man trying to come down the hillock. Wearing thick, dirty lenses, the octogenarian was carrying four bricks on his head. As I gaped at him, I saw two young men cradling Ruchira down to where we stood. She was in shock and could hardly speak. 'A few karsevaks mistook Madam for a Muslim woman and pounced on her. It could have been a disaster if we were not around,' said one of the men. We chided Ruchira for her uncalled for bravery and came back to the roof of the office.

4.30 p.m. The Final Push

What was relief half an hour ago when we left for the mosque had by now turned into celebrations. The sadhus were gambling on the exact time when the last of the domes would be razed to the ground. Sadhvi Rithambara removed Swami Dharmendra and took charge. '*Ek dhakka aur do*' (Give one more push), she roared. '*Babri Masjid tod do*' (demolish Babri Masjid), replied thousands gathered down below. As the last dome tumbled on to the ground at forty-nine minutes past four, all hell broke loose. Sadhvi jumped down from the stage and hugged Uma Bharti. And then, she kept hugging everyone whom she could find in her proximity. All the sadhus were dancing. The only man maintaining equanimity was BJP President Murli Manohar Joshi. 'No questions and no answers. Please excuse me today,' the ashen-faced Joshi mumbled.

5 p.m. The Final Act

The December afternoon was fast fading into dusk. I looked outside and saw many houses engulfed in flames. Thick black smoke was billowing from everywhere. None of the police officers had any clue of anything. A few know-all karsevaks explained, 'The Muslims are torching their own houses so that they can blame it on us.' And yet, there was no inkling of any central intervention. With a smirk on his face, Ashok Singhal returned to the roof to a fresh round of embraces. Everyone was celebrating, including police officers. One of them enquired, 'Have you noted the exact time when the mosque got demolished?' and added in the same breath, 'You are fortunate. You just saw history being made.'

The leader of RSS's think tank, Sudarshan, who did not take part in the unbridled celebrations, was sitting quietly on a chair nearby. When asked how he would explain what had happened over the past five hours, he replied in fluent Bengali, 'Just one thing. Today's incident proved that history is not made, it happens.'

Whether it was a historic moment or a historic blunder is not something I could have dwelt on then. My only concern then was how to get my copy through to my office in Kolkata. Chandan advised me against depending on the Central Telegraph Office of Faizabad and suggested that I should go back to Lucknow. 'For all you know, the telephone and telegraph lines may well be snapped just to prevent news from reaching the outside world,' he said, 'just as they did after Operation Blue Star in Golden Temple in 1984.' However, nothing like that happened.

It was important to get a reaction from Advani before I left the place. The NSG commando who was manning the door, smeared our foreheads with vermilion. He said triumphantly, it was no ordinary stuff, but extracted out of the forehead of the Ramlala idol, which was now in safe custody. We went inside into complete darkness. Two youths, sitting on a wooden platform in a corner room, were trying desperately to tune in to the news from a transistor set. The electricity connections had been snapped at the time when the domes were being pulled down, they informed. They also informed that Advani was in the next room, trying to get in touch with Delhi via telephone, in candlelight, and was all by himself.

Advani emerged after a few minutes. For the past eight years that I had known him closely, I had never seen such a nervous Advani before. It seemed that he could not digest the wild celebrations that were happening right above his head. At least, till then.

Q. Has the UP government been sacked?
A. No, not yet. However, Kalyan Singh telephoned me twice to seek my permission to offer his resignation. I have advised him against it, because if he does, central forces would immediately take over and we will see bloodbath. But by now, he might have resigned. By the time you reach Lucknow, the resignation would most probably have been accepted too.

Q. When do you plan to return to Delhi?
A. Till this morning, my plan was to take the evening flight from Lucknow. But now I must stay here for a couple of days more. I cannot leave all these people to their destiny.

Q. Could you get in touch with Delhi?
A. I have been trying for long, but cannot get through.

Q. How would you react to today's incident?
A. Unfortunate and regrettable.

A few hours later, after returning to Lucknow, we came to know that Advani changed his mind and left Ayodhya in the evening itself. Many days later, on his release from prison, Advani told journalists that he did not regret the demolition of the Babri Masjid. What he regretted was that he could not gauge the mood of the people. I was not surprised at this volte face. After all, the man was in realpolitik and had his stakes in place.

As we came out to the last rays of the setting December sun, speculating on whether Chandan's new Maruti Gypsy car could escape today's onslaught, Anju Gupta, the demure yet smart police officer with a walkie-talkie in one hand and a stick in another, met us. She drove out the crowd and whispered into Chandan's ears, 'Two photographers have been in hiding since morning in a nearby room. Mind taking them with you?' We would have been glad to do so, but a small car like his would not have been able to accommodate those two, over and above the eight that we already were, Chandan explained. Anju understood and with a shrug said, 'Don't worry. I shall take care of them.' One of the two photographers was Nitin Rai, our colleague from *Sunday* magazine. Nitin told us later that had it not been for Anju, he could have been killed that day. When the rest of the police force was enjoying the manhandling of reporters and photographers, the only *man* around was this little woman.

When we reached the main road, we found, to our surprise

and relief, that Chandan's car stood just as he had left it there in the morning. Not a scratch or a dent. The car might have escaped the madness, but not so lucky were the local Muslims. Every Muslim house was torched. A few matador vans, auto rickshaws and car tyres were also burning. The karsevaks did exactly as the leaders asked them to. They blocked the roads by felling logs and turning asphalt drums. Around these blockades the karsevaks were dancing like mad men. As we dodged and swerved to make our way through the flames and the maddening sea of humanity, shouts of '*Abhi toh yeh sirf jhaanki hain, Mathura, Kashi baaki hain*' (This is just the beginning/we will now turn our attention to Mathura and Banaras) filled the evening sky.

Curfew was already imposed in Faizabad. As we reached our hotel, Shaan-E-Awadh, we could see for ourselves how scribes had been beaten up by karsevaks. I met Alok Mitra, my photographer colleague. He looked devastated. 'Not only was I beaten to a pulp, but lost everything—two cameras and cash worth nine thousand rupees. They even snatched my gold chain,' he cried. I had no words to console him.

In the hotel lobby, there were at least fifty scribes from across the globe, all with sunken faces. We learnt that Peter Hynes Lane, of Voice of America, had suffered a serious head injury and was taken to the hospital. He was beaten with an iron rod. Former editor of *Navbharat Times*, S.P. Singh, stood next to the reception counter. 'In my twenty years as a journalist, I have never seen such manhandling of journalists,' he sounded shell-shocked. But Bob Drolin, the *Los Angeles Times* correspondent, who had come to Ayodhya, for the first time, wrote in *The Telegraph*, perhaps what was uppermost in every journalist's mind that day—'Any journalist who was not scared today was stupid.'

17
Kolkata Calling

'Mani Shankar Aiyar called you half a dozen times. Pl call him back. Urgent.' I found this note stuck on the clipboard of our Delhi office and ignored it. I can't remember the exact date today, but it was sometime in the November of 1985. I had just returned to the bureau office after a long day, and was not particularly pleased with the obvious collegial prank. Mani in those days was one of the key players of New Delhi politics and a close buddy of Prime Minister Rajiv Gandhi. Why on earth would he be desperately seeking a regional daily's correspondent?

Just as I was settling at my desk with such thoughts the phone rang, and even before I could put the receiver to my ear the blasting began from the other end: 'Where the f**k is Aveek? I am trying to reach him since early morning. None seems to have a clue as to whether he is dead or alive. Can you help?' It was a mighty agitated Mani.

I knew Aveek Babu was in Kolkata as I had spoken with him at least twice that morning and afternoon. I was confused: Why on earth was he avoiding an important call from the PMO? I knew my editor's unlisted direct number and called him. Aveek Babu himself took the call. I narrated to him verbatim what Mani asked me to convey.

'Tell him, I cannot be reached.'

'Why? What do you mean?'

'Rajiv Gandhi wants Rakhi and me to accompany him to Lakshadweep. I have received a formal invitation, they are awaiting my consent. I will not go. That is why I am avoiding them.'

Bewildered, I asked him, 'Why should you refuse the prime minister's personal invitation?'

The question angered Aveek Babu. 'Don't be stupid. I am a journalist and I must not be seen in the company of the prime minister while he is enjoying his private holidays. That's simply not done. And keep the matter confidential.' With these words he banged the phone down. I did exactly as I was told. Aveek Babu refused to be part of the prime ministerial entourage that took Lakshadweep by storm for a few days and ballooned into a major controversy.

That was quintessential Aveek Sarkar: arrogant, full of himself, combative, with a strong view on everything under the sun, yet with a tremendous pride in his profession as a journalist, a quality that has nearly vanished from the profession, with editors more often than not eating out of the hands of political bosses.

Not many people know this, but he had actually refused proposals for Rajya Sabha nominations, and even the Padma state honours, bestowed annually by the ruling government in Delhi on recipients often chosen for all other reasons than merit. Aveek Babu used to tell me often, 'More than anything else I am a journalist. Why should I compromise my position and integrity by accepting state patronage of any kind?'

Fortunately, or unfortunately, during my Delhi days I had to bear the brunt of this pride every single morning without exception. Every morning between eight and eight-thirty, I would receive a call from Aveek Babu. It became a routine affair since 1 October 1990, when I became the youngest ever chief of ABP's Delhi bureau.

Those calls were like regular college lectures when my editor would inflict on me a long monologue on a subject of his choice, in the process, invariably berating me either for my ignorance or getting something totally wrong. Often he would call me a rank illiterate or provoke me with some bizarre explanations of some events. Since I knew his tricks as also the fact that he hardly meant what he said, I would normally keep quiet and suffer his long sermons mostly in silence.

Only on rare occasions when he would get onto my nerves or I found his accusations unbearable or unsubstantiated I would hit back, turning the dialogue into a high decibel slanging match.

That morning, however, his call came earlier than usual as I slowly got out of my bed, half asleep and profusely irritated.

'Can you take this evening's flight and come to Kolkata?' He asked me matter-of-factly. This was not really unusual.

'Yes of course, but can it wait till tomorrow?' I replied sheepishly, keeping in mind my daughter's birthday celebrations that evening. She would turn seven and I could not bear the thought of leaving Delhi.

My editor understood, but before I could heave a sigh of relief he dropped the nuclear bomb on my head. 'You are being transferred to Kolkata as the News Editor and you must take charge from tomorrow itself,' he announced and hung up without even giving me an opportunity to raise any further question.

I felt miserable. It was 5 August 1993.

Going back to Kolkata while at the peak of my reporting career in the country's capital was hardly exciting. Having already spent eight long years in Delhi, I was fairly well-entrenched professionally and didn't have the slightest desire to suddenly break the status quo. More than anything else, I enjoyed writing and travelling just as I got sucked into national political dramas unfolding constantly before our eyes since Rajiv Gandhi's defeat in 1989. Following the destruction of the Babri Mosque in December 1992, politics in Delhi entered another turbulent phase, plunging the P.V. Narasimha Rao government into chaos and uncertainty. Leaving Delhi at this juncture was farthest from my imagination.

Shifting base would also mean sudden and complete disruption in my personal life. While Kasturi, my wife, would have to quit her favourite teaching job in a reputed neighbourhood school, Tupur, my daughter, would have to be drawn out of her school mid-year, a difficult prospect for the poor kid. As the reality started dawning on me, I felt angry and bitter and for a moment thought of quitting ABP to stay back in Delhi with another job somewhere.

The next morning, as I left home to catch a Kolkata-bound flight, I was determined to turn down the offer and face whatever consequences it entailed. Come rain or shine I am not returning to Kolkata, I told myself.

Aveek Babu knew I was upset and would not readily agree with his sudden decision. But he also knew my temperament that I would not shy away from accepting a professional challenge. Without mincing words, he therefore set the context of my hasty recall explaining how *Bartaman*, an upstart challenger, was coming close to ABP's circulation, almost threatening its undisputed leadership in the market. 'I am asking you to lead the paper at this critical juncture. I am confident you can deliver,' he said.

His clever ploy of massaging my bloated ego worked instantaneously and my resolve to stay back in Delhi vanished into thin air. For the first one and a half months of my new Kolkata life I was lodged in a hotel suite where my wife and child joined me a few days later. My daughter joined her new school in the new city while we were still in the hotel. Thus started a new innings, which catapulted both me and the ABP to unassailable heights, until I had to quit the organization twelve years later, in 2005, suffering inexplicable humiliation at the hands of the same man who had brought me back to Kolkata in 1993 and had given me a carte blanche to reshape his paper's destiny.

In 1985, when I was transferred to Delhi, albeit forcibly, I hardly knew Aveek Sarkar. By the time I came back eight years later I was perhaps his closest and most trusted colleague in the ABP and our bondage transcended all the barriers of an ordinary employer-employee relation. However, in ABP's Kolkata office hardly anyone welcomed the editor's sudden and dramatic choice. For one, at 36 I was considered too young and inexperienced for the job. For many colleagues, a lot more senior in age and experience, it seemed unacceptable and humiliating. Second, my claim to fame lay in writing and reporting and people wondered what I would do in the unaccustomed role of an editor. Thanks to my first guru, Gour Kishore Ghosh, I had quite a bit of desk job experience as well, since he had forced me to learn it right at the beginning of my journalistic career and it has stood me in good stead all my life. I knew I was good enough to prove all the doubting Thomases wrong. It did not take me long to actually achieve the goal.

The problem with ABP was largely twofold. First, the paper hardly carried any district news although half of its circulation came from there. *Bartaman*, with a heavy dose of district coverage, was taking advantage of the readers' growing alienation from ABP. Second, *Bartaman* was riding the Hindutva wave that touched Bengal's shores in the wake of the Ram Janmabhoomi movement and the demolition of the Babri Mosque in the late 1980s and early 1990s. The ABP refused to do the same, thanks mainly to Aveek Babu's intervention that discouraged any idea of being swayed by communal feelings.

The ABP's refusal to take advantage of the communally charged situation in those days stood in sharp contrast to not merely what *Bartaman* did in Kolkata but also a large number of Hindi publications in northern India that took a leading role in fanning communal tensions by constantly publishing distorted news that targeted the Muslim community and its political patrons. Since I covered the temple movement right from the time L.K. Advani usurped it from the VHP leadership till the destruction of the historic structure, I witnessed from close quarters how a group of Hindi newspapers in UP threw out all canons of fair journalism to generate mass hysteria in favour of the temple construction. Later, the Press Council of India conducted an investigation and published a damning report chronicling the misdeeds of these journalists and their owners.[12]

Aveek Babu's principled stand in those heady days of Hindu communal upsurge also marked a complete break from his predecessors' role in similar situations. Immediately before the Partition that followed dreadful communal bloodbath in Kolkata and many parts of East Bengal, ABP openly espoused the Hindu cause. The paper's editorial had a pronounced anti-Muslim bias and chronicled at length how the Hindu population living under the Muslim League rule was facing all kinds of hardship and discrimination. That was also the time when the paper gave up its Gandhian bias to become a champion of Subhas Chandra Bose after his unceremonious ouster from the Congress presidency. According to Aveek Babu, 'The die was cast—for both Bose and the ABP which now identified with his predicament. In a way, that was the time when the paper found its role. It became the voice of Bengal.'

After Independence, the ABP gradually shunned its Hindu communal overtone, though distrust for Muslims continued for decades thereafter. It got reflected in the paper's recruitment policy

---

[12]See 'Ayodhya Report 1990'. 'A special inquiry was set up on the Ayodhya happenings in 1990 and another in 1992. Their reports were made public in 1991 and 1993 respectively. In the first inquiry, the Council found four Uttar Pradesh dailies *Jagran*, *Aj*, *Swatantra Bharat* and *Swatantra Chetna*, guilty of publishing reports which constituted a grave violation of norms of journalistic ethics.' http://presscouncil.nic.in/OldWebsite/history.htm

that barred the entry of Muslims in the organization. Syed Mustafa Siraj, a noted Bengali writer was the first Muslim to be recruited in the ABP editorial department, at least two and a half decades after Independence. The unwritten law was changed only after Aveek Babu's era started in the organization. Thus came the celebrated M.J. Akbar as the *Sunday* editor.

As it happens in a monopoly situation, ABP's growth stagnated partly because it took its readers for granted as over the years, there was hardly any competition in the horizon. For a considerable period of time following Independence, the Bengali newspaper readership remained divided between two principal players, ABP and *Jugantar*, the Bengali daily from the Amrita Bazar Patrika group owned by Tushar Kanti Ghosh's family. As a group, Amrita Bazar was older than the ABP and historically played a more stellar role during the colonial rule. Following the proclamation of the draconian Vernacular Press Act in 1878, Amrita Bazar Patrika turned into an English daily almost overnight.

In the 1950s, *Jugantar* experienced exponential growth as it started championing the cause of the uprooted Hindu refugees from East Bengal. It happened under the leadership of Amitabha Chowdhury who later received the Ramon Magsaysay Award for his fearless journalism. Santosh Kumar Ghosh was then brought back from Delhi to take charge of ABP's news operations. Under his tutelage, *Jugantar's* challenge could easily be rebuffed. Almost forty years later, I was presented with the same kind of challenge, this time *Bartaman* replacing *Jugantar*. Again in a weird repetition of history, the guru's mantle fell on the 'chela.'

The owners of the two leading Kolkata group of newspapers were blood relations and extremely jealous of each other. In the 1984 Lok Sabha polls, I saw Aveek Sarkar helping Chitta Basu, a Forward Bloc candidate, with all kind of resources required to win the electoral contest against Tarun Kanti Ghosh, the Congress candidate and owner of the rival Amrita Bazar Patrika group.

However, that could not change the reality, as riding on the sympathy wave that swept the nation following Indira Gandhi's assassination, Tarun Kanti won easily and went to the parliament.

However, in matters of business, the Ghoshs had to concede defeat to the Sarkars and failed miserably. Ultimately, in the mid-1980s all the publications of Amrita Bazar Patrika group folded up, leaving an open field for ABP to prosper. *Bartaman*, started by Barun Sengupta in 1984, quickly occupied the vacant space and, in less than a decade, was in a position to challenge ABP's undisputed supremacy.

There was another important reason why the ABP Group survived the test of time and Amrita Bazar Patrika group did not. Seen in historical perspective, it survived because it chose to adapt constantly to remain in sync with the times. In other words, when the circumstances changed the organization changed too. In Aveek Babu's eloquent words, 'The answer is simple. When the needs of history have altered, we have reinvented ourselves.'

In many ways the ABP did pioneering work that none other could even foresee. In its effort to set standards, it made a valiant attempt to codify Bengali grammar and set standards for spelling, punctuation and usage. It was the first newspaper organization to mechanize non-Roman language. It helped create the typewriter for the use of Bengali or Hindi script and adapted the language in the keyboard so that automatic typesetting could be used in the Indian languages. As Aveek Babu would often proudly proclaim, 'We kept no patent for this pioneering work. The research was given free to the machine's American manufacturer on the condition that English and Indian language machines should be sold at the same price. We take no special credit for this, it is part of the bhadralok tradition.'

In later days, the organization worked alongside manufacturers to facilitate computerization of the Bengali language and on their own steam created a programme to run the entire language with all its conjuncts on the Windows system. The ABP created the standards that everyone else followed. In the process, it naturally emerged as the undisputed market leader and gradually became the sole spokesman of its race—the Bengalis. Like the famed rosogolla, the ABP too became synonymous with whatever was the best in Bengali culture and language.

I returned to Kolkata at a time when a similar adaptation to change was felt necessary. The change came at the attitudinal level with regard to politics and personalities. The new consensus was that we would be neither for nor against personalities. Instead, the paper must be built clearly on ideological grounds that cut across social, economic and political boundaries. Of course it was Aveek Babu's ideology and his alone that we, too, adopted. We would support the free market and the aspirations of the individual over the collective. We would openly advocate capitalism in a state run by the Left and constantly cherish the rights of the individual. And when it came to public recognition, we would endorse only those people and parties who would implement the ABP line. In setting such a lofty and ambitious goal for ourselves the first thing we did was to come out of the traditional adversarial relation with the ruling Left Front which had been showing their intent to turn right.

The new industrial policy resolution of Jyoti Basu's government, openly embracing reforms and private capital heralded a paradigm shift providing the tailwind for alteration of relationship between the Marxist rulers and their most important bourgeois adversary. The tone and tenor of ABP changed radically as a large number of Left supporters and sympathizers turned towards us forsaking tutored ideological inhibitions. During the paper's seventy-fifth anniversary celebration, held in 1997 in the presence of I.K. Gujral, the then prime minister, and P.V. Narasimha Rao, the former prime minister, Aveek Babu said rather triumphantly, 'We applaud Jyoti Basu's economic initiative because we realize that he has only been trying to implement the ABP line. On the other hand we disapprove thoroughly of his government's policies on education.' The paper's makeover exercise clearly had two aspects. While on the one hand the ABP gradually put on a new editorial avatar discarding its extreme obsession with state politics and politicking of all sorts, a parallel effort was mounted to woo larger number of readers in the districts. It was in the districts that the ABP faced the real challenge from a growing *Bartaman*.

As I started touring Bengal districts to meet newspaper readers in person to understand their needs and grievances, I realized the true strength of the brand and its stranglehold on the Bengali mind. Their main grievance was one of neglect, that ABP had been a thoroughbred Kolkata paper with very little or no concern for readers outside. Still, they read the paper because it had become, over the years, an intrinsic part of the family 'parampara', almost a part of their DNA. The common refrain I would hear from almost every reader was, 'There is nothing for us in the paper. Yet we cannot readily discard it. My grandfather read it, my father read it and now I am reading it.' As I heard them I often wondered how many newspapers in the country could command such loyalty from its readers for generations.

The ABP till the late 1990s was printed only from Kolkata. In vast areas of the northern part of the state covering seven to eight districts, the paper was available only in the afternoon. I wondered why so many thousands still bought and read a paper that had gone stale long ago. In order to stem dwindling circulation in those areas and stay afloat in competition it was decided to bring out a North Bengal edition of the paper from Siliguri with special emphasis on local news. The policy paid handsome dividends as the paper's circulation swelled in no time. At the same time we decided to customize the product on geographical basis even for districts of South Bengal. A new and robust district desk was set up in Kolkata and we recruited bright young boys from the districts to work as our retainers with handsome payouts. Districts, for the first time in ABP's history, got the necessary attention and fresh investments resulting in huge growth of the paper's circulation over a short period of time. In less than six or seven years we took the paper's circulation to a whopping million copies. I got my rewards by way of generous pay hikes every year and became the first-ever Executive Editor of ABP.

18
The Mamata Blaze

In the wee hours of 3 September 1999, a massive fire broke out at the ABP office in Kolkata that completely ravaged the top floor and heavily damaged the library on the third. One person died of asphyxiation in his sleep.

On that day I was in Solapur, Maharashtra. As I switched on a news channel immediately after checking into a hotel room I got the biggest shock of my life. I saw fire and smoke billowing out of the window of my own office room. The fire at ABP was the biggest story on all national TV channels.

I was in Maharashtra to cover the state's assembly elections. Chucking my plans, which included an interview with Sharad Pawar, the Maratha heavyweight, I rushed back to Kolkata the following morning.

I saw Aveek Babu sitting on a stool in front of our office gates as I drove straight from Kolkata airport to Prafulla Sarkar Street. An acrid smell still wafted across the area, and I saw workers chipping away at the debris. Smoke still curled out intermittently from our floor. Firefighters had cordoned off the entire affected zone. I wore a mask and, with the help of a friendly, courageous fireman, climbed up to see the devastation.

The top floor that was completely gutted housed ABP's editorial office and the circulation, advertisement and accounts departments. I came down after spending a few minutes having failed to locate even my own office on the floor, now engulfed in complete darkness, with pools of water on the floor, wood planks burnt to ashes, metal scraps lying in frightening contorted shapes and bare electric wires, with the insulation totally melted, dangling all over the place.

Both ABP and *The Telegraph* came out the following morning as all of us rose to the challenge. Overnight, our gutted office became the city's most coveted tourist spot with people pouring in from all over. They included VIPs of all kinds including, of course, politicians and ministers. Even Sonia Gandhi, then campaigning in Bellary, Karnataka, called Aveek Babu to express shock and solidarity.

∽

Aveek Babu, it became clear to me over time, had great personal rapport with the Gandhis, first with Rajiv and, after his tragic death in 1991, with Sonia. He often brought expensive chocolates from abroad for Rajiv and took them to 10 Janpath in Delhi. For the first time I saw him getting emotional in public when the news of Rajiv's assassination reached him. At Aveek Babu's behest, Sonia wrote and arranged a pictorial biography of her husband a few months after Rajiv's death. I, too, was invited to its ceremonial release function at the Rashtrapati Bhavan. Aveek Babu's closeness to the Gandhi family landed me in an extremely embarrassing situation a few days before the 2001 Assembly polls in West Bengal.

'I am assigning to you an extremely sensitive task. And confidential,' Aveek Babu chuckled mischievously as he prepared to leave office for the day. That night he was scheduled to fly out to the US. Hence he chose me to carry out the job.

'Sonia Gandhi called a while ago. She is sending Kamal

Nath to Kolkata for a secret dialogue with Mamata Banerjee regarding electoral adjustments. She requested me for help,' my editor continued.

'That's all right. But what am I supposed to do?'

'Two things. Inform Mamata that the meeting will take place at my residence tomorrow night. Kamal will take a late-night flight and reach there straight from the airport. You reach my home early, receive both of them and play a good host. Remember, I won't be there and I don't want Rakhi to be involved,' said my editor, explaining the nature of the job.

It was immediately after the dates had been announced for the polls.

I was aware that the Trinamool Congress head, Mamata Banerjee, was seeking an alliance with her parent party having left Atal Bihari Vajpayee's NDA government in a huff in early 2001 demanding Defence Minister George Fernandes's resignation from the central cabinet over *Tehelka's* exposure of corruption in defence procurements. The exposé put Bangaru Laxman, the then BJP president, in a spot as he was shown accepting bundles of currency notes on camera. He vacated his party post and went to jail, but Fernandes, with Vajpayee's blessing, survived the storm.

On learning about the corruption charges, Mamata, then a cabinet minister, put in her papers in Delhi, disregarding the collective wishes of her MPs and other political associates. I was watching a scintillating India–Australia test cricket match from the upper-tier club house of the Eden Gardens in Kolkata. At tea break, an official of the Cricket Association of Bengal came to me to inform, in a whisper, that a very important phone call had come for me from Delhi at Jagmohan Dalmiya's office downstairs. Flabbergasted, I rushed to attend the call.

It was Sudip Bandyopadhyay at the other end. He was calling from Mamata's ministerial room in the parliament. He sounded helpless and desperate, 'Mamata is not listening to any one of us. She is determined to resign and leave the NDA. I am giving the phone to her, please tell her not to commit this hara-kiri.'

It was impossible to reason with Mamata as she was screaming at the top of her voice abusing BJP leaders and George Fernandes. She shouted, 'Please don't request me to stay in the cabinet of thieves. I don't believe in valueless politics. For me a cabinet berth means nothing as I am not crazy for power.' I threw up my hands and went back to see the remaining day's play, where Rahul Dravid and V.V.S. Laxman were putting up a valiant show against the Aussies. By then I knew the lady well and understood that Mamata would not budge an inch from her position. She did not. That night itself she flew back to Kolkata declaring her decision to come out of the NDA coalition.

Sudip had sought my help during those critical hours as he knew of my closeness to Mamata. While in Delhi, I had seen her as a first-time MP. She was a dynamic young woman who left no opportunity of making noise or staging strong protests on any issue related to the demands of her own state. Her tantrums were ridiculed by most, and particularly by the Left leaders. But Mamata remained unfazed. Soon she became a favourite of Rajiv, causing tremendous heartburns. Geeta Mukherjee, a veteran CPI leader, was the first to spot Mamata's potential when she said publicly, 'This girl will go very far. I just wonder why she should be in the Congress camp and not with us.' Not many agreed with her though.

Mamata's meteoric rise has few parallels in Indian politics. In the 1984 Lok Sabha polls, the state Congress bigwigs had given her a party ticket from a traditional Left bastion against the Left heavyweight, barrister Somnath Chatterjee, more out of compassion than any real expectation of winning the seat. As Subrata Mukherjee, her mentor in Congress politics, told me later, 'Mamata came from very humble backgrounds. I thought she would be able to keep for herself and her family a portion of the electoral fund that the party would provide her. No one imagined she would emerge victorious, trouncing a CPM heavyweight like Somnath Babu.' The electoral results of 1984, even in West Bengal, were replete with such surprises, thanks to the sympathy wave for the deceased Indira Gandhi. However, Mamata could not retain her seat in the next election in 1989 and shifted to a safer South Kolkata seat that she retained continuously from 1991 to 2011, when she entered the Writers' Buildings triumphantly as the state's first woman chief minister.

We grew really close after my return to Kolkata in September 1993. She would come to my home, often unannounced, and spend hours with me or my wife. She was then both an MP and a junior minister in charge of sports and youth affairs in P.V. Narasimha Rao's cabinet. I realized soon enough that during the years I was in Delhi, Mamata had emerged as the most popular opposition face in the state, overshadowing almost all the senior Congress leaders including Pranab Mukherjee, A.B.A. Ghani Khan Choudhury and Priya Ranjan Dasmunsi. Because of her antics, unpredictable behaviour and maverick style of functioning, Mamata always meant a good copy, constantly drawing media attention. Our relation was based on an unstated quid pro quo as both realized the importance of each other. In those days there were no news television channels and Mamata needed me for her publicity. I needed her as the most saleable product in the state's news market. The understanding, therefore, worked well for both of us.

Mamata's usual style of facing adverse situations was to lock herself in her bedroom for days together, snapping all ties with the world outside. I was the only person who would be allowed access to her room during those trying times. She would let me in but won't speak a word for hours. She would either scribble or draw pictures of flowers and I would pretend to marvel at her artistic genius in a desperate effort to assuage her frayed tempers. There were days and nights, both in Kolkata and Delhi, when I confronted the angry woman in such an unenviable situation and my strike rates were comparable to the best batsman in one-day cricket.

Even though Mamata became a junior minister in the central cabinet, she concentrated mostly on West Bengal, taking her anti-Left crusade to every corner of the state. She would be the first person to reach a troubled spot involving party men or commoners, demanding ready justice. Her visits almost always were full of drama, often landing the police forces in nightmarish situations. Over a short period of time, her brand of combative politics paid her rich dividends, as Mamata emerged not merely as an incorrigible street fighter but also the most credible Congress leader against the ruling Left. Her humble background, spartan lifestyle and impeccable honesty stood in sharp contrast to the other state Congress leaders, most of whom were either in cahoots with the ruling Left or had lost their popular appeal. Mamata openly called the state Congress the B team of the CPI(M) and the Left-leaning Congress leaders soon earned from her the sobriquet of 'watermelon'—a green (meaning Congress) exterior with a concealed deep red (indicating communist sympathies) inside. In less than ten years following her emergence as a giant killer in the 1984 elections, she became famous as West Bengal's universal Didi (elder sister). By the time I returned to Kolkata taking charge of ABP's news operations, Mamata Banerjee was West Bengal's unchallenged face of the state's political opposition to the unassailable Left.

The deal I struck with Mamata was simple. She would give exclusive stories and information only to the ABP. In return we would give her as much coverage as possible. I must concede that almost always she kept her part of the bargain giving me exclusive stories. Soon I was impressed with the lady's news sense.

From 1991 onwards till she left the Congress in December 1997, Mamata fought her battle simultaneously on two fronts, against the ruling Left and the ruling faction in the PCC led by

Somen Mitra. Even as her popularity index soared continuously, she failed in her mission to wrest control of the state Congress. Rajiv Gandhi's untimely death followed by Sonia's decision to stay indoors for almost seven years contributed greatly to her discomfiture within the organization as the central Congress leadership in Delhi, whether during Narasimha Rao or Sitaram Kesri's time, remained completely under the influence of Somen's all-powerful mentor Pranab Mukherjee, who disliked Mamata for her antics and irresponsible behaviour.

Yet the indefatigable Didi showed no signs of relenting, taking in her stride the upsets and defeats within the organization. She virtually ran a parallel Congress organization with the support of the media as also the diehard anti-Left sections within the Congress. The ABP, too, fell for her and started projecting her as the reincarnation of Joan of Arc who would soon deliver the state from the Left misrule. I played the conductor's role in the jugalbandi between her and my organization.

In 1996, Lok Sabha and Assembly polls were held simultaneously in West Bengal. Predictably, the ruling clique in the state Congress had a clear edge in the nomination of party candidates, giving tickets to some with disreputable backgrounds. Losing her cool and all sense of proportion, an enraged and defiant Mamata created an ugly ruckus and staged an unprecedented drama that continued for almost forty-eight hours. Yet again, almost inexorably I was drawn into it.

Mamata's protests and tantrums were making headlines as usual. Close to the last date of filing nomination papers, I received a call from her on my direct line in office at around one-thirty in the morning. I was then about to leave, having put the last edition of next morning's paper to bed. What she said on phone forced me to issue immediate instructions to the press to stop printing. The front page needed to change as the most important news had just come in.

Mamata said, 'I have just decided not to contest the elections. Enough is enough.'

'Are you kidding at this hour of the night? Do you want me to write the story for tomorrow's paper?' I questioned Mamata equally agitated.

She replied coolly, 'Why else would I bother you so late at night? This is my final decision and I am not going to budge from there. You can quote me and write the story.'

I did, and the exclusive story predictably generated a political storm in the state next morning. But Mamata went into hiding even before the paper hit the stands adding another exciting dimension to the scintillating drama. She had left her home at the crack of dawn hoodwinking even her security guards. None in the family knew where she had gone absconding.

That put me into a great deal of embarrassment as everyone thought and believed I would be privy to this classified information. Even my editor thought so, as did almost all important Congress leaders in the state who kept calling me in turns to ask the same question. I cursed Mamata for giving me the story.

Late in the evening I received a call from Gautam Bose, a friend from my Presidency College days. He was then acting as Mamata's private secretary. Gautam whispered on the phone, 'Don't tell anyone, Didi is hiding at my place. She wants you to come here on your way back home.'

In order to avoid further embarrassment, I kept the information to myself and chose not to write a single line for the paper. I thought that would also be a breach of trust.

I went to Gautam's place close to midnight to discover Didi in a completely different mood. She looked happy and contented and greeted me with a disarming smile. For the one hour I was there she did not utter a word about her decision or the reactions it had generated outside. Instead, she asked me personal questions, narrated some unknown stories of her childhood, persuading me to have dinner there. Her unexpected metamorphosis overnight rattled me. She even asked for her small synthesizer to sing a couple of Rabindra Sangeet songs. All the while I thought I am in a theatre hall watching a surreal drama. As I drove back I thought she must have got a signal from Delhi that the controversial candidates would be dropped from the list. Otherwise what else could have explained this unbelievable transformation?

I was wrong. Mamata came out of her hibernation after about thirty hours, more bitter, as neither her threat nor her hard bargains yielded the desired result. The PCC leadership put up a valiant fight and agreed finally to drop just one candidate from the list. Tying her shawl into a knot around her neck she told her wailing supporters, 'I would rather die than accept things lying down. I am not going to backtrack on my words.'

But backtrack she did and finally submitted her nomination papers without any more fuss. Predictably the Left Front won as usual with a huge margin. Those Congress candidates Mamata branded as 'criminal' also won, adding salt to Didi's grievous injuries.

From early 1997 it was becoming clear that she wanted to quit the Congress and float her own outfit. During the AICC session held in August that year in Kolkata, Didi staged another round of defiant drama by organizing a huge rally near the venue of the session. She named her outfit 'Trinamool Congress' and gave a clarion call to all Congressmen to rally under her banner. Most of the eminent Congress leaders, except for Ajit Panja, stayed away from Mamata's rally. But a large section of the party's rank and file responded to her call. The countdown for the split began in right earnest.

The Congress's decision to withdraw support from the I.K. Gujral-led National Front government necessitated another general election in early 1998. Mamata flung herself into the last round of battle with the state Congress leadership asking for a controlling position in matters of nomination of party candidates. After rounds and rounds of discussion in Delhi it was decided that she would be made the chairperson of the state election committee and 50 per cent of candidates would be her nominees. I was present in Delhi to watch the drama from close quarters and report for my paper.

On the night Mamata was told of the compromise formula, she went to call on Sonia Gandhi at her 10 Janpath residence around midnight. I too accompanied her in the car. There was no formal appointment and no other Congressperson would have dared to go there at such an unearthly hour to meet Rajiv's widow. But no rule ever applied to Mamata. As we left her Baba Kharak Singh Marg residence, Mamata said, 'Let me try my luck. I think it is my duty to see Soniaji before I leave for Kolkata tomorrow morning. These old jokers would not have come to this compromise if she had not intervened in my favour.'

How true her premonition was! Sonia had already gone to bed and the man at the reception did not know what to do in such an unexpected and unsavoury situation. Finally he yielded to Didi's constant prodding and agreed to pass on the message of her arrival to Sonia's bedroom. Seconds later, Mamata was asked to go in as I waited in the reception. A few minutes later Didi came out triumphantly, saying, 'Soniaji was in her nightgown. Still she came out of her bedroom to bless me!'

Mamata came back to Kolkata the following morning and the AICC press release based upon the compromise formula was to come in the afternoon. It did not come, raising fresh apprehensions in the Mamata camp. Her associates made frantic calls to Delhi to ascertain the reasons for the delay as an angry Mamata again disappeared from public view to lock herself up in her bedroom. The AICC communique that was finally issued the following day had the clear stamp of betrayal, only saying that Mamata would be the chairman of the party's campaign committee and not of the election committee, which was entrusted with the nomination of candidates. Didi lost no time to split the party and declared the birth of the All India Trinamool Congress. From now on it would be Didi versus the Left. Period.

In the National Democratic Alliance led by Atal Bihari Vajpayee, Mamata was a welcome ally as it provided the BJP a toehold, for the first time, in West Bengal riding on Didi's popularity. Mamata, on the other hand, was a little unsure of her political future and felt comfortable in the company of an all-India party. She was made the first woman railway minister of the country that provided Didi the first great opportunity to shower her own state with new trains, new lines and new projects, some feasible but most unfeasible. As a railway minister she was brazenly partisan towards her own state and populist to the detriment of the economy.

Both Vajpayee and Advani, the two pillars of the BJP and the first NDA, were personally fond of Mamata. Vajpayee even paid a visit to Mamata's house during one of his Kolkata tours and touched her mother's feet in front of countless cameras. Both of them were therefore upset when Mamata, instead of showing solidarity in moments of crisis, chose the confrontational path against her own government demanding George Fernandes's resignation even though the *Tehelka* exposure had nothing to do with the defence minister personally.

Many years later, Mamata admitted quitting NDA in 2001 had been a mistake on her part. But that was not how she viewed her decision immediately after quitting the central cabinet, dubbing it an instance of practising value-based politics. Grown in a Congress culture that put emphasis on pluralism and secular values, Mamata also felt a little uncomfortable in the company of stalwarts of the saffron brigade. For her then, alliance with the BJP was nothing but a temporary marriage of convenience providing her a breathing space after the momentous decision of quitting Congress.

One night, shortly after quitting the central cabinet, Mamata and Sudip Bandyopadhyay came to my Kolkata residence seeking help in a possible adjustment with the Congress for the ensuing assembly elections. They requested me to persuade Aveek Sarkar to put in a word on their behalf to Sonia Gandhi. I heard them out, understood their desperation and sense of urgency but purposely did not broach the matter to my editor. My journalistic vanity stood in the way.

Yet when Aveek Babu himself told me to play host to a secret midnight meeting between Mamata and Sonia's envoy at his residence I heaved a sigh of relief. For me the job was a bit self-demeaning. But I could not say no to my boss, also I was curious to know what transpired in the ice-breaking parleys.

The midnight meeting proved somewhat of a disaster as Mamata started bargaining hard, claiming in several districts even those seats that went Congress's way in the last elections. Every time Kamal Nath asked her to be reasonable, the decibel level of Mamata's voice increased, causing further embarrassment to the Congress leader. I had no role in the discussion but from the adjacent room I could clearly hear Didi threatening to leave the room over and over again whenever the Congress's proposals seemed unacceptable to her. After about an hour, the meeting ended and remained inconclusive. I could hear Kamal Nath say, 'I have to protect the interest of my party even as we are interested in having an alliance with you. I will have to speak with Soniaji before I can come back with appropriate answers.'

Kamal remained seated on the couch for a few more minutes after a grumbling Mamata left Aveek Babu's home.

He looked crestfallen and exasperated. Then, in a whisper, he asked me, 'How do you guys manage this lady year after year?'

―◆―

19
Bengal's Chanakya and Chavez

Didi has a penchant for doing many things not regularly associated with a politician. She is a self-proclaimed poet, lyricist and prolific writer. Come every celebrated Kolkata Book Fair she publishes a host of her books. She claims to survive the whole year with the royalties these books generate for her. She has no other declared source of income. A practitioner of probity in public life she maintains a frugal, almost ascetic existence. She does not accept either official salary or conveniences. When in stress she draws colourful flowers and composes limericks. Also, political slogans.

Before the 2001 elections, Mamata Bandyopadhyay coined a slogan, '*Ebar noyto never*' (Now or Never). Once the results came out, however, 'never' seemed a more distinct possibility. The slogan haunted her for a long time after the disaster.

A shattered Mamata blamed the state Congress leadership for sabotaging the alliance, and, in her characteristic style, attributed Left victory to their 'scientific rigging', which meant subtle tampering with the electoral process at every level with the precision of a scientific experiment. In reality, though, the Left, notwithstanding manipulations here and there, indeed had the popular mandate to rule.

Sonia Gandhi was upset when, despite her discreet intervention, Mamata had to leave the Congress in 1997. Like her husband, Sonia too was fond of Mamata and admired her indefatigable spirits. Thus, when in 2001 an occasion arose for bringing the estranged leader closer to the Congress, Sonia, as the party president, ignored the legitimate claims of her state party colleagues and signed on the dotted line forwarded by Mamata in matters of ticket sharing.

The saga, as I saw it unfolding before my eyes, looked bizarre and unbelievable. Kamal Nath's visit to Kolkata to have secret parleys with Didi was kept a closely guarded secret from all the important state Congress leaders. I too had to swear an oath of secrecy to both Aveek Babu and Kamal. None of the other state leaders was given access to their discussions, not even Pranab Mukherjee or Priya Ranjan Dasmunsi. Even their legitimate claims and recommendations, if they came in conflict with Didi's wishes, were promptly discarded. Kamal's brief from Sonia appeared crystal clear: whatever the price, an alliance with Didi had to be forged.

Hearing from Kamal that Mamata claimed majority of the Assembly seats in his Lok Sabha constituency, a traditional Congress stronghold, where Mamata's party did not have anything more than a notional presence, a distraught Dasmunsi sought my help to reach Didi and pleaded his case. I felt bad to see him virtually begging her to be reasonable at least with regard to his constituency. Mamata yielded to Dasmunsi but remained adamant about Congress claims elsewhere.

The hurriedly crafted alliance proved disastrous for both the parties, more for Mamata, as her stakes were higher. An alliance foisted from above did not percolate to the grassroots and remained largely on paper. The disgruntled Congressmen refused to share the dais with TMC leaders. Denied of tickets, a large number of sitting Congress MLAs fought as independent candidates to spoil the alliance's victory. The battle was lost even before it began.

Yet the media, including my own paper, went gung-ho in their partisan coverage predicting a regime change in the state after twenty-four years. Their optimism, like Mamata's, was based on a few calculations that seemed quite reasonable before the polls. After two and a half decades in power it was easier for the united Opposition to whip up the latent anti-incumbency sentiments about the Left Front government. Moreover, Jyoti Basu had stepped aside from chief ministership six months before the polls, creating a distinct void in Left leadership. Buddhadeb Bhattacharjee, who succeeded him, was known for his arrogance and dogmatism and did not have an iota of Basu's charisma. It was not very unreasonable for Didi to believe that her turn had indeed arrived. In a Mamata versus Buddhadeb battle there would be no prize for guessing who would be the winner.

The all-round euphoria generated around the possibility of a regime change rattled even the CPI(M) state leadership. Even they were apprehensive of an eventual electoral debacle. Caught in this air of uncertainty, Anil Biswas, the CPI(M) state secretary, invited me over to his flat one night for dinner. I came back with the impression that Alimuddin Street, Kolkata's Kremlin, was trembling in fear.

Like Pranab Mukherjee, Anil Biswas too was my father's student, a qualification that greatly neutralized the communist's ire and dislike towards a bourgeois journalist. Anil Da's fondness for me served as my entry permit to many Left quarters that otherwise remained closed to media persons. I respected him a great deal as I was aware of his battle against poverty in childhood as also his journey from being a cadre at the grassroots level to the most important party post in the state, which had the world's longest ruling elected communist party in power.

Anil Da came to Krishnagar Government College, where

my father taught, from Karimpur, a backward village near the Bangladesh border. I learnt from my father that he just had one shirt and a pair of pyjamas. He washed them every night to wear them next morning. He was an active member of the students union of the undivided communist party and later went to jail for eleven months as a result of his involvement in some violent demonstrations. My father used to carry food and books for his favourite student to jail. He was not a brilliant student but had a sharp mind.

With Anil Da, my father remained in touch till the day his student breathed his last in a city nursing home just before the 2006 Assembly polls. On the day he became the state secretary of his party he called my father first thing in the morning to seek his blessings. A Left-minded person all his life, my father started disliking the CPI(M) and its activities from the late 1980s. However, his love and affection for his student remained unwavering till the last.

Frail and short, Anil Biswas was an unassuming, reticent Bengali bhadralok, and had a cool and amiable temperament that endeared him to everyone. Till he took the reins of the party in 1998 he was the editor of its daily organ, *Ganashakti Patrika*. As such he knew the newspaper trade inside out and had a natural bonhomie with the journalist tribe. During the Left regime he favoured a number of Kolkata journalists in various ways without asking for anything in return. This was where the two students of my father, Pranab and Anil, both short and wily as politicians, had one thing in common.

The media dubbed him as CPI(M)'s modern-day Chanakya because of his quiet organizational skills, his unflappable temperament and his ability in conflict management.

I was once a key witness to this particular skill of the CPI(M)'s highest organizational post holder in a high-voltage clash between Jyoti Basu, at that point of time the state's chief minister as well as the unchallenged patriarch of the party, and Viren J. Shah, then the governor of the state. Not only was it a high-voltage clash, it was over so sensitive an issue that none of those involved in it risked leaking it to the media, a usual practice by politicians to score points in such situations.

I knew Shah very well even before he landed in West Bengal as the governor. He was a Rajya Sabha MP when I was in Delhi. Since I covered the Upper House for my paper, I knew him personally and had struck a working rapport with him. The relation was further cemented as his company, Mukand Steel, was trying hard to take over the IISCO steel plant at Burnpur near Asansol. When his name was announced as governor in 1999, I travelled to Mumbai to interview him and then accompanied him to the steel plant where he had his farewell lunch with the workers.

Shah's nomination as the governor of a Left-ruled state surprised many but had the support and nod of the ruling party, particularly Anil Biswas. The party calculated that they could count on Shah's help and experience in bringing fresh investment to the state. Shah maintained cordial relations with Jyoti Basu and invited him to Raj Bhavan frequently, offering choice alcohol and delicious Gujarati food.

Such camaraderie notwithstanding, Basu refused to see eye to eye with Shah, when the chief minister learnt that a female employee of Raj Bhavan, the governor's residence and office, had brought a charge of sexual harassment against the governor. She was well-connected with the state CPI(M) bigwigs who took up the matter in right earnest. Important party leaders such as Buddhadeb Bhattacharjee and Shyamal Chakrabarty saw red and advised the chief minister to shine the red light on the governor. Jyoti Basu, himself also furious, went to Raj Bhavan and told Shah to resign and leave the state immediately.

Shocked, embarrassed and clueless as to how he would save

his face and extricate himself from this situation, Shah sent for me. He took me into confidence, narrated his version of the sex scandal as also the details of Jyoti Babu's ultimatum. He then grabbed my hand and pleaded, 'You are like my son. I beseech you to help me in this trouble.'

I did my own investigation and found that Shah was not totally innocent. I could have broken the story in ABP and ensure his unceremonious exit from the state. But my own closeness to Shah and his emotional appeal to me obviously had disabled my sense of justice momentarily. I felt sorry for the old man and sought Anil Da's intervention in the messy affair. Anil Da smiled and after a few days, a jubilant Shah called me over yet again for a wonderful Gujarati dinner. I did not ask Anil Da how he went about it nor did he reveal the details to me. I hardly cared beyond the fact that the storm had blown over.

The CPI(M)'s all-powerful Chanakya, however, was not being Shah's saviour just for the heck of it. In reality, he was returning a favour of sorts. Anil Da was criticized in the media for his party's overwhelming interference in the field of education, from the primary to the university levels. We called it 'Anilayan' in Bengali, meaning 'Anilization', much in the form and shape of Stalinization in erstwhile Soviet Union. Even as he was quite pragmatic regarding various other issues, including opening up the state more and more before private capital, in matters of controlling the educational sector he was dogmatic and followed the rule books of a loyal communist. As a result, the quality of education in West Bengal gradually declined, robbing the state of its traditional good name and reputation.

As the governor, Shah became the ex officio chancellor of all state universities. The first conflict between Shah and the CPI(M) had brewed over the nomination of the Calcutta University vice chancellor, a high-profile academic chair that had fallen vacant. As per rule, the chancellor has the right to choose any of the three names that are being sent to him for his final approval. The names of the academicians sent to Shah's office, with the nod of the ruling party, for picking the next vice chancellor were all CPI(M) loyalists. Anil Da, however, wanted the governor to pick the first name in the list. As the news travelled to him that Shah might choose the second name instead of the first, Anil Da smelt a rat and sent for me. 'Go and tell your friend to nominate the first name in the list. If he does otherwise I will take it as a hostile act that will have its consequences.' Shah could have stuck to his guns, and the CPI(M)'s overwhelming power in the state, notwithstanding, a clash over the issue could have resulted in uncomfortable media exposure for Anil Da, already criticized for ensuring the party's undue influence over the state's education system. Shah, however, didn't precipitate the clash, and had quietly signed on dotted line.

Managing the 2001 elections against heavy odds and constant adverse media propaganda was a Himalayan task that fell squarely on Anil Da's shoulders. He presented a stellar performance, but from behind the curtain, silently and secretly.

The man who ripped the dividend of his friend's hard labour was Buddhadeb Bhattacharjee, who had succeeded Basu six months ago and now, in 2001, got the popular mandate to rule. Anil Da provided the new chief minister unstinted party support as the latter embarked on an unprecedented reform agenda that sought to change the face of the Left in West Bengal. In that sense, Buddhadeb was luckier than his predecessor who had to face party opposition in various critical matters during his long tenure. Once Anil Da was gone from the scene, in early 2006, Buddhadeb bungled majorly on various fronts, including in Singur and Nandigram, and ultimately precipitated the end of Left rule in West Bengal in 2011.

But in 2001, post Assembly polls, Mamata stood marginalized and, following the electoral drubbing in the 2004 Lok Sabha polls when only she could retain her parliamentary seat, almost faded into oblivion. Some political pundits even published her political epitaph.

Before he became the chief minister, Buddhadeb Bhattacharjee, till 2001, had remained largely aloof from the media glare, and was seen as arrogant and dogmatic. At a personal level, Buddhadeb and I hated each other in equal measures. In my weekly column in ABP, I used to take regular pot-shots at him, ridiculing him for his intellectual pretensions. He used to retaliate by calling me names in open press conferences. I enjoyed the battle, and so did ABP's readers. Buddhadeb hardly moved beyond his charmed circle of self-seeking writers, poets and film-makers and he made headlines only for arrogant or stupid remarks. Personally, I was a bit apprehensive when he was chosen as Basu's successor. How mistaken I was!

It seemed that just like the real Buddha, he too underwent 'nirvana' to emerge in a completely new avatar as his role changed. In a way unseen and unheard in the annals of the communist history, Buddhadeb went out of his way to befriend the state media for support and the big moneybags for capital and investment in the state. After a while, it became difficult to distinguish him from the chief ministers of other political parties. Over time, his ratings went sky-high in the media world. Buddhadeb emerged as the most industry-friendly chief minister in the country. My relation with him became warm, friendly and cordial. Once the hatchet got buried, my paper offered him unconditional support in his new initiatives to transform the image of West Bengal from a laggard to an economically forward moving state.

One early morning as I was driving to drop my son to his school, I received a call on my mobile, a gadget that had just hit the city. The conversation with the caller went like this:

'This is Buddhadeb speaking.'
'Which Buddhadeb? I know at least a dozen.'
'I am Buddhadeb Bhattacharjee.'
'All right, but what do you want from me?'
'Perhaps you are unable to recognize my voice. I am Buddhadeb Bhattacharjee, chief minister of West Bengal.'

Stunned and embarrassed I did not know how to react. The last thing I ever expected was a call from Buddhadeb. He was modest and gentlemanly. In the ABP, we were then carrying a serialized story on the plight of the tribal people working in the tea gardens in North Bengal that he said was helping the secessionist forces working there. Neither did he request me to stop publishing the series nor did he express his unhappiness. He just requested me to keep this point in mind in future.

I was mighty impressed with him in my first telephonic encounter. Aveek Sarkar was floored. Immediately after meeting the CM for the first time my editor called me to say, 'I am convinced this man is the last hope for West Bengal.'

As I got to know him better, Buddhadeb admitted to me many of the mistakes he and his party had committed in the past. Coming to me personally he would say, 'I used to hate you and your paper for what you wrote against me and my party. Then gradually I realized your criticism had some merits. I understand now that you had no personal agenda and that you too wanted welfare and development of West Bengal. In my own way I have learnt to be realistic and tolerant towards other viewpoints.'

It sounded almost like the Satan chanting scriptures. At the same time his metamorphosis into a liberal, kindred soul was also very genuine. The earlier ill feelings disappeared on both sides and we became friends in no time.

It was not as if Buddhadeb opened only to me or my paper, even though he understood ABP's importance as the market leader. Jyoti Basu was hardly available for the media, not so

Buddhadeb. Except for his home, one could reach him anywhere over phone, in his office at the state secretariat, in party office, even in Nandan, a modern theatre complex that he built as the state's culture minister mainly for screening of movies. On his way back home from the Writers' Buildings he would go there to unwind in the company of a chosen few, discuss the latest trends in postmodern literature in Latin America or parallel cinema in Europe. Not for him the popular culture, literature or cinema of which he would be quietly dismissive. For Tagore and his songs, like any other Bengali, he had a blind adulation.

When in a lighter mood, he would discuss cricket very enthusiastically. It was a game he played during his schooldays and the passion stayed with him permanently. That was about the only bourgeois passion he had enjoyed. He was a great patron and admirer of Sourav Ganguly. When India beat Pakistan in the World Cup held in South Africa, Sourav, as the captain, received calls from only two Indian political leaders, L.K. Advani and Buddhadeb Bhattacharjee.

A man of impeccable personal honesty and integrity, Buddhadeb, even as the state chief minister, continued to live in his modest two-room government flat in South Kolkata that remained out of bounds for everyone. He would often say, 'Unlike other chief ministers, I cannot invite guests at home, it's so small. That, however, I will not change. What if I don't remain the CM tomorrow? Where will I go? I have no private property.'

His open denunciation of the party's earlier mistakes or courting of the media and industry with open arms sent jitters among the conservative section of his party colleagues, but Buddhadeb remained nonchalant. He openly criticized the government employees—most of whom owed allegiance to his party's trade union—for fostering a slow and tardy work culture impeding timely, efficient governance and development. Once, in an industry meet, he castigated his own party for still believing that 'bandh' (shutting down of everything, including factories, private offices, educational institutions, shops and even transport) remained an effective instrument in the hands of the working class.

It wasn't that the party digested everything he did or said but it was also true that he got away almost always with minor reprimands. In the state, Anil Biswas extended full-throated support to the chief minister, and, in Delhi, Prakash Karat had been non-interfering. Even those comrades who opposed him in the party forums did not question the honesty of his intentions. Buddhadeb Bhattacharjee was a man in a great hurry to implement his liberal and reformist agenda.

The same mentality also got reflected in his dealings with the NDA government at the Centre, particularly with Deputy Prime Minister L.K. Advani. Buddhadeb had no qualms in openly acknowledging the help and cooperation he received continuously from Advani and his government. Unlike Jyoti Basu, his successor, he did not allow ideological divergences to come in the way of executive functioning.

Advani too was fond of the West Bengal chief minister. Once during a conversation in his Home Ministry office, the BJP stalwart narrated to me what he perceived to be the basic difference between Basu and Bhattacharjee: 'Jyoti Babu would be very reluctant to meet us publicly. Once before the formation of the Janata Party Government in 1977, he wanted to meet me but with a clear rider, the meeting had to be in a secret place and kept completely confidential. It seemed to me he was somewhat afraid of meeting us in public. Buddhadeb does not have such hang-ups or inhibitions.'

For Buddhadeb, anyone who would lend a helping hand had to be counted as a friend notwithstanding his political background. Thus he had no problems raising a toast with Ratan Tata in Kolkata or sharing lassi with Advani in Delhi. After the UPA came to power in Delhi in 2004, Buddhadeb lost no time in striking a quick rapport with everyone important in the new dispensation. He found a friend and admirer in Prime Minister Manmohan Singh who would go to town praising the West Bengal chief minister. With Pranab Mukherjee, he played the Bengali card and started calling him Dada as the Congressmen did. Even Pranab was pleasantly amused and surprised with his open-arm strategy. When Buddhadeb befriended even Montek Singh Ahluwalia, the deputy chairman of the Planning Commission, I congratulated him for his public relations skills with a jibe, 'So for you Montek is no longer a lackey of the World Bank and the IMF!'

Buddhadeb Bhattacharjee would be remembered in history as a small Bengali version of Den Xiaoping. In this respect, Buddhadeb has, till date, no parallel in the chequered history of the communists in India. He made the right noises at the right time, made the right moves and charted the right vision for Bengal's development. It was another matter that his moves in Singur and Nandigram floundered, paving the way for his eventual ouster in 2011. Yet posterity would remember him as the state's best chief minister since Bidhan Chandra Roy.

He would vehemently protest if I called him our Margaret Thatcher in dhoti. To that extent, he was still a communist. He also refused to be compared with Deng Xiaoping, although I found his denial inexplicable. He told me he would be happy if someone compared him with Hugo Chavez of Venezuela. It is a strange coincidence that both of them today stand at the margins of history.

20
Job Lost, Battle Won

'I hear that you have told Aveek Sarkar and his folks that I am the most dishonest journalist in town. Have you really?' A certain day in April 2006 had found me distraught enough to accost the chief minister of the state with such a question. I was in Buddhadeb Bhattacherjee's office to interview him for the news channel that I had joined after quitting ABP Group on 1 October 2005. It was just as we were preparing for the take, that I couldn't resist myself from shooting this question. In hindsight today, it does sound extraordinarily silly, particularly because of being targeted at a chief minister. But for me the circumstances were not ordinary either.

Since the moment I quit ABP, the Sarkars had started badmouthing me with all the vengeance at their command. I had ignored it until I came to know that in private conversations, they were also quoting the chief minister to give the dog a bad name, indeed even after shooting it! It hurt me the most, because by that time I had known Bhattacharjee enough to be certain that he was not a man to lie. Bhattacharjee, of course, in keeping with my expectations dismissed it as 'utter rubbish'.

Six years later, when I joined *Ei Samay*, the first Bengali daily from *The Times of India* stable, I was amazed to learn such canards had also reached the highest echelons of the Bennett, Coleman

& Co. Group. After I learnt about that, it occurred to me that I do owe the not-so-small number of my dedicated readers I had been able to nurture over my long journalistic career—not only across West Bengal, but Bengalis in other parts of India and even abroad— my side of the story about what really went wrong between me and the newspaper with whose fortune my life was intricately entwined for more than two decades.

I believe it would be fitting to end my story with that.

ω

For ten years after I came back to Kolkata from Delhi in 1993 responding to Aveek Babu's distress call, I had no problems with my editor or with anyone. This had been the most successful decade in my career, during which the ABP also grew from strength to strength, finally reaching the magic circulation figure of one million copies per day. Simultaneously, my authority and power in the organization also rose as also my salary and perks. I must admit that during this period I was given complete liberty to run the newspaper as I wished. I do not remember any occasion when Aveek Babu turned down any request I made in the interest of the paper. I basked in his glory, was known and recognized as Aveek Babu's alter ego, his man Friday, both within and outside the organization. It was the most happening, also the happiest, decade of my life.

Aveek Babu was aware of my perceived importance in the external world and I had no occasion to feel he was resenting my larger-than-life image as the ABP's ambassador. Indeed, I was convinced that he really enjoyed it. He took a great deal of pride in grooming and shaping me as a journalist. There were a number of occasions when he publicly acknowledged that I had more power than him in the ABP in deciding what would be printed. As an employer he seemed thoroughly self-assured, a guru who took enormous pride in the disciple's growing excellence.

Once, in front of the top-ranking sanyasis of Belur Math I faced an embarrassing situation. One of the sanyasis went up to Aveek Babu, handed over a piece of paper for publication in ABP. Without mincing words, Aveek Babu directed him towards me, saying in half-jest, 'Maharaj! Go to him if you really want it published. In ABP, he is the real boss. Even I cannot negate what he decides.' That was a typical way of Aveek Babu pulling my leg in public.

He had a mind-boggling collection of books in his personal library at home and I had the liberty to pick any book on the explicit condition that it would be returned. When I took to playing golf and became an addict he gifted me his own expensive old set instead of selling it to a friend who was begging him for it. I also got my first Montblanc pen from him as a gift. I bought for him a few cigars when I went to Rangoon on an airlines junket. From Jamaica, I got him a few packets of Blue Mountain coffee, his favourite and by default, mine also.

I always felt a touch of personal care and affection in everything he did for me. A health freak with the firm notion that most of the food available and cooked in India is simply inedible, Aveek Babu survived on plain dosa even when he lived in the most expensive suites of five-star hotels. Since I resented his food habit and made no bones about it, he would order for me my favourite Chinese food with a rider: 'Bangals (meaning people from East Bengal) would remain Bangals for eternity.'

Once I was with Aveek Babu in Davos, Switzerland. I had gone there as a member of P.V. Narasimha Rao's media entourage while he was there as a delegate. During lunch break he took me to a pastry shop, an idea I did not like at all. Seeing my reticence he rebuked me politely, 'You may not have such quality pastry ever in your life. So please stop whining.' I felt ashamed after I devoured half a dozen in less than fifteen minutes.

On another occasion I had gone to New York, again with Narasimha Rao. Aveek Babu was already there. He came to my hotel soon after I checked in at the end of a long and tiring journey. We then went for a walk in Manhattan following which he took me to a Chinese restaurant for dinner. He knew only Chinese food could lift my spirits. To my amazement, he ordered an eight-course dinner. When the food came in, trolley after trolley, my host announced every morsel was for my consumption. I failed to do justice to the delectable offerings and most of the food was wasted. Dinner over, Aveek Babu walked me back to my hotel.

Once I went to Wagah border near Amritsar to receive him as he was returning from Lahore after a brief visit to Pakistan. He was to fly to Manila that night and there was no flight connection to Delhi that day. I was told to take with me two cars in case one developed snags on the road in the terrorist-infested areas. Siddhartha Shankar Ray was then Punjab's governor who made all arrangements for Aveek Babu to facilitate his hassle-free entry. I stayed overnight at a hotel in Amritsar and left early the following morning to receive him. As the governor's guest I was given VIP treatment by the jawans and their officers and watched the spectacular change of guard ceremony on both sides of the border from very close quarters. It slipped from everyone's mind that Delhi could also be reached by plane from Amritsar. I took my editor promptly to the Amritsar airport, introduced Aveek Babu as the governor's first cousin to wangle two tickets. We left the two cars at the airport to reach Delhi before noon. He patted my back for hoodwinking Indian Airlines officials with a small, innocent, yet necessary, lie.

There were many occasions when I would have heated arguments with him. But I knew Aveek Babu would take everything in his stride and would forget the episode as soon as he left the office. He was the finest editor a working journalist could aspire for.

Come 2004, the scenario changed drastically. I was partly responsible for my own discomfiture. Once ABP's circulation crossed the one million mark, I started feeling somewhat restless having achieved my goal. A feeling crept into me that I had reached a plateau and had nothing more to contribute to the newspaper except doing the holding operations. The spectre of doing just the same thing for another thirteen years seemed dreadful.

The success of my former senior colleague, Barun Sengupta, in launching a new daily, *Bartaman*, kindled my imagination to try and do the same. But, as I got into the act and started sounding some businessmen friends in Kolkata, I realized soon enough the futility of the enterprise, for none of them was willing to invest in a newspaper business where the gestation period was long and return unattractive. My probing mission ended in a whimper.

The biggest act of indiscretion on my part was to take into confidence a few of my colleagues and share with them details of my secret initiative. A few of them had also accompanied me when had I discussed the project with probable investors. They stabbed me in the back and promptly reported everything to Aveek Babu. He was told exaggerated stories of my desperation to break away with a number of colleagues and that I was out to wreck ABP from within. Right at that moment, for me, the die was cast in the ABP.

I noticed Aveek Babu's attitude towards me had suddenly undergone a dramatic change. He would hardly speak with me even in editorial meetings and his eyes reflected quiet anger and suspicion. Even in the newsroom I saw and felt some colleagues consciously distancing themselves from me. In my own habitat that I painstakingly built over the last one decade I felt like a pariah. I went into severe depression.

The ABP was then planning to launch its Bengali news television channel from Kolkata after acquiring majority stakes in Rupert Murdoch's Star News. They were looking for a leader. In sheer desperation I asked Aveek Babu if I could be chosen for the job. The proposal suited both of us. Aveek Babu was keen that I disengage myself from ABP and I wanted reprieve from the stifling and humiliating atmosphere.

On the day I walked up to Aveek Babu's room with my prayer, he broke his silence and came clean. 'You have to decide what you want to do. Many people tell me you are planning to launch your own newspaper.'

'I am aware who have tried to poison your mind. It is true that I tried to explore the possibility but I gave up soon thereafter. I would not have come to you with this new proposal if I were determined to go my way.'

I left 6 Prafulla Sarkar Street in October 2004 and headed straight for Mumbai. My destination: Star News headquarters. A complete stranger to the new medium I was told to undergo a comprehensive month-long training. In a weird circumstance, my life suddenly took a new turn.

I struck an immediate rapport with Uday Shankar, then boss of Star News. He was a live wire, educated, smart, although a bit overbearing. In the national Hindi news channel world, Uday was already a big name having successfully launched Zee News and Aaj Tak before that. He was younger and less experienced than I was, but I had no qualms in accepting him as my leader in a totally new and unknown trade. Uday, too, embraced me with open arms and taught me the mantra of television journalism—'Nautanki'. It was not enough to peddle credible information round the clock. Then it would be like Doordarshan, no one will watch your channel. You would be required to create some drama around the story, with sound, music, voice-over and telling footage. Unlike in a newspaper, television is a team game where so many people—the reporter, the cameraperson, the editor, the graphic artist and finally the anchor—contribute, perhaps in equal measure, to the making and broadcasting of a story. One's failure cannot be made up by the other.

It was a medium where look and feel overshadowed everything

else. Everything you showed on television must be pretty and beautiful. The bottom line, you had to create an illusory image of the reality where nothing was dark and dirty.

It took us five months to launch the Bengali channel that was named Star Ananda, using the brand names of the two joint venture partners. Uday gave me a free hand in matters of recruitment and we got together a young crop, most of them in their twenties. A group of American television journalists was hired to give us hands-on training for almost a month that I attended religiously along with others. I got familiar with various acronyms prevalent in the world of visual media. For example, if a reporter spoke in front of the camera from a spot it was called PtoC, meaning Piece to Camera. Likewise, a VOT meant Voice on Tape as SOT stood for Sound on Tape, so on and so forth. I learnt what a 'good story' on television really meant.

For a few months our small office turned into my home where I slept on the floor every night using a bundle of newspapers as a pillow. It reminded me of my *Aajkaal* days when we had done a similar exercise before the launch of the paper. The difference being I was only 24 when *Aajkaal* saw the light of the day and now my age was just double.

Star Ananda was launched in March 2005 without any fanfare. On the morning of the launch, Uday and I, along with several others, went to the Kali temple in Kalighat to seek the goddess's blessings. Uday was keen that I appeared before the camera on every important occasion, as he believed every successful channel depended on some popular, credible faces. I did not know that Aveek Babu wanted just the opposite as he had never told me that. Thus began a bizarre chapter when Uday and Aveek Babu were working on cross-purposes, and I, caught in the middle, was reaping all the humiliation.

Here's an example: Star Ananda was launched a few days before the Kolkata Corporation polls providing us a tailwind to quickly popularize the channel. Uday asked me to follow what he did during election times in his own Hindi channel. It was a debating show where all the major contestants of a particular constituency would be invited to have a free-for-all debate over one hour. These debates would be in public places, and not indoor, with local audience in attendance. We called the programme, 'Bolun Councillor' (Speak up Mr Councillor). It became an instant rage as the Bengali audience had never before been exposed to such live drama on television. Soon the debating venues, in places, turned into battlefields with supporters of the contending candidates shouting, screaming and fighting among themselves. We showed the high-drama live in the quest of better television rating points. So the situation came to such a pass that the Kolkata Police commissioner called me to stop the programme as it was leading to law-and-order problems. I refused to oblige.

Uday repeatedly asked me to moderate the last debate in the series that was organized on the lawns of the posh Calcutta Club, and I agreed. The contenders for the mayoral post participated in it in front of several hundred Club members. Even Aveek Babu sat in the audience. Once the debate got over he called me aside to say, 'You are not supposed to moderate these things. Ask others to do it.' I told him I did not do it on my own and requested him to speak to Uday to resolve the problem.

Aveek Babu called me next afternoon in office again to convey a similar message in harsher words. 'Let me make one thing clear to you. Henceforth, I will not allow anyone to achieve stardom in my organization. Look at what Rajdeep (Sardesai) has done to Prannoy (Roy).'

I did not understand what prompted Aveek Babu to speak with me like that without any apparent provocation. Humiliated, I called Uday in Mumbai to narrate what I heard from him. Uday asked me ignore such stupid tantrums.

When finally the Left Front won the Corporation elections

with a comfortable majority, I called Buddhadeb Bhattacharjee and persuaded him to give an exclusive interview for our channel. He agreed on one condition that I myself would take the interview and would not embarrass him with bouncers. Uday too gave me the go-ahead from Mumbai.

Excited, I went to the CPI(M)'s state headquarters with my crew. My colleagues back in office put up a promo announcing the event. Half an hour before the chief minister was to arrive at the venue of the interview, Aveek Babu called to bar me from taking the interview. I then sent for a younger colleague who arrived moments before Buddhadeb. The chief minister was surprised that I was not speaking with him. To his pointed questions I kept silent in utter humiliation.

The proverbial last straw came over another programme that I had painstakingly planned.

In August 2005, Eunan O'Halpin, an Irish historian who has written a number of books on British Intelligence, came to Kolkata's Netaji Bhawan to deliver a sensational lecture. He carried with him an official document that showed, for the first time, that the British wanted to assassinate Subhas Chandra Bose once he sought the support of the Axis powers in the Second World War for India's liberation. The order was issued in 1941 after the British intercepted Italian diplomatic communication and came to know Bose was in Kabul, planning to reach Germany through the Middle East. Two Special Operations Executive (SOE)[13] operatives working in Turkey were instructed by their headquarters in London to intercept Bose and kill him before he reached Germany. The attempt failed since Bose reached Germany

---

[13] In the days that followed the fall of France, a new volunteer fighting force was hastily improvised to wage a secret war against Hitler's armies. This force was called the Special Operations Executive (SOE) and their mission was sabotage and subversion behind enemy lines. The SOE was set up in July 1940.
Source: http://www.bbc.co.uk/history/worldwars/wwtwo/soe_01.shtml

through Central Asia and not West Asia. But the order remained in place for a long time thereafter.

I planned an hour-long programme on this sensational revelation as I knew the Bengalis' love and passion for their tragic hero. Sugata Bose, the grand-nephew of Subhas Chandra Bose, a renowned historian himself, thought the document shed light on an unknown aspect of the British attitude towards Bose. O'Halpin thought the order was extraordinary, unusual and rare because it clearly demonstrated that the English took Bose far more seriously than was known. Leonard Gordon, a Columbia University history professor and the biographer of the Bose brothers, echoed O'Halpin's views. Personally, I had a great deal of interest in Netaji since my college days when Sugata and I had jointly translated from English into Bengali two major books of Bose. Even I thought this order had very few parallels in history. It appeared to be a last desperate measure against someone who had thrown the Empire in complete panic. Excited, I decided to go to town with the story with all kinds of visual embellishments.

Aveek Babu saw the promo we had prepared with great care and called me immediately in a fit of rage. 'What is this stupid programme? Take it off-air.'

I tried to explain to him the planned programme. He refused to listen and said, 'How do you know this document is authentic? Anybody masquerading as a historian can claim anything to draw attention. Are we to fall in his trap?'

I replied, 'The historian concerned teaches at Trinity College Dublin and is an acknowledged scholar in British military history. Two historians who have vetted the document are from Harvard and Columbia universities.'

Then I lost my cool and continued, 'As an employee of your organization I am obliged to carry out your order. But for heaven's sake don't try to teach me history as you are the least qualified to do so.'

I came out of my room to announce the boss's order. Everyone was shocked.

A few days later, I sent in my resignation letter and went incommunicado for a few days. A Bengali entrepreneur was planning to float a news channel and asked me to lead it. I took up the challenge, roped in Aparna Sen and launched Kolkata TV in March 2006 that took the city by the storm. There was large-scale desertion from Star Ananda to Kolkata TV that neither Aveek Babu nor Uday could prevent. All of us preferred uncertainty and adventure over insult and constant humiliation.

During the last few months of my association with him, Aveek Babu harped on one theme continuously, that brand was always more important than an individual and that there should not be any star performer in an organization. I neither disputed nor questioned the merit of his argument realizing the futility of such an exercise. I realized he was out to clip my wings in whatever manner he could. My job in his channel would be to remain in the background and never appear before the camera. I had no problems accepting that proposition either. My problem was that I was getting conflicting signals from my editor and owner over which I had no control. What I found unacceptable was the crude and vulgar way Aveek Babu was trying to establish his writ over his own channel. This new and unknown avatar of Aveek Babu shocked and surprised me. I kept wondering what prompted him to act and behave with me in such an ugly manner.

In this battle between the brand and the individual, the outcome must have gravely disappointed Aveek Babu as most of my colleagues from Star Ananda resigned in favour of an individual. The lure of working for the two redoubtable brands, ABP and Star, proved inadequate. I lost the job but won the battle.

Index

Aaj Tak, 268
Aajkaal, 39, 44–45, 49, 51, 53–54, 67, 218, 269
Abdi, S.N.M., 213
Advani, L.K., 213, 215–16, 218–21, 225–26, 233, 249, 260–61
Afghan policy of Zia-ul-Haq, 156
Agnihotri, Ram Shankar, 210
Ahluwalia, Montek Singh, 262
Ahluwalia, Surendrajeet Singh, 32
Ahmed, Muzaffar, 81
Air Raid Precaution Unit, 38
Aiyar, Mani Shankar, 95, 98, 101, 228
Akal Takht, 85–86, 88, 92
Akali Dal leadership, 89
Akbar, M.J., 52, 59, 69, 75, 116, 234
Al-Aqsa Mosque, 125
Alekhya, 35
Ali, Syed Mujtaba, 171
All India Congress Committee (AICC), 62
All India Sant Committee, 208
All India Sikh Students Federation, 85
All India Trinamool Congress, 249
Amrita Bazar Patrika, 73, 234–35
Anachronism, 199
Anandabazar Patrika (ABP), 12, 18, 34, 39, 41–44, 49–52, 54–56, 58, 61–62, 64–65, 67–69, 71–73, 75–76, 95, 98, 101, 106, 113, 115, 119, 130, 141, 144, 171, 229, 231–40, 244–45, 256, 258–59, 263–68, 273
Anti-incumbency, 253
Anti-Sikh pogrom, 11, 68, 73
Anushilan Samiti, 203
Asiaweek, 38
Avaidyanath, Mahant, 220
Aveek Babu, 43, 51–53, 56, 66, 68, 71, 73, 76, 78, 81–82, 102, 105–106, 113–15, 156, 228–29, 231–36, 239–40, 250, 252, 264–73
Awami National Party (ANP), 158, 165

Babri Masjid demolition, 42,
  208–09, 223–24, 226, 230, 232
Babur-nama: Babur's Memoirs,
  205
Badal, Prakash Singh, 88
Bahujan Samaj Party, 105
Bamdev, Acharya, 207–08, 210
Bandmaster, 12
Banerjee, Mamata, 70, 127, 239,
  241–53, 258
Bangladesh, birth of, 2
Bannerjee, Ajay, 29
Bannerjee, Ranjan, 48
Barnala, Surjit Singh, 85, 89, 92
Bartaman, 51, 66, 218, 231–32,
  234–35, 237, 267
Barua, Dev Kanta, 135
Basu, Jyoti, 63, 69, 81, 97, 101,
  114–15, 117, 125, 129, 133–34,
  236, 253–55, 261
Bengal Renaissance, 26
Bengal Tenancy Act (1885), 25
Bhakra-Nangal dam, 78
Bhatia, Shekhar, 192
Bhattacharjee, Buddhadeb,
  116, 120, 124, 157, 253, 255,
  257–263, 271
Bhattacharya, Debasis, 218
Bhatti, Razia, 165
Bhindranwale, Jarnail Singh, 86
Bhowmick, Nani, 202
Bhutto, Benazir, 159–170
Bhutto, Zulfikar Ali, 154,
  159–160, 168
Biswas, Anil, 253–255, 261
Bofors Scandal, 77, 104, 166
Bose, Baninath, 6
Bose, Gautam, 246
Bose, Jagadish Chandra, 26
Bose, Satyendranath, 26
Bose, Subhas Chandra, 26, 53,
  68, 116, 150, 233, 271–72
Bourgeois elitism, 26
Brahmachari, Tapananda, 222
Brezhnev, Leonid, 199
Bruce, Robert, 3
Bulganin, Nikolai, 2
Burman, Rahul Dev, 5
Business India, 223
Business Standard, 72, 75, 87

Campbell, George, 25
Capitalism, 121, 202, 236
Carnegy, P., 205
Chakrabarty, Shyamal, 255
Chakrabarty, Subhas, 81
Chakraborty, Bhaskar, 31
Chakraborty, Hirendranath, 29
Chakraborty, Nirendranath, 56,
  61
Chakraborty, Gopen, 203
Chandi Bibi, 155
Chandra, Prabodh, 4
Chatterjee, Gouri, 190
Chatterjee, Somnath, 116, 120,
  242
Chattopadhyay, Bankim
  Chandra, 3, 19
Chattopadhyay, Sarat Chandra,
  19
Chattopadhyay, Shakti, 12, 56, 60
Chattopadhyay, Sunil, 3–4, 28,
  39
Chautala, Om Prakash, 78

Chhatra Parishad, 30–32
Chidambaram, P., 137
Childhood, 5, 13, 18, 24, 55–57, 106, 108, 124, 134, 138, 246, 253
Choudhury, A.B.A. Ghani Khan, 71, 132, 243
Chowdhury, Amitabha, 234
Civil disobedience movement, 32
Clinton, Bill, 125
Communist oligarchy, 202
Communist Party of Great Britain (CPGB), 119
Communist Party of India (Marxist) (CPI[M]), 11, 40, 203
Communist Party of the Soviet Union (CPSU), 190
Congress Party System, 24
Cowasjee, Ardeshir, 166

Dakshini Barta, 33
Dalmiya, Jagmohan, 241
Darkness at Noon, 193
Das, C.R., 122
Das, Haricharan, 211
Das, Paramhans Ramchandra, 207–08
Dasgupta, Asim, 124
Dasgupta, Manimoy, 213
Dasgupta, Swapan, 207
Dasmunsi, Priya Ranjan, 33, 70, 97, 101, 115, 130, 243, 252
Datta, Jyotirmoy, 34, 43, 61
Datta, Minakshi, 46
Delinquency, 20
Deshe Bideshe, 171

Dharmendra, Acharya, 219
Dharmendra, Swami, 223–24
Digambar Akhara, Ayodhya, 208
Dikshit, Shrish Chandra, 212
Dixit, Mani, (J.N. Dixit) 152–153
Dostum, Abdul Rashid, 185
Drolin, Bob, 227
Dubs, Adolph, 174
Dutta, Amlan, 41
Dutta, Satyendra Nath, 142
Dzerzhinsky, Feliks, 194

Editors Guild of India, 69
Ei Samay, 263
Electoral adjustments, 241
Emergency, 32–36, 43, 66–67, 70, 96, 99, 123

Fair journalism, canons of, 233
Faizabad District Gazetteer, 205
Farakka agreement, 123
Fearless journalism, 42, 234
Fernandes, George, 249
Feudalism, 50
Ford, Gerald, 162
Frontier Gandhi, 158

Ganashakti Patrika, 254
Gandhi, Indira, 1–2, 11, 32–35, 62–63, 68, 70, 73, 76, 86–87, 103, 134, 156, 235, 243
Gandhi, Mohandas Karamchand, 53
Gandhi, Rajiv, 32, 62–63, 69, 86, 91, 95, 97–98, 100–02, 104–05, 113, 115, 129–30, 132, 147, 152, 156, 165–66, 191, 205–06,

228–30, 245
Gandhi, Sanjay, 32–33
Gandhi, Sonia, 101, 136, 138, 140, 196, 240, 248, 250, 252
Gangopadhyay, Sunil, 12, 56, 59
Ghatak, Ritwik, 11–12, 18
Ghosal, Khitindra Chandra, 35
Ghosh, Arunava, 31
Ghosh, Gautam, 124
Ghosh, Gour Kishore, 34, 38–46, 48–51, 54–55, 62, 64, 67, 232
Ghosh, Sankha, 26
Ghosh, Santosh Kumar, 39, 50, 55, 57, 60, 64, 234
Ghosh, Sunit, 75–77
Gill, K.P.S., 93
Golden Temple, 68, 70, 84, 86–89, 93, 225
Gorbachev, Mikhail, 178, 191, 193–194, 196, 198–200
Gorkha National Liberation Front (GNLF), 102
Gowda, H.D. Deve, 117, 123
Great Soviet Encyclopedia, 197
Green Revolution, 78
Gujral, I.K., 236, 247
Gupta, Shekhar, 175, 184

Hasina, Sheikh, 124
Hekmatyar, Gulbuddin, 156, 175
Himalayan Mountaineering Institute, 102
Hindu communal upsurge, 233
Hindu Kush, 173, 184
Hindu refugees, 234
The Hindu, 104, 171, 173, 205–06, 223, 232–33
Hindustan Standard, 18, 39, 55
Hindustan Times, 81, 223
Hindutva wave, 232
Hussain, Altaf, 164
Hussain, Begum Abida, *See* Chandi Bibi

Idiosyncrasies of languages, 2, 28
The Illustrated Weekly, 131, 213
India Today, 62–63, 175
The Indian Express, 104
Indian National Congress, 68, 160
Indian Newspaper Society (INS), 75
An Indian Pilgrim, 150
Indo-Soviet Treaty of Friendship, 1
Indo-US relations, 122
International Monetary Fund (IMF), 137, 262

Jaffna Tamils, 145
Jahenda Bala festival, 185
Jain, Prabhas, 220
Janatha Vimukthi Peramuna (JVP), 152
Jayawardene, J.R., 152
Jethmalani, Ram, 104
Jinnah, Mohammad Ali, 167
Joshi, Murli Manohar, 213, 215–216, 219, 224
Jugantar, 234

Kabuliwala, 171–72, 179–83, *See also* Tagore, Rabindranath
Kairon, Pratap Singh, 78

Kali Sarkar, 144
Kali temple, 6, 269
Kalighat brothel, 12–13
Kanti, Tarun, 234–235
Karat, Prakash, 116, 261
Karseva, 206–212, 215–17, 219–20
Karsevaks, 204, 206, 208–17, 219–24, 227
Kasturi, 28, 73, 122, 231
Katiyar, Vinay, 209, 215–16, 219, See also Vishva Hindu Parishad (VHP)
Kesri, Sitaram, 245
KGB, 179, 191, 193–94, 199–201
KHAD (state Intelligence agency), 179–80
Khalistan, resolution on, 85
Khalistani aspirations, 85, 92, See also Bhindranwale, Jarnail Singh
Khan, Arif Mohammad, 104
Khan, Khan Abdul Wali, 158–59, 165
Khan, Khan Abdur Ghaffar, See Frontier Gandhi
Khan, Saadat Ali, 204
Khrushchev, Nikita, 2
Khyber Pass, 158, 177
Koestler, Arthur, 193
Kolkata (magazine), 61
Kothari, Rajni, 24
Kryuchkov, Vladimir, 194, 200

Lahiri, Avijit, 218
Lal, Bhajan, 91
Lal, Devi, 78
Laxman, Bangaru, 241
Le Monde, 199
Left Front, 26, 115, 127, 236, 247, 253, 270
Left movement, 118
Leftist ideology, 6
Lepcha delegation, 102
Liberation Tigers of Tamil Eelam (LTTE), 141–43, 145, 149, 151
Lok Sabha elections (1984), 131
London Times, 44
Los Angeles Times, 227
Lynch, Merrill, 121

Mahajan, Pramod, 219–220
Mahalanobis, Prasanta Chandra, 26
Mahato, Sagina, 40
Maksimovna, Raisa, 199
Male-dominated polity, 167
Malik, Ashok, 213
Margdarshak Mandal, 207
Marx, Karl, 42
Massoud, Ahmed Shah, 177, 184
Mazar-i-Sharif, 184–86
Mazumdar, Charu, 42
Mega scandals of Zardaris, 166
Mini-Bharat, 11
Misra, Jagannath, 131
Misra, Sripat, 131
Mitra, Ashok, 63, 119
Mitra, Chandan, 84, 93, 223
Mitra, Somen, 245
Modern India, 25
Mohammad, Nur, 179–80
Mountbatten Declaration, 17

MRD (Movement for Restoration of Democracy), 160
Muhajirs, 163–64
Mujahideen, 151, 156, 173, 175–80, 186
Mukherjee, Ajoy, 24
Mukherjee, Geeta, 242
Mukherjee, Pranab, 5, 41, 51, 71, 96, 101, 129–40, 243, 245, 252–53, 262
Mukherjee, Subrata, 242
Mukhopadhyay, Ashutosh, 26
Muslim League, 116, 233
Mustafa, Seema, 77, 91
Muttahida Quami Movement (MQM), 163–65

Nagar, Maraimalai, 105
Najibullah, 173, 175–78, 180, 183, 185
Namboodiripad, E.M.S., 24
Nandi, Dwijen, 81
Nandigram, 120, 257, 262, *See also* Singur
Narayan, Jayaprakash, 32
Narendra Ramakrishna Mission College, 35
Nath, Kamal, 240–241, 250, 252
National Democratic Alliance, 249
National Front government, 247
Nauroz festival, 184, 186
Navbharat Times, 218, 227
Navnirman agitation, 32, *See also* Narayan, Jayaprakash
Nawaz, Sarfraz, 161
Naxal movement, 6, 26, 42

Naxalism, 31
Naxals, 6–7, 11
Nehru, Arun, 130–31, 133
Nehru, Jawaharlal, 133, 160
Nehru, Motilal, 75, 133
Nehruvian era, 75
Nepotism, 27
Nevill, H.R., 205
New Industrial Policy, 120, 236
Newsline, 165
Nixon, Richard, 1
Non-cooperation, 32

O'Halpin, Eunan, 271–272
Operation Black Thunder, 93
Operation Blue Star, 69, 85–88, 93, 225

Padma state honours, 229
Pakistan Muslim League (PML), 160
Pakistan Peoples Party (PPP), 159–161, 163, 165–166, 168
Panja, Ajit Kumar, 36, 247
Panjshir Valley, 184
Partisan political position, 105
Pawar, Sharad, 214
People's Democratic Party of Afghanistan (PDPA), 175
Permanent Settlement Act, 25
Personal space, 16
Pioneer, 218, 220
Planning Commission, 262
Polit Bureau, 116, 119, 198–99
Prabhakaran, Velupillai, 145–46, 149–50, *See* Liberation Tigers of Tamil Eelam (LTTE)

Pradesh Congress Committee
    (PCC), 97
Prasad, Rajendra, 26
Pravda, 196–198
Premadasa, Ranasinghe, 152
Presidencian, 26, 33
Presidency College, 5, 25–26, 35, 37–38
Press Council of India, 233
Press Information Bureau (PIB), 141, 149
Pseudo-secular press, 215
Punjab Accord, 87–88, 90
Puri, Hardeep, 153

Quest, 45, 270

Rabindra Parishad, 32
Radical Democratic Party, 41
Rahman, Sheikh Mujibur, 2–3
Rahman, Ziaur, 48
Rajdahani Rajneeti, 76
Raje, Vasundhara, 216
Rajiv Gandhi–Harchand Singh Longowal agreement, 86
Rajya Sabha nominations, 229
Ram Janmabhoomi Movement, 206–07, 212, 216, 220, 232
Ram Janmabhoomi Nyas, 208
Ram Janmabhoomi Salvation Committee, 208
Ram, Kanshi, 105
Ramon Magsaysay Award, 234
Rao, P.V. Narasimha, 120, 122, 137, 194, 214, 231, 236, 243, 245, 265–66
Rao, R. Gundu, 131

Ray, D.B., 217
Ray, Satyajit, 4–5, 45, 53
Ray, Shiv Narayan, 41
Ray, Siddhartha Shankar, 7, 26, 34, 36, 66, 122, 134, 266
Refugees, 1, 164, 182
Rithambara, Sadhvi, 207, 215, 219, 222, 224
Roy, Annada Shankar, 34
Roy, Bidhan Chandra, 133–34, 262
Roy, Kamini, 16
Roy, Leela, 34
Roy, M.N., 41, 45
Roy, Manabendra Nath, 203
Roy, Prafulla Chandra, 26
Roy, Prannoy, 270
Roy, Tushar, 12
RSS, 206, 210–15, 217, 220, 224
Rupadarshi, 34
Russian revolution, 195
Saffron Brigade, 105, 249
Saha, Meghnad, 26
Sahay, Mohan, 218
Sanando, 54, 58
Sangh Parivar, 204
Sardesai, Rajdeep, 270
Sarkar, Ashok, 56–57, 76
Sarkar, Sushobhan, 29
Sattar, Abdul, 168
Satyayug, 41
Scindia, Vijaya Raje, 215
Sen, Amartya, 26
Sen, Aparna, 273
Sen, Satyen, 33
Sengupta, Barun, 34, 43, 51, 65, 67, 76, 235, 267

Seshadri, H.V., 215
Shah Bano case, 205
Shah, Viren J., 255
Shantiniketan, 5, 53
Shekhar, Chandra, 72
Shiromani Akali Dal, 86
Siddharthan, Geetha, 214
Sikh Gurdwara Prabandhak Committee (SGPC), 89
Sikh nationalism, 84
Simla Agreement, 1
Singh, Ajay, 218
Singh, Arjun, 89, 216
Singh, Balwant, 89–91
Singh, Bhim, 212, 214
Singh, Buta, 86
Singh, Joginder, 88
Singh, Kalyan, 210, 219, 222, 225
Singh, Maharaja Ranjit, 86
Singh, Mahesh Narayan, 214
Singh, Manmohan, 77, 101, 136–37, 262
Singh, Mulayam, 214, 219
Singh, Ranjit, 86, 182
Singh, S.K., 168
Singh, S.P., 227
Singh, V.P., 51, 113, 131, 166, 214
Singh, Zail, 86
Singha, Timir Baran, 26
Singhal, Ashok, 207, 213, 215–16, 220, 224, *See also* Vishva Hindu Parishad (VHP)
Singur, 120, 257, 262, *See also* Nandigram
Sinha, Bidhan, 67
Siraj, Syed Mustafa, 56, 234

Slums, 8, 10–11
Socialism, 197
Socialist revolution, 197
The Sole Spokesman, 167, 236
Star Ananda, 269, 273
The Statesman, 34, 43, 45–46, 49, 76, 84, 218
Student Federation of India, 157
Sudarshan, K.S., 215, 224
Sunday magazine, 59, 226
Sunday Mail, 214

Tagore, Rabindranath, 19, 53, 107, 171
Taliban, 176
Tamil militancy, 146, 152
Tankhaya, 85–86, 92
Tehelka, 241, 249
Telegraph, 52, 59, 75–77, 86, 91, 151, 192, 206, 213, 225, 227, 240
Tenure of Land in India, 25
Thackeray, Bal, 221
The Times of India, 41, 81, 263
Tohra, Gurcharan Singh, 88
Tokenism, 209
Toshniwal, B.P., 209
Trinamool Congress, 27, 127, 241, 247
2G scam, 137

Uday Shankar, 268
Uma Bharti, 215, 217, 219, 224
UNHCR, 3
Union of Victims of Unjustified Repression, 201
United Liberation Front of

Assam (ULFA), 72
United States Information
 Service (USIS), 39
UPA-I, 139
US bipartisan leadership, 122
US imperialism, 65

Vajpayee, Atal Bihari, 125, 216, 241, 249
Value-based politics, 249
Velvettithurai, 145
Venkatraman, R., 156
Verma, Kewal, 77
Vernacular journalism, 38
Vernacular Press Act, 234
Vietnam War, 178
Vishva Hindu Parishad (VHP), 206, 208, 210, 212–13, 215, 233
Vivekananda, Swami, 26

West Bengal College Service
 Commission, 39
West Bengal Industrial
 Development Corporation, 120
West Bengal politics, 132
World Bank, 137, 262
World War II, 17

Yeltsin, Boris, 176, 192–200, 202

Zaidi, Akbar, 157
Zakaria, Kuruvilla, 29
Zedong, Mao, 42
Zia-ul-Haq, 154–55, 159